A DEFENCE OF VIRGINIA

A DEFENCE OF VIRGINIA

Robert Lewis Dabney

Little Boy Publishing

New York
1867

CONTENTS

PREFACE.

To the conquerors of my native State, and perhaps to some of her sons, a large part of the following defence will appear wholly unseasonable. A discussion of a social order totally overthrown, and never to be restored here, will appear as completely out of date to them as the ribs of Noah's ark, bleaching amidst the eternal snows of Ararat, to his posterity, when engaged in building the Tower of Babel. Let me distinctly premise, that I do not dream of affecting the perverted judgments of the great anti-slavery party which now rules the hour. Of course, a set of people who make success the test of truth, as they avowedly do in this matter, and who have been busily and triumphantly engaged for so many years in perfecting a plain injustice, to which they had deliberately made up their minds, are not within the reach of reasoning. Nothing but the hand of a retributive Providence can avail to reach them. The few among them who do not pass me by with silent neglect, I am well aware will content themselves with scolding; they will not venture a rational reply.

But my purpose in the following pages is, first and chiefly, to lay this pious and filial defence upon the tomb of my murdered mother, Virginia. Her detractors, after committing the crime of destroying a sovereign and co-equal commonwealth, seek also to bury her memory under a load of obloquy and falsehood. The last and only office that remains to her sons is to leave their testimony for her righteous fame— feeble it may be now, amidst the din of passion and material power, yet inextinguishable as Truth's own torch. History will some day bring present events before her impartial bar; and then her ministers will recall my obscure little book, and will recognize in it the words of truth and righteousness, attested by the signatures of time and events.

Again: if there is indeed any future for civilized government in what were the United States, the refutation of the abolitionist postulates must possess a living interest still. Men ask, "Is not the slavery question dead? Why discuss it longer?" I reply: Would God it were dead! Would that its mischievous principles were as completely a thing of the past as our rights in the Union in this particular are! But in the Church, abolitionism lives, and is more rampant and mischievous than ever, as infidelity; for this is its true nature. Therefore the faithful servants of the Lord Jesus Christ dare not cease to oppose and unmask it. And in the State, abolitionism still lives in its full activity, as Jacobinism; a fell spirit which is the destroyer of every hope of just government and

Christian order. Hence, the enlightened patriot cannot cease to contend with it, until he has accepted, in his hopelessness, the *nefas de republica desperandi*. Whether wise and good men deem that this discussion is antiquated, may be judged from the fact that Bishop Hopkins (one of the most revered divines among Episcopalians) judged it proper, in 1864, and Dr. Stuart Robinson, of Louisville, (equally esteemed among Presbyterians,) in 1865, to put forth new and able arguments upon this question.

It should be added, in explanation, that, as a son of Virginia, I have naturally taken her, the oldest and greatest of the slaveholding States, as a representative. I was most familiar with her laws. In defending her, I have virtually defended the whole South, of which she was the type; for the differences between her slave institutions and theirs were in no respect essential.

The most fearful consequence of the despotic government to which the South is now subjected, is not the plundering of our goods, nor the abridgment of privileges, nor the death of innocent men, but the degrading and debauching of the moral sensibilities and principles of the helpless victims. The weapon of arbitrary rulers is physical force; the shield of its victims is usually evasion and duplicity. Again: few minds and consciences have that stable independence which remains erect and undebauched amidst the disappointments, anguish, and losses of defeat, and the desertion of numbers, and the obloquy of a lost cause. Hence it has usually been found, in the history of subjugated nations, that they receive at the hands of their conquerors this crowning woe—a depraved, cringing, and cowardly spirit. The wisest, kindest, most patriotic thing which any man can do for his country, amidst such calamities, is to aid in preserving and reinstating the tottering principles of his countrymen; to teach them, while they give place to inexorable force, to abate nothing of righteous convictions and of self-respect. And in this work he is as really a benefactor of the conquerors as of the conquered. For thus he aids in preserving that precious seed of men, who are men of principle, and not of expediency; who alone (if any can) are able to reconstruct society, after the tumult of faction shall have spent its rage, upon the foundations of truth and justice. The men at the North who have stood firmly aloof from the errors and crimes of this revolution, and the men at the South who have not been unmanned and debauched by defeat—these are the men whom Providence will call forth from their seclusion, when the fury of fanaticism shall have done its worst, to repair its mischiefs, and save

America from chronic anarchy and barbarism; if, indeed, any rescue is designed for us. It is this audience, "few but fit," with which I would chiefly commune. They will appreciate this humble effort to justify the history of our native States, and to sustain the hearts of their sons in the hour of cruel reproach.

Hampden Sidney, Virginia, June, 1867.

CHAPTER I.
INTRODUCTORY.

To the rational historian who, two hundred years hence, shall study the history of the nineteenth century, it will appear one of the most curious vagaries of human opinion, that the Christianity and philanthropy of our day should have given so disproportionate an attention to the evils of African slavery. Such a dispassionate observer will perceive that, while many other gigantic evils were rampant in this age, there prevailed a sort of epidemic fashion of selecting this one upon which to exhaust the virtuous indignation and sympathies of the professed friends of human amelioration. And he will probably see in this a proof that the Christianity and benevolence of the nineteenth century were not so superior, in wisdom and breadth, to those of the seventeenth and eighteenth, as the busy actors in them had persuaded themselves; but were, in fact, conceited, overweening, and fantastic.

It will appear to him a still stranger fact, that this zeal against African slavery was so partial in its exhibition. Up to this day, not only the Southern States of the late American Union, but the Brazilian, Turkish, and Spanish empires, among civilized nations, and many barbarous people, have continued the explicit practice of slavery, in so stern a form, that the institution in the Confederate States was, by comparison, extremely mild. Yet, throughout the Northern States of America and Europe, it is upon the devoted heads of Southern masters almost exclusively that the vials of holy wrath are poured out. Renascent Spain is quite a pet among Yankees and Europeans, though tenaciously clinging, in her colonies, to a system of slavery at whose barbarities the public sentiment of these Southern States would shudder, and though persistently winking at the African Slave Trade in addition. Slaveholding Brazil is on most pleasing terms with the United States and the European governments, which vie in soliciting her commercial intercourse and friendship with most amiable suavity. But when the sounding lash of the self-constituted friend of man is raised to chastise "the wickedness of slavery," all Yankeedom and all Europe seem to think only of us sinners. And yet here, of all places where it prevailed, African bondage was most ameliorated and most justifiable! Indeed, not a few of these consistent reformers have ten-fold as much patience with that demon of slaveholders, the King of Dahomey, than with the benignant Christian master in Virginia; and go to that truculent savage to request him not to cut the throats of another thousand of his inoffensive slaves in a "grand custom," with far more of courtesy, forbearance, and amiability, than they can exercise towards us, when they come to reason with us touching the rights of our late peaceful and well-fed domestics. We see no reason for this partiality, but that the King of Dahomey is himself of that colour, which seems to be the only one acceptable to the tastes of this type of philanthropists. An Abolitionist poet has sung of our oppressing our brother man, because he was "guilty of a skin." To give the contrast, these persons act as though, in their view, the King of Dahomey's meritorious possession of the skin of approved colour, were enough to cover his multitude of sins! Now, if the rest of Christendom have determined to take slaveholders for their pet objects of abuse, we may justly demand of them, at least, to distribute their hard words more generally, and give all a share.

This injustice is to be accounted for, in part, by the greater prominence which the late United States held before the world, making all their supposed sins more prominent; and in part by the zeal of our late very amiable and equitable partners, the Yankee people. They reserved their abuse and venom on this subject for their Southern fellow-citizens alone. They made it their business to direct the whole storm of odium, from abroad and at home, on our heads. They, having the manufacture of American books chiefly in their hands, took pains to fill Europe and their own country with industrious slanders against their own brethren: and so occupied the ear of the world with abuse of us, as to make men almost forget that there were any other slaveholders. For this they had two motives, one calculated, and the other passionate and instinctive. The latter was the sectional animosity which was bred by the very intimacy of their association under one government, with rival interests. The man who has learned to hate his brother, hates him, and can abuse him, more heartily than any more distant enemy. The deliberative motive was, to reduce the South to a state of colonial dependency upon themselves, and exclude all other nations from the rich plunder which they were accustomed to draw from the oppressed section, by means of the odium and misunderstanding which they created concerning us. The South was their precious gold mine, from which they had quarried, and hoped yet again to quarry, hoards of wealth, by the instruments of legislative and commercial jugglery. From this precious mine, they wished to keep other adventurers away by the customary expedient of spreading an odious character for moral *malaria* and pestilential vices around it. It did not suit their selfish purposes, that Europe should know, that in this slaveholding South was the true conservative power of the American Government, the most solid type of old English character, the greatest social stability and purity, and above all, the very fountain of international commerce and wealth; lest Europe should desire to visit and to trade with this section for itself. And the readiest way to prevent this, was to paint the South to all the rest of the world, in the blackest colours of misrepresentation, so as to have us regarded as a semi-barbarous race of domestic tyrants, whose chief occupations were chaining or scourging negroes, and stabbing each other with bowie-knives. The trick was a success. The Yankee almost monopolized the advantages of Southern trade and intercourse.

But the South should have been impelled by the same facts to defend its institutions before the public opinion of the civilized world; for *opinion* is always omnipotent in the end, whatever prejudices and physical powers may oppose it. If its current is allowed to flow unchecked, its silent waters gradually undermine the sternest obstacles. This great truth men of thought are more apt to recognize than men of action. While the true statesman is fully awake to it, the mere politician is unconscious of its power; and when his expedients—his parties and his statutes—have all been silently swept away by the diffusion of abstract principles opposed to them, he cannot understand his overthrow. If the late Confederate States would have gained that to which they aspired, the position of a respectable and prosperous people among the nations of the world, it was extremely important that they should secure from their neighbours a more just appreciation of their institutions. A respectful and powerful appeal in defence of those institutions was due to our neighbours' opinions, unfair and unkind as they have been to us; and due to our own rights and self-respect.

Our mere politicians committed an error in this particular, while we were still members of the United States, by which we should now learn. They failed to meet the Abolitionists with sufficient persistence and force on the radical question—the righteousness of African servitude as existing among us. It is true that this fundamental point has received a discussion at the South, chiefly at the hands of clergymen and literary men, which has evoked a number of works of the highest merit and power, constituting almost a literature on the subject. One valuable effect of this literature was to enlighten and satisfy the Southern mind, and to produce a settled unanimity of opinion, even greater than that which existed against us in other States. But such is the customary and overweening egotism of the Yankee mind, that none of these works, whatever their merit, could ever obtain general circulation or reading in the North. People there were satisfied to read only their own shallow and one-sided arguments, quietly treating us as though our guilt was too clear to admit of any argument, or we were too inferior to be capable of it. The consequence was, that although the North has made the wrongs of the African its own peculiar cause—its great master-question—it is pitiably ignorant of the facts and arguments of the case. After twenty-five years of discussion, we find that the staple of the logic of their writers is still the same set of miserable and shallow sophisms, which Southern divines and statesmen have threshed into dust, and driven away as the chaff before the whirlwind, so long ago, and so often, that any intelligent man among us is almost ashamed to allude to them as requiring an answer. When the polemic heat of this quarrel shall have passed away, and the dispassionate antiquary shall compare the literature of the two parties, he will be amazed to see that of the popular one so poor, beggarly, and false, and that of the unpopular one so manly, philosophic, and powerful. But at present, such is the clamour of prejudice, our cause has not obtained a hearing from the world.

The North having arrogated to itself the name of chief manufacturer of literary material, and having chief control of the channels of foreign intercourse, of course our plea has been less listened to across the Atlantic than in America. The South has been condemned unheard. Well-informed men in Great Britain, we presume, are ignorant of the names and works of the able and dignified advocates to whom the South confidently and proudly committed her justification; and were willing to render their verdict upon the mere accusations of our interested slanderers. But while the United States yet existed unbroken, there was one *forum*, where we could have demanded a hearing upon the fundamental question: the Federal Legislature. From that centre of universal attention, our defence of the righteousness of the relation of master and slave, as existing among us, might have been spread before the public mind; and the abstract question having been decided by triumphant argument, the troubles of our Federal relations might possibly have been quieted. There were two courses, either of which might have been followed by our politicians, in defending our Federal rights against Abolitionism. One plan would have been, to exclude the whole question of slavery persistently from the national councils, as extra-constitutional and dangerous, and to assert this exclusion always, and at every risk, as the essential condition of the continuance of the South in those councils. The other plan was, to meet that abstract question from the first, as underlying and determining the whole subject, and to debate it everywhere, until it was decided, and the verdict of the national mind was passed upon it. Unfortunately, the Southern men did neither persistently. After temporary resistance, they permitted the debate; and then failed to conduct it on fundamental principles. With the exception of Mr. Calhoun, (whom events have now shown to have been the most far-seeing of our statesmen, notwithstanding the fashion of men to depreciate him as an "abstractionist" while he lived,) Southern politicians usually satisfied themselves with saying, that the whole matter was, according to the Constitution, one of State sovereignty; that Congress had no right to legislate concerning its merits; and that therefore they would not seem to admit such a right, by condescending to argue the matter on its merits. The premise was true; but the inference was practically most mischievous. If the Congress had no right to legislate about slavery, then it should not have been permitted to debate it. And Southern men, if they intended to make their stand on that ground, should have exacted the exclusion of all debate, at every cost. But this was perhaps impossible. The debate came; and, of course, the principles agitated ran at once back of the Constitution, to the abstract ethical question: "Is the holding of an African slave in the South a moral wrong in itself?" Southern men should have industriously followed them there; but they did not do it: and soon the heat and animosity of an aggressive and growing faction hurried the country beyond the point of calm consideration. A moment's reflection should have shown that the decisive question was the abstract righteousness of the relation of master and slave. The Constitution gave to the Federal Government no power over that relation in the States. True; but that Constitution was a compact between sovereign commonwealth: it certainly gave recognition and protection to the relation of master and slave; and if that relation is intrinsically unrighteous, then it protected a wrong. Then the sovereign States of the North were found in the attitude of protecting a wrong by their voluntary compact; and therefore it would have been the duty of all citizens of those States to seek, by all righteous means, the amendment or repeal of that compact. They would not, indeed, have been justified to claim all the benefits of the compact, and still agitate under it a matter which the compact excluded. But they would have been more than justified, they would have been bound to clear their skirts of the wrong, by surrendering the compact, if necessary. There was no evasion from the duty, except by proving that the Constitution did nothing unrighteous by protecting the relation; in other words, that the relation was not unrighteous. Again, on the subject of the "Higher Law," our conservative statesmen and divines threw up a vast amount of pious dust. This partially quieted the country for a time; but, as might have been foreseen, it was destined to be inevitably blown away. There *is a higher law*, superior to constitutions and statutes; not, indeed, the perjured and unprincipled cant which has no conscience against swearing allegiance to a Constitution and laws which it declares sinful, in order to grasp emoluments and advantages, and then pleads "conscience" for disobeying what it had voluntarily sworn to obey; but the everlasting law of right in the word of God. Constitutions and laws which contravene this, ought to be lawfully amended or repealed; and it is the duty of all citizens to seek it. Let this be applied to the Fugitive Slave Law. If the bondage was intrinsically unrighteous, then the Federal law which aided in remanding the fugitive to it, legalized a wrong. It became, therefore, the duty of all United States officers, who were required by statute to execute this law—not, indeed, to hold their offices and emoluments, and swear fidelity, and then plead conscientious scruples for the neglect of these sworn functions, (for this is a detestable union of theft and perjury with hypocrisy,)—but to resign those offices wholly, with their profits and their sinful functions. It would have become the duty of any private citizen, who might have been summoned by a United States officer, to act in a *posse*, guard, or any other way in enforcing this law, to decline obedience; and then, in accordance with Scripture, to submit meekly to the legal penalty of such a refusal, until the unrighteous law were repealed. But, moreover, it would have become the right and duty of these and all other citizens to seek the repeal of that law, or, if necessary, the abrogation of that Federal compact which necessitated it. But on the other hand, when we proved that the relation of master and slave is not unrighteous, and that therefore the Fugitive Slave Law required the perpetration of no wrong, and was constitutional, it became the clear moral duty of every citizen to concur in obeying it.

Once more: the true key of the more commanding question of *free soil* was in the same abstract ethical point. If the relation of master and servant was unrighteous, and the institution a standing sin against God and human rights, then it was not to be extended at the mere dictate of convenience and gain. Although Northern men might be compelled to admit that, in the States, it was subject to State control alone, and expressly exempted from all interference of the Federal Government by the Constitution; yet, outside of the States, that Constitution and Government, representative as it was as a majority of free States, ought not to have been prostituted to the extension of a great moral wrong. Those free States ought, if their Southern partners would not consent to relinquish their right by a peaceable amendment of the Constitution, to have retired from the odious compact, and to have surrendered the advantages of the Union for conscience' sake. If, on the contrary, African slavery in America was no unrighteousness, no sin against human rights, and no contradiction to the doctrines of the Constitution, then the general teachings of that instrument concerning the absolute equality of the States and their several citizens under it, were too clear to leave a doubt, that the letter and spirit of the document gave the slaveholder just the same right to carry his slaves into any territory, with that of the Connecticut man to carry his clock-factory. Hence the ethical question, when once the slavery agitation became inevitable, should have been made the great question by us. The halls of Congress should have rung with the arguments, the newspaper press should have teemed with them. But little was done to purpose in this discussion, save by clergymen and literary men; and for reasons already indicated they were practically unheard. After it was too late to stem the torrent of passion and sectional ambition pouring against us, politicians did indeed awake to a tardy perception of these important views; but the eyes of the Northern people were then obstinately closed against them by a foregone conclusion.

We have cited these recent and striking illustrations of the fundamental importance of the ethical discussion, to justify the task we have undertaken. Some may suppose that, as the United States are no more as they were, and slaveholding is absolutely and finally ended, the question is obsolete. This is a great mistake. The status of the negro is just beginning to develop itself as an agitating and potent element in the politics of America. It will still continue the great ground of contrast, and subject of moral strife, between the North and the South. We have attempted to indicate the potency of the slow and silent but irresistible influence of opinion over human affairs. Let our enemies claim the triumph without question in the field of opinion; let them continue to persuade mankind successfully that we were a people stained by a standing social crime; and we shall be continually worsted by them. In order to be free, we must be respected: and to this end we must defend our good name. We need not urge that instinctive desire for the good opinion of our fellow-men, and that sense of justice, which must ever render it painful to be the objects of undeserved odium. Instead, therefore, of regarding the discussion of the rightfulness of African slavery as henceforth antiquated, we believe that it assumes, at this era, a new and wider importance. While the swords of our people were fighting the battles of a necessary self-defence, the pens of our statesmen should have been no less diligent in defending us against the adverse opinion of a prejudiced world. Every opening should have been seized to disabuse the minds of Europeans, a jury to which we have hitherto had no access, although condemned by it. The discussion should everywhere have been urged, until public opinion was effectually rectified and made just to the Confederate States.

At the first glance, it appears an arduous, if not a hopeless undertaking, to address the minds of such nations as the North and Great Britain in defence of Southern slavery. We have to contend against the prescriptive opinions and prejudices of years' growth. We assert a thesis which our adversaries have taken pains to represent as an impossible absurdity, of which the very assertion is an insult to the understanding and heart of a freeman. Ten thousand slanders have given to the very name of Southern slaveholder a colouring, which darkens every argument that can be advanced in his favour. Yet the task of self-defence is not entirely discouraging. Our best hope is in the fact that the cause of our defence is the cause of God's Word, and of its supreme authority over the human conscience. For, as we shall evince, that Word is on our side, and the teachings of Abolitionism are clearly of rationalistic origin, of infidel tendency, and only sustained by reckless and licentious perversions of the meaning of the Sacred text. It will in the end become apparent to the world, not only that the conviction of the wickedness of slaveholding was drawn wholly from sources foreign to the Bible, but that it is a legitimate corollary from that fantastic, atheistic, and radical theory of human rights, which made the Reign of Terror in France, which has threatened that country, and which now threatens the United States, with the horrors of Red-Republicanism. Because we believe that God intends to vindicate His Divine Word, and to make all nations honour it; because we confidently rely in the force of truth to explode all dangerous error; therefore we confidently expect that the world will yet do justice to Southern slaveholders. The anti-scriptural, infidel, and radical grounds upon which our assailants have placed themselves, make our cause practically the cause of truth and order. This is already understood here by thinking men who have seen Abolitionism bear its fruit unto perfection: and the world will some day understand it. We shall possess at this time another advantage in defending our good name, derived from our late effort for independence. Hitherto we have been little known to Europeans, save through the very charitable representations of our fraternal partners, the Yankees. Foreigners visiting the United States almost always assumed, that when they had seen the North, they had seen the country, (for Yankeedom always modestly represented itself as constituting all of America that was worth looking at.) Hence the character of the South was not known, nor its importance appreciated. Its books and periodicals were unread by Europeans. But now the very interest excited by our struggle has caused other nations to observe for themselves, and to find that we are not *Troglodytes* nor *Anthropophagi*.

Another introductory remark which should be made is, that this discussion, to produce any good result, must distinctly disclaim some extravagant and erroneous grounds which have sometimes been assumed. It is not our purpose to rest our defence on an assumption of a diversity of race, which is contradicted both by natural history and by the Scripture, declaring that "God hath made of one blood all nations of men for to dwell on all the face of the earth." Nor does the Southern cause demand such assertions as that the condition of master and slave is everywhere the normal condition of human society, and preferable to all others under all circumstances. The burden of odium which the cause will then carry, abroad, will be immeasurably increased by such positions. Nor can a purpose be ever subserved by arguing the question by a series of comparisons of the relative advantages of slave and free labour, laudatory to the one part and invidious to the other. There has been hitherto, on both sides of this debate, a mischievous forgetfulness of the old adage, "comparisons are odious!" When Southern men thus argued, they assumed the disadvantage of appearing as the propagandists, instead of the peaceful defenders, of an institution which immediately concerned nobody but themselves; and they arrayed the self-esteem of all opponents against us by making our defence the necessary disparagement of the other parties. True, those parties have usually been but too zealous to play at this invidious game, beginning it in advance. We should not imitate them. It is time all parties had learned that the lawfulness and policy of different social systems cannot be decided by painting the special and exceptional features of hardship, abuse, or mismanagement, which either of the advocates may imagine he sees in the system of his opponent. The course of this great discussion has too often been this: Each party has set up an easel, and spread a canvas upon it, and drawn the system of its adversary in contrast with its own, in the blackest colours which a heated and angry fancy could discover amidst the evils and abuses imputed to the rival institution. The only possible result was, that each should blacken his adversary more and more; and consequently that both should grow more and more enraged. And this result did not argue the entire falsehood of either set of accusations. For, unfortunately, the human race is a fallen race—depraved, selfish, unrighteous and oppressive, under all institutions. Out of the best social order, committed to such hands, there still proceeds a hideous amount of wrongs and woe; and that, not because the order is unrighteous, but because it is administered by depraved man. For this reason, and for another equally conclusive, we assert that the lawfulness, and even the wisdom or policy of social institutions affecting a great population, cannot be decided by these odious contrasts of their special wrong results. That second reason is, that the field of view is too vast and varied to be brought fairly under comparison in all its details before the limited eye of man. First, then, if we attempt to settle the matter by endeavouring to find how much evil can be discovered in the working of the opposite system, there will probably be no end at all to the melancholy discoveries which both parties will make against each other, and so no end to the debate: for the guilty passions of men are everywhere perpetual fountains of wrong-doing. And second, the comparison of results must be deceptive, because no finite mind can take in all the details of both the wholes. Our wisdom, then, will be to take no extreme positions, and to make no invidious comparisons unnecessarily. It is enough for us to place ourselves on this impregnable stand; that the relation of master and slave is recognized as lawful in itself by a sound philosophy, and above all, by the Word of God. It is enough for us to say (what is capable of overwhelming demonstration) that for the African race, such as Providence has made it, and where He has placed it in America, slavery was the righteous, the best, yea, the only tolerable relation. Whether it would be wise or just for other States to introduce it, we need not argue.

And in conclusion, we would state that it is our purpose to argue this proposition chiefly on Bible grounds. Our people and our national neighbours are professedly Christians; the vast majority of them profess to get their ideas of morality, as all should, from the Sacred Scriptures. A few speculative minds may reason out moral conclusions from ethical principles; but the masses derive their ideas of right and wrong from a "Thus saith the Lord." And it is a homage we owe to the Bible, from whose principles we have derived so much of social prosperity and blessing, to appeal to its verdict on every subject upon which it has spoken. Indeed, when we remember how human reason and learning have blundered in their philosophizings; how great parties have held for ages the doctrine of the divine right of kings as a political axiom; how the whole civilized world held to the righteousness of persecuting errors in opinion, even for a century after the Reformation; we shall feel little confidence in mere human reasonings on political principles; we shall rejoice to follow a steadier light. The scriptural argument for the righteousness of slavery gives us, moreover, this great advantage: If we urge it successfully, we compel the Abolitionists either to submit, or else to declare their true infidel character. We thrust them fairly to the wall, by proving that the Bible is against them; and if they declare themselves against the Bible (as the most of them doubtless will) they lose the support of all honest believers in God's Word.

This discussion will therefore be, in the main, a series of expositions. The principles of scriptural exposition are simply those of common sense; and it will be the writer's aim so to explain them that they shall commend themselves to every honest mind, and to rid them of the sophisms of the Abolitionists.

But before we proceed to this discussion we propose to devote a few pages to the exposition of the historical facts which place the attitude of Virginia in the proper light.

CHAPTER II.
THE AFRICAN SLAVE TRADE.

This iniquitous traffick, beginning with the importation of negroes into Hispaniola in 1503, was first pursued by the English in 1562, under Sir John Hawkins, who sold a cargo at the same island that year. The news of his success reaching Queen Elizabeth, she became a partner with him in other voyages. Under the Stuart kings, repeated charters were given to noblemen and merchants, to form companies for this trade, in one of which, the Duke of York, afterwards James II., was a partner. The colony of Virginia was planted in 1607. The first cargo of negroes, only twenty in number, arrived there in a Dutch vessel in 1620, and was bought by the colonists. All the commercial nations of Europe were implicated in the trade; and all the colonies in America were supplied, to a greater or less extent, with slave labour from Africa, whether Spanish, Portuguese, English, French, or Dutch. But England became, on the whole, the leader in this trade, and was unrivalled by any, save her daughter, New England.

The happy revolution of 1688, which placed William and Mary on the throne, arrested for a time the activity of the royal company for slave trading, by throwing the business open to the whole nation. For one of the reforms, stipulated with the new government, was the abolition of all monopolies. But the company did not give up its operations; and it even succeeded in exacting from Parliament an indemnity of £10,000 *per annum* for the loss of its exclusive privilege. But the most splendid triumph of British enterprise was that achieved by the treaty of Utrecht, 1712, between Queen Anne and Spain. By a compact called the *Asiento* treaty, the Spanish monarch resigned to the English South Sea Company, the exclusive slave trade even between Africa and the Spanish colonies. Four thousand eight hundred slaves were to be furnished to the Spanish colonies annually, for thirty years, paying to the King of Spain an impost of thirty-three and a third dollars per head; but the company had the privilege of introducing as many more as they could sell, paying half duty upon them. The citizens of every other nation, even Spaniards themselves, were prohibited from bringing a single slave. The British Queen and the King of Spain became stockholders in the venture, to the extent of one-fourth each; the remainder of the stock was left to British citizens. And Anne, in her speech from the throne, detailing to her Parliament the provisions of the treaty of Utrecht, congratulated them on this monopoly of slave trading, as the most splendid triumph of her arms and diplomacy. Meantime, the African Company, with private adventurers at a later day, plied the trade with equal activity, for furnishing the British colonies. Finally, in 1749, every restriction upon private enterprise was removed; and the slave trade was thrown open to all Englishmen; for, says the statute: "the slave trade is very advantageous to Great Britain." But every resource of legislation, and even of war, was employed during the eighteenth century to secure the monopoly of the trade to British subjects, and to enlarge the market for their commodity in all the colonies. To this end, the royal government of the plantations, which afterwards became the United States, was perseveringly directed. The complaint of Hugh Drysdale, Deputy Governor of Virginia, in 1726, that when a tax was imposed to check the influx of Africans, "the interfering interest of the African company has obtained the repeal of the law," was common to him and all the patriotic rulers of the Southern colonies.

Reynal estimates the whole number of negroes stolen from Africa before 1776 at nine millions; Bancroft at something more than six millions. Of these, British subjects carried at least half: and to the above numbers must be added a quarter of a million thrown by Englishmen into the Atlantic on the voyage. As the traffick continued in full activity until 1808, it is a safe estimate that the number of victims to British cupidity taken from Africa was increased to five millions. The profit made by Englishmen upon the three millions carried to America before 1776, could not have been less than four hundred millions of dollars. The negroes cost the traders nothing but worthless trinkets, damaged fire-arms, and New England rum: they were usually paid for in hard money at the place of sale. This lucrative trade laid the foundation, to a great degree, for the commercial wealth of London, Bristol, and Liverpool. The capital which now makes England the workshop and *emporium* of the world, was in large part born of the African slave trade. Especially was this the chief source of the riches which founded the British empire in Hindostan. The South Sea and the African Companies were the prototypes and pioneers of that wonderful institution, the East India Company; and the money by which the latter was set on foot was derived mainly from the profitable slave-catching of the former. When the direct returns of the African trade in the eighteenth century are remembered; when it is noted how much colonial trade has contributed to British greatness, and when it is considered that England's colonial system was wholly built upon African slavery, the intelligent reader will be convinced that the slave trade was the corner-stone of the present splendid prosperity of that Empire.

But after the nineteenth century had arrived, the prospective impolicy of the trade, the prevalence of democratic and Jacobin opinions imported from France, the shame inspired by the example of Virginia, with (we would fain hope) some influences of the Christian religion upon the better spirits, began to create a powerful party against the trade. First, Clarkson published in Latin, and then in English, his work against the slave trade, exposing its unutterable barbarities, as practised by Englishmen, and arguing its intrinsic unrighteousness. The powerful parliamentary influence of Wilberforce was added, and afterwards that of the younger Pitt. The commercial classes made a tremendous resistance for many years, sustained by many noblemen and by the royal family; but at length the Parliament, in 1808, declared the trade illicit, and took measures to suppress it. Since that time, the British Government, with a tardy zeal, but without disgorging any of the gross spoils with which it is so plethoric, wrung from the tears and blood of Africa, has arrogated to itself the special task of the catchpole of the seas, to "police" the world against the continuance of its once profitable sin. Its present attitude is in curious contrast with its recent position, as greedy monopolist, and queen of slave traders; and especially when the observer adverts to her activity in the Coolie traffick, that new and more frightful form, under which the Phariseeism of this age has restored the trade, he will have little difficulty in deciding, whether the meddlesome activity of England is prompted by a virtuous repentance, or by a desire to replace the advantages of the African commerce with other fruits of commercial supremacy.

The share of the Colony of Virginia in the African slave trade was that of an unwilling recipient; never that of an active party. She had no ships engaged in any foreign trade; for the strict obedience of her governors and citizens to the colonial laws of the mother country prevented her trading to foreign ports, and all the carrying trade to British ports and colonies was in the hands of New Englanders and Englishmen. In the replies submitted by Sir William Berkeley, Governor, 1671, to certain written inquiries of the "Lords of Plantations," we find the following statement: "And this is the cause why no great or small vessels are built here; for we are most obedient to all laws, while the men of New England break through, and trade to any place that their interest leads them." The same facts, and the sense of grievance which the colonists derived from them, are curiously attested by the party of Nathaniel Bacon also, who opposed Sir William Berkeley. When they supposed that they had wrested the government from his hands, Sarah Drummond, an enthusiastic patriot, exclaimed: "Now we can build ships, and like New England, trade to any part of the world." But her hopes were not realized: Virginia continued without ships. No vessel ever went from her ports, or was ever manned by her citizens, to engage in the slave trade; and while her government can claim the high and peculiar honour of having ever opposed the cruel traffick, her citizens have been precluded by Providence from the least participation in it.

The planting of the commercial States of North America began with the colony of Puritan Independents at Plymouth, in 1620, which was subsequently enlarged into the State of Massachusetts. The other trading colonies, Rhode Island and Connecticut, as well as New Hampshire (which never had an extensive shipping interest), were offshoots of Massachusetts. They partook of the same characteristics and pursuits; and hence, the example of the parent colony is taken here as a fair representation of them. The first ship from America, which embarked in the African slave trade, was the *Desire*, Captain Pierce, of Salem; and this was among the first vessels ever built in the colony. The promptitude with which the "Puritan Fathers" embarked in this business may be comprehended, when it is stated that the Desire sailed upon her voyage in June, 1637. The first feeble and dubious foothold was gained by the white man at Plymouth less than seventeen years before; and as is well known, many years were expended by the struggle of the handful of settlers for existence. So that it may be correctly said, that the commerce of New England was born of the slave trade; as its subsequent prosperity was largely founded upon it. The Desire, proceeding to the Bahamas, with a cargo of "dry fish and strong liquors, the only commodities for those parts," obtained the negroes from two British men-of-war, which had captured them from a Spanish slaver.

To understand the growth of the New England slave trade, two connected topics must be a little illustrated. The first of these is the enslaving of Indians. The pious "Puritan Fathers" found it convenient to assume that they were God's chosen Israel, and the pagans about them were Amalek and Amorites. They hence deduced their righteous title to exterminate or enslave the Indians, whenever they became troublesome. As soon as the Indian wars began, we find the captives enslaved. The ministers and magistrates solemnly authorized the enslaving of the wives and posterity of their enemies for the crimes of the fathers and husbands in daring to defend their own soil. In 1646, the Commissioners of the United Colonies made an order, that upon complaint of a trespass by Indians, any of that plantation of Indians that should entertain, protect, or rescue the offender, might be seized by reprisal, and held as hostages for the delivery of the culprits; in failure of which, the innocent persons seized should be slaves, and be exported for sale as such. In 1677, the General Court of Massachusetts ordered the enslaving of the Indian youths or girls "of such as had been in hostility with the colony, or had lived among its enemies in the time of the War." In the winter of 1675-6, Major Waldron, commissioner of the General Court for that territory now included in Maine, issued a general warrant for seizing, enslaving, and exporting every Indian "known to be a manslayer, traitor, or conspirator." The reader will not be surprised to hear, that so monstrous an order, committed for execution to any or every man's irresponsible hands, was employed by many shipmasters for the vilest purposes of kidnapping and slave hunting. But in addition, in numerous instances whole companies of peaceable and inoffensive Indians, submitting to the colonial authorities, were seized and enslaved by publick order. In one case one hundred and fifty of the Dartmouth tribe, including their women and children, coming in by a voluntary submission, and under a general pledge of amnesty, and in another instance, four hundred of a different tribe, were shamelessly enslaved. By means of these proceedings, the numbers of Indian servants became so large, that they were regarded as dangerous to the Colony. They were, moreover, often untameable in temper, prone to run away to their kinsmen in the neighbouring wilderness, and much less docile and effective for labour than the "blackamoors." Hence the prudent and thrifty saints saw the advantage of exporting them to the Bermudas, Barbadoes, and other islands, in exchange for negroes and merchandise; and this traffick, being much encouraged, and finally enjoined, by the authorities, became so extensive as to substitute negroes for Indian slaves, almost wholly in the Colony. Among the slaves thus deported were the favourite wife and little son of the heroic King Philip. The holy Independent Divines, Cotton, Arnold, and

Increase Mather, inclined to the opinion that he should be slain for his father's sins, after the example of the children of Achan and Agag; but the authorities probably concluded that his deportation would be a more profitable, as well as a harsher punishment. These shocking incidents will no longer appear incredible to the reader, when he is informed that the same magistrates sold and transported into foreign slavery two English children, one of them a girl, for attending a Quaker meeting; while the adult ladies present were fined £10 each, and whipped.

In pleasing contrast with these enormities, stands the contemporaneous legislation of the Colony of Virginia touching its Indian neighbours. By three acts, 1655 to 1657, the colonists were strictly forbidden to trespass upon the lands of the Indians, or to dispossess them of their homes even by purchase. Slaying an Indian for his trespass was prohibited. The Indians, provided they were not armed, were authorized to pass freely through the several settlements, for trading, fishing, and gathering wild fruits. It was forbidden to enslave or deport any Indian, no matter under what circumstances he was captured; and Indian apprentices or servants for a term of years could only be held as such by authority of their parents, or if they had none, of the magistrates. Their careful training in Christianity was enjoined, and at the end of their terms, their discharge, with wages, was secured by law.

The second, and more potent cause of development of the New England slave trade, was the commerce between those colonies and the West Indies. Each of the mother countries endeavoured to monopolize to herself all the trade and transportation of her own colonies. But it was the perpetual policy of Great Britain to intrude into this monopoly, which Spain preserved between herself and her colonies, while she jealously maintained her own intact. This motive prompted her systematic connivance at every species of illicit navigation and traffick of her subjects in those seas. The New England colonies were not slow to imitate their brethren at home; and although their maritime ventures were as really violations of the colonial laws of England, as of the rights of Spain, the mother country easily connived at them for the sake of their direction. The Spanish Main was consequently the scene of a busy trade during the seventeenth century, which was as unscrupulous and daring as the operations of the Buccaneers of the previous age. The only difference was, that the red-handed plunder was now perpetrated on the African villages instead of the Spanish, and for the joint advantage of the New England adventurers and the Spanish and British planters. At length, the treaty of Utrecht, in 1712, recognized this encroaching trade, and provided for its extension throughout the Indies. New England adventure, as well as British, thus received a new *impetus*. The wine-staves of her forests, the salt fish of her coasts, the tobacco and flour of Virginia, were exchanged for sugar and molasses. These were distilled into that famous New England rum, which, as Dr. Jeremy Belknap, of Massachusetts, declared, was the foundation of the African slave trade. The slave ships, freighted with this rum, proceeded to the coast of Guinea, and, by a most gainful traffick, exchanged it for negroes, leaving the savage communities behind them on fire with barbarian excess, out of which a new crop of petty wars, murders, enslavements, and kidnappings grew, to furnish future cargoes of victims; while they wafted their human freight to the Spanish and British Indies, Virginia, the Carolinas, and their own colonies. The larger number of their victims were sold in these markets; the less saleable remnants of cargoes were brought home, and sold in the New England ports. But not seldom, whole cargoes were brought thither directly. Dr. Belknap remembered, among many others, one which consisted almost wholly of children.

Thus, the trade of which the good ship Desire, of Salem, was the harbinger, grew into grand proportions; and for nearly two centuries poured a flood of wealth into New England, as well as no inconsiderable number of slaves. The General Court of Massachusetts recognized the trade as legal, imposing a duty of £4 per head on each negro sold in the province, with a drawback for those resold out of it, or dying in twelve months. The weight of this duty is only evidence of a desire to raise revenue, and to discourage the settlement of numbers of negroes in Massachusetts; not of any disapproval of the traffick in itself, as a proper employment of New England enterprise. The government of the province preferred white servants, and was already aware of the unprofitable nature of African labour in their inhospitable climate; but the furnishing of other colonies with negroes was a favoured branch of commerce. The increase of negro slaves in Massachusetts during the seventeenth century was slow. But the following century changed the record.

In 1720, Governor Shute states their numbers at two thousand. In 1754, a census of negroes gave four thousand five hundred; and the first United States census, in 1790, returned six thousand.

Meantime, the other maritime colonies of Rhode Island and Providence Plantations, and Connecticut, followed the example of their elder sister emulously; and their commercial history is but a repetition of that of Massachusetts. The towns of Providence, Newport, and New Haven became famous slave trading ports. The magnificent harbour of the second, especially, was the favourite starting-place of the slave ships; and its commerce rivalled, or even exceeded, that of the present commercial metropolis, New York. All the four original States, of course, became slaveholding.

No records exist, accessible to the historian, by which the numbers of slaves brought to this country by New England traders can be ascertained. Their operations were mingled with those of Englishmen from the mother country. While the total of the operations of the latter, including their importations into the Spanish colonies, was greatly larger than that of the New Englanders, the latter probably sustained at least an equal share of the trade to the thirteen colonies, up to the time of the Revolution; and thenceforward, to the year 1808, when the importations were nominally arrested, they carried on nearly the whole. So that the presence of the major part of the four millions of Africans now in America, is due to New England. Some further illustrations will be given of the method and spirit in which that section conducted the trade. The number of The Boston Post-Boy and Advertiser for September 12th, 1763, contains the following:

"By a gentleman who arrived here a few days ago from the coast of Africa, we are informed of the arrivals of Captains Morris, Ferguson, and Wickham, of this port, who write very discouraging accounts of the trade upon the coast; and that upwards of two hundred gallons of real rum had been given for slaves per head, and scarcely to be got at any rate for that commodity. This must be sensibly felt by this poor and distressed Government, *the inhabitants whereof being very large adventurers in the trade, having sent and about sending upwards of twenty sail of vessels*, computed to carry in the whole about nine thousand hogsheads of rum, a quantity much too large for the places on the coast, where that commodity has generally been vended. We hear that many vessels are also gone and going from the neighbouring Governments, likewise from Barbadoes, from which place a large cargo of rum had arrived before our informant left the coast, of which they gave two hundred and seventy gallons for a prime slave."

When it is remembered that the Massachusetts ports were then small towns, the fact that they had more than twenty ships simultaneously engaged in the trade to the Guinea coast alone, clearly reveals that it was the leading branch of their maritime adventure, and main source of their wealth. The ingenuous lament of the printer over the increasing cost of "a prime slave," gives us the correct clue to the change in their views concerning the propriety of the trade. When the negro rose in value to two hundred gallons "of real rum" (the sable slave hunters were becoming as acute as Brother Jonathan himself, touching the adulterated article), the conscience of the holy adventurer began to be disturbed about the righteousness of the traffick. When the slave cost two hundred and fifty gallons, the scruples became troublesome; and when his price mounted up towards three hundred, by reason of the imprudence of the naughty man with his large cargo, from Barbadoes, the stings of conscience became intolerable. By the principles of that religion which "supposeth that gain is godliness," the trade was now become clearly wrong.

The following extracts are from the letter of instructions given by a leading Salem firm to the captain of their ship, upon its clearing for the African coast:

"CAPTAIN———: Our brig, of which you have the command, being cleared at the office, and being in every other respect complete for sea, our orders are, that you embrace the first fair wind, and make the best of your way to the coast of Africa, and there invest your cargo in slaves. As slaves, when brought to market, like other articles, generally appear to the best advantage; therefore too critical an inspection cannot be paid to them before purchase, to see that no dangerous distemper is lurking about them, to attend particularly to their age, to their countenances, to the straightness of their limbs, and, as far as possible, to the goodness or badness of their constitution, etc., etc., will be very considerable objects. Male or female slaves, whether full grown or not, we cannot particularly instruct you about; and on this head shall only observe that prime male slaves generally sell best in any market."

"Upon your return, you will touch at St. Pierre's, Martinico, and call on Mr. John Mounreau for your further advice and destination. We submit the conducting of the voyage to your good judgment and prudent management, not doubting of your best endeavours to serve our interest in all cases; and conclude with committing you to the almighty Disposer of all events."

The present commercial and manufacturing wealth of New England is to be traced, even more than that of Old England, to the proceeds of the slave trade, and slave labour. The capital of the former was derived mainly from the profits of the Guinea trade. The shipping which first earned wealth for its owners in carrying the bodies of the slaves, was next employed in transporting the cotton, tobacco, and rice which they reared, and the imports purchased therewith. And when the unjust tariff policy of the United States allured the next generation of New Englanders to invest the swollen accumulations of their slave trading fathers in factories, it was still slave grown cotton which kept their spindles busy. The structure of New England wealth is cemented with the sweat and blood of Africans.

In bright contrast with its guilty cupidity, stands the consistent action of Virginia, which, from its very foundation as a colony, always denounced and endeavoured to resist the trade. It is one of the strange freaks of history, that this commonwealth, which was guiltless in this thing, and which always presented a steady protest against the enormity, should become, in spite of herself, the home of the largest number of African slaves found within any of the States, and thus, should be held up by Abolitionists as the representative of the "sin of slaveholding;" while Massachusetts, which was, next to England, the pioneer and patroness of the slave trade, and chief criminal, having gained for her share the wages of iniquity instead of the persons of the victims, has arrogated to herself the post of chief accuser of Virginia. It is because the latter colony was made, in this affair, the helpless victim of the tyranny of Great Britain and the relentless avarice of New England. The sober evidence of history which will be presented, will cause the breast of the most deliberate reader to burn with indignation for the injustice suffered by Virginia, and the profound hypocrisy of her detractors.

The preamble to the State Constitution of Virginia, drawn up by George Mason, and adopted by the Convention June 29th, 1776, was written by Thomas Jefferson. In the recital of grievances against Great Britain, which had prompted the commonwealth to assume its independence, this preamble contains the following words: "By prompting our negroes to rise in arms among us; those very negroes whom, by an inhuman use of his negative, he had refused us permission to exclude by law." Mr. Jefferson, long a leading member of the House of Burgesses, and most learned of all his contemporaries in the legislation of his country, certainly knew whereof he affirmed. His witness is more than confirmed by that of Mr. Madison, who says: "The British Government constantly checked the attempts of Virginia to put a stop to this infernal traffick." Mr. Jefferson, in a passage which was expunged from the Declaration of Independence by New England votes in the Congress, strongly stated the same charge. And George Mason, perhaps the greatest and most influential of Virginians, next to Washington, reiterated the accusation with equal strength, in the speech in the Federal Convention, 1787, in which he urged the immediate prohibition of the slave trade by the United States. See Madison Papers, vol. iii., pp. 1388-1398. A learned Virginian antiquary has found, notwithstanding the destruction of the appropriate evidences, which will be explained anon, no less than twenty-eight several attempts made by the Burgesses to arrest the evil by their legislation, all of which were either suppressed or negatived by the proprietary or royal authority. A learned and pious Huguenot divine, having planted his family in the colony, in the first half of the last century, bears this testimony: "But our Assembly, foreseeing the ill consequences of importing such numbers among us, hath often attempted to lay a duty upon them which would amount to a prohibition, such as ten or twenty pounds a head; but no governor dare pass such a law, having instructions to the contrary from the Board of Trade at home. By this means they are forced upon us, whether we will or not. This plainly shows the African Company hath the advantage of the colonies, and may do as it pleases with the ministry." These personal testimonies are recited the more carefully, because the Vandalism of the British officers at the Revolution annihilated that regular documentary evidence, to which the appeal might otherwise be made. Governor Dunmore first, and afterwards Colonel Tarleton and Earl Cornwallis, carried off and destroyed all the archives of the colony which they could seize, and among them the whole of the original journals of the House of Burgesses, except the volumes containing the proceedings of 1769 and 1772. The only sure knowledge which remains of those precious records is derived from other documents and fragmentary copies of some passages, found afterwards in the desks of a few citizens. The wonderfully complete collection of their laws edited by Hening, under the title of "Statutes at Large," was drawn from copies and collections of the acts which, having received the assent of the governors and kings, were promulgated to the counties as actual law. Of course the suppressed and negatived motions against the slave trade are not to be sought among these, but could only have been found in the lost journals of the House. But enough of the documentary evidence remains, to substantiate triumphantly the testimony of individuals.

The first act touching the importation of slaves, which was allowed by the royal governor and king, was that of the 11th William III., 1699, laying an impost of twenty shillings upon each servant or African slave imported. The motive assigned is the raising of a revenue to rebuild the Capitol or State House, lately burned down; and the law was limited to three years. This impost was renewed for two farther terms of three years, by subsequent Assemblies. Before the expiration of this period, the Assembly of 1705 laid a permanent duty of sixpence per head on all passengers and slaves entering the colony; and this little burthen, the most which the jealousy of the British slave traders would permit, was the germ of the future taxes on the importation. This impost was increased by the Assembly of 1732, to a duty of five *per centum ad valorem*, for four years. Subsequent Assemblies continued this tax until 1740, and then doubled it, on the plea of the war then existing. During the remainder of the colonial government, the impost remained at this grade, ten *per centum* on the price of the slaves, and twenty *per centum* upon those imported from Maryland or Carolina. As the all-powerful African Company in England was not concerned in maintaining a transit of the slaves from one colony to another, after they were once off their hands, they permitted the Burgesses to do as they pleased with the Maryland and Carolina importations. Here, therefore, we have an unconfined expression of the sentiments of the Assemblies; and they showed their fixed opposition to the trade by imposing what was virtually a prohibitory duty. In 1769, the House of Burgesses passed an act for raising the duty on all slaves imported, to twenty *per centum*. The records of the Executive Department show that this law was vetoed by the king, and declared repealed by a proclamation of William Nelson, President of the Council, April 3d, 1771. The Assembly of 1772 passed the same law again, with the substitution of a duty of £5 per head, instead of the twenty *per centum*, on slaves from Maryland and Carolina; and it received the signature of

Governor Dunmore. It may well be doubted whether it escaped the royal veto.

But the House now proceeded to a more direct effort to extinguish the nefarious traffick. Friday, March 20th, 1772, it was "Resolved, that an humble address be prepared to be presented to his Majesty, to express the high opinion we entertain of his benevolent intentions towards his subjects in the colonies, and that we are thereby induced to ask his paternal assistance in averting a calamity of a most alarming nature; that the importation of negroes from Africa has long been considered as a trade of great inhumanity, and under its present encouragement may endanger the existence of his American dominions; that self-preservation, therefore, urges us to implore him to remove all restraints on his Governors from passing acts of Assembly which are intended to check this pernicious commerce; and that we presume to hope the interests of a few of his subjects in Great Britain will be disregarded, when such a number of his people look up to him for protection in a point so essential; that when our duty calls upon us to make application for his attention to the welfare of this, his antient colony, we cannot refrain from renewing those professions of loyalty and affection we have so often, with great sincerity, made, or from assuring him that we regard his wisdom and virtue as the surest pledges of the happiness of his people."

"Ordered, That a Committee be appointed to draw up an address to be presented to his Majesty, upon the said resolution." And a Committee was appointed of Mr. Harrison, Mr. Carey, Mr. Edmund Pendleton, Mr. Richard Henry Lee, Mr. Treasurer, and Mr. Bland.

"Wednesday, April 1st, 1772: Mr. Harrison reported from the Committee appointed upon Friday, the twentieth day of last month, to draw up an address to be presented to his Majesty, that the Committee had drawn up an address accordingly, which they had directed him to report to the House; and he read the same in his place; which is as followeth," etc. The address is so nearly in the words of the resolution, that the reader need not be detained by its repetition. The House agreed, *nemine contradicente*, to the address, and the same Committee was appointed to present an address to the Governor, asking him to transmit the address to his Majesty, "and to support it in such manner as he shall think most likely to promote the desirable end proposed." This earnest appeal met the fate of all the previous: Mammon and the African Company were still paramount at Court, over humanity and right. But the Revolution was near at hand, bringing a different redress for the grievance.

On the 15th of May, 1776, Virginia declared her independence of Great Britain, and the Confederacy, following her example, issued its declaration on the 4th of July of the same year. The strict blockade observed by the British navy, of course arrested the foreign slave trade, as well as all other commerce. But in 1778, the State of Virginia, determined to provide in good time against the resumption of the traffick when commerce should be reopened, gave final expression to her will against it. At the General Assembly held October 5th, Patrick Henry being Governor of the Commonwealth, the following law was the first passed:

AN ACT FOR PREVENTING THE FARTHER IMPORTATION OF
SLAVES.[35]

"I. For preventing the farther importation of slaves into this Commonwealth: *Be it enacted by the General Assembly*, That from and after the passing of this act, no slave or slaves shall hereafter be imported into this Commonwealth by sea or land, nor shall any slaves so imported be bought or sold by any person whatsoever.

"II. Every person hereafter importing slaves into this Commonwealth contrary to this act, shall forfeit and pay the sum of one thousand pounds for every slave so imported, and every person selling or buying any such slaves, shall in like manner forfeit and pay the sum of five hundred pounds for every slave so bought or sold, one moiety of which forfeitures shall be to the use of the Commonwealth, and the other moiety to him or them that will sue for the same, to be recovered by action of debt or information in any court of record.

"III. *And be it further enacted*, That every slave imported into this Commonwealth, contrary to the true intent and meaning of this act, shall, upon such importation, become free."

The remaining sections of the law only proceed to exempt from the penalty citizens of the other United States, coming to live as actual residents with their slaves in the Commonwealth, and citizens of Virginia bringing in slaves from other States of the Union by actual inheritance.

Thus Virginia has the honour of being the first Commonwealth on earth to declare against the African slave trade, and to make it a penal offence. Her action antedates by thirty years the much bepraised legislation of the British Parliament, and by ten years the earliest movement of Massachusetts on the subject; while it has the immense advantage, besides, of consistency; because she was never stained by any complicity in the trade, and she exercised her earliest untrammelled power to stay its evils effectually in her dominions. Thus, almost before the Clarksons and Wilberforces were born, had Virginia done that very work for which her slanderers now pretend so much to laud those philanthropists. All that these reformers needed to do was to bid the British Government go and imitate the example which Virginia was the first to set, among the kingdoms of the world. It is true that the first Congress of 1774, at Philadelphia, had adopted a resolution that the slave trade ought to cease; but this body had no powers, either federal or national; it was a mere committee; and its inspiration upon this subject, as upon most others, came from Virginia. In 1788, Massachusetts passed an act forbidding her citizens from importing, transporting, buying, or selling any of the inhabitants of Africa as slaves, on a penalty of fifty pounds for each person so misused, and of two hundred pounds for every vessel employed in this traffick. Vessels which had already sailed were exempted from all penalty for their present voyages. It is manifest from the character of the penalties, that this law was not passed to be enforced; and the evidence soon to be adduced will show, beyond all doubt, that this is true. The act was one of those cheap tributes which Pharisaic avarice knows so well how to pay to appearances. Connecticut passed a very similar law the same year, prohibiting her citizens to engage in the slave trade, and voiding the policies of insurance on slave ships. The slave trade of New England continued in increasing activity for twenty years longer.

It may be said, that if the government of Virginia was opposed to the African slave trade, her people purchased more of its victims than those of any other colony; and the aphorism may be quoted against them, that the receiver is as guilty as the thief. This is rarely true in the case of individuals, and when applied to communities, it is notoriously false. All States contain a large number of irresponsible persons. The character of a free people as a whole should be estimated by that of its corporate acts, in which the common will is expressed. The individuals who purchased slaves of the traders were doubtless actuated by various motives. Many persuaded themselves that, as they were already enslaved, and without their agency, and as their refusal to purchase them would have no effect whatever to procure their restoration to their own country and to liberty, they might become their owners, without partaking in the wrong of which they were the victims. Many were prompted by genuine compassion, because they saw that to buy the miserable creatures was the only practicable way in their reach to rescue them from their pitiable condition; for tradition testifies that often when the captives were exposed in long ranks upon the shore, near their floating prisons, for the inspection of purchasers, they besought the planters and their wives to buy them, and testified an extravagant joy and gratitude at the event. All purchasers were, perhaps, influenced partly by the convenience and advantage of possessing their labour. Had every individual in Virginia been as intelligent and virtuous as the patriots who, in the Burgesses, denounced the inhuman traffick, the colony might perhaps have remained without a slave, notwithstanding the two centuries of temptation during which its ports were plied with cargoes seeking sale. But a commonwealth without a single weak, or selfish, or bad man, is a Utopia. The proper rulers were forbidden by the mother country to employ that prohibitory legislation which is, in all States, the necessary guardian of the publick virtue; and it is therefore that we place the guilt of the sale where that of the importation justly belongs. Doubtless many an honourable citizen, after sincerely sustaining the endeavour of his Burgess to arrest the whole trade, himself purchased Africans, because he saw that their general introduction into the country was inevitable, without legislative interference; and his self-denial would only have subjected him to the severe inconveniences of being without slaves in a community of slaveholders, whilst it did not arrest the evil.

The government of Virginia was unquestionably actuated, in prohibiting the slave trade, by a sincere sense of its intrinsic injustice and cruelty. Mr. Jefferson, a representative man, in his "Notes on Virginia," had given indignant expression to this sentiment. And the reprobation of that national wrong, with regret for the presence of the African on the soil, was the universal feeling of that generation which succeeded the Revolution; while they firmly asserted the rightfulness of that slavery which they had inherited. But human motives are always complex; and along with the moral disapprobation for the crime against Africa, the Burgesses felt other motives, which, although more personal, were right and proper. They were sober, wise and practical men, who felt that to protect the rights, purity, and prosperity of their own country and posterity, was more properly their task, than to plead the wrongs of a distant and alien people, great although those wrongs might be. They deprecated the slave trade, because it was peopling their soil so largely with an inferior and savage race, incapable of union, instead of with civilized Englishmen. This was precisely their apprehension of the enormous wrong done the colony by the mother country. They understood also the deep political motive which combined with the lust of gain to prompt the relentless policy of the Home Government. With it, the familiar argument was: "Let us stock the plantations plentifully with Africans, not only that they may be good customers for our manufactures, and producers for our commerce; but that they may remain dependent and submissive. An Englishman who emigrates, becomes the bold assertor of popular and colonial rights; but the negro is only fit for bondage." For the same reason, the colonies felt that the forcing of the Africans upon them was as much a political as a social wrong. But that righteous Providence, whose glory it is to make the crimes of the designing their own punishment, employed African slavery in the Southern colonies as a potent influence in forming the character of the Southern gentleman, without whose high spirit, independence, and chivalry, America would never have won her freedom from British rule.

This contrast between the policy and principles of Virginia and of the New England colonies will be concluded with two evidences. The one is presented in the history of the Declaration of Independence. Mr. Jefferson, the author, states that he had inserted in the enumeration of grievances against the King of Great Britain, a paragraph strongly reprobating his arbitrary support of the slave trade, against the remonstrances of some of the colonies. When the Congress discussed the paper, this paragraph was struck out, "in complaisance," he declares, "to South Carolina and Georgia, who had never attempted to restrain the importation of slaves, and who, on the contrary, still wished to continue it. Our Northern brethren also, I believe, felt a little tender under these censures; for though their people had very few slaves themselves, yet they had been pretty considerable carriers of them to others." Thus New England assisted to expunge from that immortal paper a testimony against the slave trade, which Virginia endeavoured to place there.

The other evidence is presented by a case much more practical. In the Convention of 1787, which framed the Constitution of the United States, two questions concerning African slaves caused dissension. Upon the supreme right of the States over the whole subject of slavery within their own dominions, upon the recognition of slaves as property protected by the federal laws, wherever slavery existed, and upon the fugitive slave law, not a voice was raised in opposition. But the Convention presumed (what subsequent history did not confirm,) that the main expenses of the federal government would be met by direct taxation; and some principle was to be adopted, for determining how slaves should rank with freemen, in assessing capitation taxes, and apportioning representation. The other question of difficulty was the suppression of the African slave trade, which, upon the return of peace, had been actively revived by New England, with the connivance of Carolina and Georgia. The Southern States, who expected to have nearly the whole tax on slaves to pay, desired to rate them very low; some members proposed that five slaves should count as equal to only one white freeman; others, that three slaves should count for one. The New England colonies generally desired to make a negro count as a white man, both for representation and taxation! After much difference, the majority of the Convention agreed to a middle conclusion proposed by Mr. Madison, that five negroes should count for three persons. But the other question was not so easily arranged. The Committee of eleven appointed to draw up a first draught of a constitution had proposed that in Art. vii., § 4, of their draught, Congress should be prohibited from laying any import duty on African slaves brought into the country. The effect of this, so far as the federal government was concerned, would be to legalize the slave trade forever, and protect it from all burdens. Maryland (by her legislature, then sitting,) to her immortal honour, and Pennsylvania and Virginia, exhibited a determination to change this section, so as to arrest the trade through the action of the federal government, either by prohibition or tax. The New England States, South Carolina, and Georgia, opposed them, and advocated the original section, assigning various grounds. The difference threatened to make shipwreck of the whole work of the Convention, when Gouverneur Morris adroitly proposed to commit the subject, along with that of the proposed navigation law, in order that disagreeing parties might be induced, by private conference, to combine mutual concessions into a sort of bargain. The subjects were accordingly committed to a Committee of one from each State. This Committee reported, August 24th, "in favour of not allowing Congress to prohibit the importation of slaves before 1800, but giving them power to impose a duty at a rate not exceeding the average of other imports." South Carolina (through General Pinckney) moved to prolong the importation from 1800 to 1808, *and Massachusetts* (through Mr. Gorham) *seconded the motion.* It was then passed, as last proposed, *New Hampshire, Massachusetts, Connecticut,* (the only New England States then present,) Maryland, North Carolina, and South Carolina, voting in the affirmative, and New Jersey, Pennsylvania, Delaware, and Virginia in the negative. The maritime States soon after gained their point, of authorizing Congress to pass, by a majority vote, a navigation law for their advantage.

Thus, by the assistance of New England, the iniquities of the African slave trade, and the influx of that alien and savage race into America, were prolonged from the institution of the federal government until 1808. Is it said, that New England had at this time no interest in slavery, did not value it, and was already engaged in removing it at home? This is true; and it is so much the worse for her historical position. It only shows that she desired to fix that institution which she had ascertained to be a curse to her, upon her neighbours, for the sake of keeping open twenty years longer an infamous but gainful employment, and of securing a legislative bounty to her shipping. In other words, her policy was simply mercenary. And these votes for prolonging the slave trade effectually rob her of credit for emancipation at home; proving beyond all peradventure, that the latter measure was wholly prompted by her sense of her own interests, and not of the rights of the negro. For if the latter motive had governed, must it not have made her the equal opponent of the increase of slavery in Carolina and Georgia?

But the agency of New England in that increase was still more active and direct. As though to "make hay while the sun shone," the people of that section renewed their activity on the African coast, with a diligence continually increasing up to 1808. Carey, in his work upon the slave trade, estimates the importations into the thirteen colonies between 1771 and 1790, (nineteen years,) at thirty-four thousand; but that between the institution of the federal government and 1808, he places at seventy thousand. His estimate here is unquestionably far too low; because forty thousand were introduced at the port of Charleston, South Carolina, alone, the last four years; and within the years 1806 and 1807, there were six hundred arrivals of New England slavers at that place. The latter fact shows that those States must have possessed nearly the whole traffick. And the former bears out Mr. De Bow, in enlarging the total of importations under the federal government to one hundred and twenty-five thousand, at least. For the average at one port was ten thousand per year. In 1860, there were ten-fold as many Africans in the United States as had been originally brought thither from Africa. But as many of these had been multiplying for four, or even five generations, this rate of increase is too large to assume for the importations of 1800, whose descendants had only come to the third generation. Assuming the half as nearly correct, which seems a moderate estimate, we find their increase five-fold. So that there were, in 1860, six hundred and twenty-five thousand more slaves in the United States than would have been found here, had not New England's cruelty and avarice assisted to prolong the slave trade nineteen years after Virginia and the federal government would otherwise have arrested it.

After the British, and even after the other governments of Europe, had abolished the trade in name, it continued with a vast volume. Whereas at the time of the abolition, in 1808, eighty-five thousand slaves were taken from Africa annually, nearly fifty thousand annually were still carried, as late as 1847, to Brazil and the Spanish Indies. In this illicit trade, no Virginian (and, indeed, no Southern) ship or shipmaster has ever been in a single case implicated, although our State had meantime begun no inconsiderable career of maritime adventure. But adventurers from New England ports and New York were continually found sharing the lion's portion of the foul spoils. And to the latest reclamations of the British Government upon the Brazilian, for violations of the treaties and laws against the slave trade upon the extended shores of that empire, the answer of its noble Emperor has still been, that if Britain would find the real culprits, she must go to the ports of Boston and New York to seek them.

But one more fact remains: When the late Confederate Government adopted a constitution, although it was composed exclusively of slaveholding States, it voluntarily did what the United States has never done: it placed an absolute prohibition of the foreign slave trade in its organic law.

CHAPTER III.
LEGAL STATUS OF SLAVERY IN THE UNITED STATES.

It has been a favourite and persistent assertion of Abolitionists, that slavery in America was an exceptional institution, and contrary to the law of nature and nations. They represent it as owing its existence solely to the *lex loci* of the States where it was legalized by their own legislation; and hence they draw the conclusion, that the moment a slave passed out of one of these States into a free State, or into the territories of the United States, his bondage terminated of itself. Hence, also, they argue that slaveholders had no right to the protection of that species of property in the territories, which were the common possession of the citizens of all the States; and that the federal government could not properly permit the growth of, or recognize, new slave States. Their party cry was: "Freedom is national; slavery is local." It is plain that this proposition is the premise necessary to all the above assumptions. It will now be shown that this proposition is untrue. Slavery in the United States, instead of being the mere creature of *lex loci*, was founded on a basis as broad as that of the American Union, was in full accordance with the law of nature and nations as then recognized by the States and the federal government, and had universal recognition by the force of general law. The exclusion of slavery from any State was legally the exception, owing its validity purely to the *lex loci*, and to the recognized sovereignty of the States over their own local affairs. Hence, the rights of slaveholders stood valid, of course, in all the common territories of the United States, and everywhere, save where the sovereignty of a non-slaveholding State arrested them within its own borders. This representation is established by the following facts:

First. When the federal government was formed, all the family of European nations was slaveholding; and they all alike held the Africans as unquestioned and legitimate subjects of bondage. The slave trade was held by publick law as legitimate as the trade in corn. It was the subject of treaty stipulations between the several powers; and slave trading companies were formally chartered and protected by all the leading powers. Slaves were declared by the English judges to be merchandise. They were universally held legal prize of war when taken on the high seas. They were recognized subjects of reclamation in forming and executing treaties. Thus, not to go outside of our own history, we find General Washington, in 1783, by order of Congress, remonstrating with the British commander evacuating New York city, because certain officers of the retiring forces carried away with them the fugitive slaves of American citizens; and the latter was compelled to surrender the attempt, as an unauthorized spoliation of property. In 1788, the Government of the United States claimed of Spain the return of fugitive slaves from the Spanish colony of Florida; and our government promised, in return, the rendition of Spanish slaves found in the United States. It is well known that the treaty of the United States with Great Britain, negotiated by Mr. Jay, and ratified by President Washington, and the treaty of Ghent, in 1815, both secured indemnities for slaves of American citizens abducted during the two wars; thus treating them as property under the protection of national law in America, and of the law of nations. In face of this array of facts, we boldly ask, with what face it can be asserted that slavery was not recognized by international law? Whether it is not as consonant with the law of nature as of nations, will appear at another place.

Second. During the whole planting and growth of the British colonies in America, and at the time when they passed from that government into the federal Union, the Empire of Great Britain was slaveholding in all its parts. The obvious consequence is, that the government formed by the thirteen colonies in a part of the territory of that empire, inherited the legal condition of their mother, in this particular. In seceding from that empire, they brought away the slaveholding *status*; and this subsisted *ipso facto*, except where it was changed by the *lex loci*. All the original territory of the American Union was slave territory, as was that subsequently acquired from France. Hence slave owners of course possessed their rights in all this territory, unless they were expressly restrained by special legislation of the States, sovereign each one within its own borders. The consequence cannot be denied, if the premise be admitted. Let the reader consider the following evidences of it:

In 1772, only four years before the Declaration of Independence, Lord Mansfield, in the Court of King's Bench, decided the famous Somersett case, by which, it has usually been asserted, slavery was forever terminated in England, and the principle was settled that this relation was inconsistent with her free laws. Mr. Stewart, a citizen of Virginia, going to England on business, carried with him a negro slave,

Somersett, whom he had bought in Jamaica. After a time he indicated a purpose to return home, carrying his slave with him; whereupon the negro absconded. His master had him seized, and placed on board a ship in the Thames, to be forcibly carried to Jamaica and sold. The negro then sued out an application for *habeas corpus*, which being argued at a previous term, was finally decided by Lord Mansfield, at the Trinity term, 1772. The true extent of that decision will hereafter be shown. Our purpose here is to cite the admissions made by the court, as to the existing state of English laws. It is noticeable, that this tribunal exhibited a great reluctance to decide the case, declaring that it was attended with great, and almost inextricable difficulties, and that Lord Mansfield proposed to evade a decision by recommending a compromise between Mr. Stewart and the black. This not being done, the court stated that there were then fifteen thousand negro slaves in England, worth not less than seven hundred thousand pounds sterling. It also recognized the decisions of Sir Philip Yorke, and Lord Chief Justice Talbot, confirmed in 1749, by that of the chancellor, Lord Hardewicke, that if a slave, brought by his master to England, should be detained from him, an action of *trover* for his recovery would lie; and the decision of Lord Talbot, that a negro slave brought by his master to England from a colony, or baptized by the clergy, did not thereby gain his liberty; and the opinion of the latter that while the Statute of Tenures had abolished manorial villeinage, a white man might still become a *villein in gross*, by the laws of England. The court declared farther, that the slave property of a debtor was undoubtedly liable to action in the English courts, to recover the sums due a creditor. But after all these admissions, which clearly amount to a recognition of the fact that England itself was then by law a slaveholding country, Lord Mansfield proceeds to settle the principle (the only one, as he carefully declares, to which his decision extends) that the power of the writ of *habeas corpus*, not being limited to free persons by express statute, should, as he thinks, in England be extended to slaves, when they invoke it, and should be held to override the rights of the master under the laws; because those rights were now regarded as odious and excessive by current publick opinion. Such, and no more, is the extent of this much be praised, and much misunderstood decision! It is plain to common sense, that if it is not an instance of the judicial abuse of making, instead of expounding, law, it only establishes the fact that the laws of slaveholding England were then in a ridiculously inconsistent state.

In fact, not only were there then fifteen thousand negro slaves in England, but they were publickly bought and sold in the markets of London. The prevalence of slavery is attested by another species of historical evidence, very different from that of learned judges, but at least as authentick. The pictures by which Hogarth has fixed the follies and peculiarities of fashionable life on his immortal canvass, frequently contain the African valet; showing that the possession of this species of servants was demanded by high life. From the Normans, those noted slaveholders, to 1775, no statute had been passed upon the subject of personal slavery. There then existed, in the northern part of the kingdom of Great Britain, from thirty thousand to forty thousand persons, of whom the Parliament said, "Many colliers, coal-heavers, and salters, are in a state of slavery, or bondage, bound to the collieries or salt-works where they work, for life, transferable with the collieries and salt-works, when their original masters have no use for them." Again in 1799, they declare that "many colliers and coal-heavers still continue in a state of bondage."

Thus it appears that England was itself slave territory, at the time the thirteen colonies, declaring their independence, brought away her laws and institutions. But our argument of this fact is *ex abundantia*; it may be waived, and still our conclusion holds, because, by existing laws, all the plantations and colonies of England in America were then, yet more indisputably, slave territory. No stronger proof of this proposition can be imagined, than the manner in which slavery was planted in these communities. Not only were all the thirteen colonies, and all the West India plantations, slaveholding; but it required no statute, either of Parliament or of colonial legislature, to introduce African slavery, or to establish the right of the owner, because it was already established by imperial law and usage. The first negroes were bought in Virginia in 1620; the first act touching their bondage was passed by the Burgesses in 1659; and this does not enact their slavery, but recognizes it as existing. It was not until 1670, that any law was passed which expressly enacted their slavery. But for fifty years they had been unquestioned slaves, had paid impost duty as such, had been bought and sold, had been bequeathed, had been subject of suits. By what law? Obviously by the general law of the British Empire, and of nations. The manner of the introduction of slavery into Massachusetts was the same. "The involuntary servitude of Indians and negroes in the several colonies originated under a law not promulgated by legislation, and rested upon prevalent views of universal jurisprudence, or the *law of nations*, supported by the express or implied authority of the Home Government." But the "canny" Puritans, more careful than the Virginians to fortify their slave property, enacted slavery of both classes, in their earliest codes of laws, 1641 and 1660.

That African slavery was the universal law of the British colonial empire, is equally plain from the facts already given concerning the legalizing of the slave trade. The treaty of Utrecht secured to Britain a monopoly of that traffick. The Parliament chartered the African Company, with the right to trade in slaves to all the colonies. The Parliament then by statute threw the trade open to all British subjects. The Parliament, by express law, made the property in slaves held in the colonies subject of action in English courts. The Solicitor-General, with Chancellor after Chancellor, decided that residence in England did not emancipate the slave upon his return to his colonial home. The General Court of Massachusetts enacted the same rule, as did the Burgesses of Virginia, again and again; and were never disallowed therein by the king. Even so late as 1827, fifty-five years after the Somersett case, Lord Stowell decided, in the case of the slave Grace, from Antigua, that on her return to the colony, her condition as a slave for life was fully revived. And in the correctness of this decision, we find Mr. Justice Story concurring.

The argument then is, that at the American Revolution all the territory claimed by the thirteen colonies was, by the law of the Empire, and of nations, slaveholding territory. The colonies, in assuming their independence, brought away the rights and institutions which they had inherited as colonial parts of that empire; and whatever prescriptive right was not expressly changed by law, was universally held to survive, as of course. Hence all the territory of the American Union was slave territory; and the only mode by which any part became non-slaveholding, was by the exercise of State sovereignty enacting a *lex loci*, which was only operative within the bounds of the State itself.

Third. The chief territory which the United States acquired between the Revolution and the Mexican war, was Louisiana. This vast region was gained by treaty from France in 1803. It was then a single province and government of the French Republick, and was, through all its extent, a slaveholding country. In the third article of the treaty for its purchase, between the United States and the First Consul, it was stipulated that until the ceded territory should be incorporated, as States, in the Union, all its citizens should be "in the mean time maintained and protected in the free enjoyment of their liberty, property, and the religion which they profess." The settled doctrine of the courts of Louisiana has always been, that this guarantee covered all the citizens emigrating into any part of the territory before its erection into a State, as fully as those living in Louisiana in 1803. Thus, the rights of slave owners in the whole of the Louisiana purchase were guaranteed to them by treaty, until such time as the part they inhabited became a sovereign State, and thus assumed plenary power over the subject. But, by Article 6th, § 2d, of the Constitution of the United States, all treaties made by the authority of the United States are declared to be the supreme law of the land. Thus the rights of the master in all this region were placed above the power of the legislature itself.

Fourth. The federal constitution recognized and protected property in slaves, in every way which was competent to a federative compact of this kind. The slaveholding States had representation for three-fifths of their slaves. The slaves were made subjects of direct taxation, as property. The constitution provided expressly for a fugitive slave law, which was soon passed by the Congress, and continued to be the law of the land until the termination of the government. By the constitution, property in slaves was created like any other property; and no ground can be found for the assertion that its rights were more restricted than rights in cattle or lands. But the fundamental idea of that instrument was the impartial equality of all the citizens before the law. Whatever authority Congress had over the common territories, was as trustee for all the citizens of the United States equally. Hence it seems obvious that this body was bound to recognize in all the citizens equal rights, in going into those territories with any species of property which they might hold by the laws of any State, or of Congress, and to protect them in those rights while the country was in a territorial condition.

Finally, these principles have been expressly decided by the highest constitutional authority in the land, as well as by the voice of the most enlightened founders of the government. When the mischievous contest concerning the admission of Missouri was rising in 1819, Mr. Madison declared, concerning the article of the constitution which conferred on Congress its powers over the territories, (Art. 4, § 3,) that "it cannot be well extended beyond a power over the territories *as property*, and the power to make provisions really needful or necessary for the government of settlers, until ripe for admission into the Union." The Supreme Court of the United States, in the well-known case of Dred Scott, decided that Africans were not citizens of the United States in the meaning of the constitution; that property in African slaves was on the same footing under that instrument with other legal property; that the residence of a slave in a territory of the United States did not emancipate him, nor did his residence in a non-slaveholding State for a time, prevent the recurrence of his state of bondage, on his return to the State in which he had been a slave; and that Congress had no power to use its authority to exclude slavery from any part of the territories.

Thus the main proposition with which we set out is abundantly sustained by the history and legislation of the country. Three evasions from this conclusion have been attempted, of which the first is from the language of the Declaration of Independence, in which these famous words occur: "We hold these truths to be self-evident: that all men are created equal; that they are endowed by their Creator with certain unalienable rights; that among them are life, liberty, and the pursuit of happiness," etc. The inference is, that the Declaration intended to imply that the slavery of the Africans was a natural wrong incapable of being legalized; and it is claimed that this document is of the organic force of constitutional law to the confederation which then asserted its independence. Both these suppositions are erroneous. As to the latter, it may be justly argued, that the Declaration of Independence was simply what it calls itself: a *declaration*, a justificatory statement addressed to the world without, and not an act of organic legislation ascertaining the rights of the citizens within. The evidence is, that it *enacts nothing* save the one point of the independence of the colonies. Neither the Confederation nor the new Union formed in 1787 ever based any legislation upon it, save as their acts involved the fact of independence. The constitution made no reference to it; did not ground itself upon it, and did not reënact it. Hence, let its meaning be what it may, it legislates nothing for or against slavery.

But it is too clear to be disputed, that the enslaved African race were not intended to be included, and formed no part of the people who asserted their rights in this Declaration. The evidence is, that if the men who framed it had intended to refer to African slavery, they would have completely stultified themselves. For the majority of them, and of the States which they represented, continued to hold Africans in bondage just as before. A few years after, the same men met in federal convention, and framed the late constitution of the United States; by which property in slaves was protected and perpetuated as before, and traffick in Africans was prolonged until 1808, and made subject of taxation like other merchandise. The States which were emancipating their own Africans, equally with those which retained them in bondage, retained their laws prohibiting the marriage of Africans with whites. Connecticut, until 1796, prohibited free negroes from travelling beyond their township without a pass. New Hampshire, and Congress itself, precluded negroes from serving in the militia. The Declaration of Independence was therefore intended by its framers to assert the liberties of civilized Americans and Englishmen, and not of African barbarians held in bondage. Whether their consistency therein can be defended, is a separate question, to which attention will be given in the proper place. But all publicists are agreed, that the meaning of a document is the document; and that this meaning is to be ascertained by the intentions of those who frame and adopt it.

The second objection to our conclusion is grounded upon the Ordinance of the Confederation, in 1787, by which slavery was prohibited in the North-western Territory ceded to the United States by Virginia. This magnificent domain, including the present States of Ohio, Indiana and Illinois, was conquered from the public enemy in the years 1778-9, by the Commonwealth of Virginia. She sent out her own troops, at her own charges, without either authority or assistance from the Confederation, then also engaged in a war with Great Britain, under her own commission to her heroick son, General George Rogers Clarke. Upon the conquest of the country, she disposed by her own State action of the prisoners of war captured, and annexed the territory to the State of Virginia, which then also included Kentucky. The other States, and the Confederation, uniformly recognized this region as legitimately a part of Virginia. But during and after the war, the States which owned no unsettled territory grew exceedingly jealous of those which possessed such regions, and especially of Virginia. They feared her ulterior grandeur and power. But their expressed plea was, that she, and other States possessed of vacant lands, could pay their share of the common war debt, without taxation, by the sale of these lands, which, as they claimed, were the fruits of the common exertions of the States, while the others would be subjected to an onerous taxation. The North-west Territory had, in fact, been won by Virginia, with her own bow and spear; but at the request of the Congress of the

Confederation, she magnanimously laid the splendid prize upon the altar of the common cause, ceding it in 1784 to Congress, for the common behoof of the United States. The Congress of the Confederation passed a long enactment, known as the Ordinance of 1787, providing, in many articles, for its settlement, for its government while a territory, and for the sale of lands. Among these was a clause prohibiting slavery in it. But meantime, the Confederation was superseded by the general government organized under the new constitution of 1787. The first Congress during the administration of General Washington, acting under the article of the constitution already cited for taking and managing the "territory and other property" of the Confederation, passed an act, (August 7th, 1789,) for putting in effect the Ordinance of the Congress of the Confederation, now extinct.

Such is the history of the case. The inference of the objector is, that because the Congress of 1789, acting under the late constitution, claimed power to execute the ordinance of 1787, (passed by the previous and different general government,) with its anti-slavery clause included, therefore that constitution gave it power to exclude slavery from any other territory. But the inference is worthless. For, first, the Congress of the old Confederation had not a particle of constitutional power to adopt such an anti-slavery clause. So declared Mr. Madison emphatically: and so has decided the Supreme Court of the United States. Both these high authorities declare, that if the clause had any validity, it derived it only from the assent of Virginia, who had full sovereignty over the territory, and who accepted and ratified the exclusion by act of her General Assembly, as well as by the mouths of her representatives in the Confederation. And the Congress of 1789, in accepting the conditions imposed by the Ordinance of 1787 on the territory, as valid and abiding, undertook to change nothing, because it regarded that validity as the result of treaty stipulations between Virginia and the other twelve States represented by the old Congress. It conceived itself as having inherited from a previous and different government powers over this particular territory, which it could by no means have originated by its own constitutional authority. Second: The government framed under the new constitution was one of limited powers; and Congress was expressly inhibited, by the instrument which created it, from exercising any authority not granted. But such a power as that to exclude citizens of any of the United States from the common territory, because they proposed to carry there property legalized both by the Constitution of the United States and of their own State, was not granted to Congress. That a government whose very foundation was the equality of the States, should thus attempt to disfranchise some States of a part of their rights, was a solecism too monstrous for these able and enlightened men. Third: When similar cessions of territory were afterwards made by North Carolina and Georgia, these States refused to Congress the privilege of appending to their laws touching these lands, the exclusion of slavery; and Congress obeyed, so framing their enactments as to admit and protect slave-owners. This proves that the exclusion derived its force from the consent of the Sovereign State, and not from the power of Congress.

The third ground of objection which has been advanced against our main proposition, is the doctrine said to have been decided by the Supreme Court of the United States, (as in the case of Prigg against the State of Pennsylvania,) that according to recognized international laws, a nation which does not hold slaves itself is not bound to recognize property in slaves in neighbouring nations, when those slaves come into its borders; and that if a rendition is claimed, it must be asked of comity, or of special stipulation, and not as of international right. The answer is clear and facile. The States of the American Union were, initially, as independent nations to each other; and then they were all slaveholding. Each one of them recognized in its own citizens the right of property in slaves; and therefore, if the above doctrine be granted, they could not then, by international law, refuse to recognize it in nations living at amity with them. Again: When they passed out of this condition of absolute independence, into that of federal union, their relations, so far as they ceased to be international, were regulated exclusively by the constitution; and by this constitution the property in slaves was expressly recognized, the rendition of fugitive slaves was expressly required of all the States, whether themselves holding slaves or not; and all the common territory of the Union was originally slave territory until it became free territory by sovereign State action. Plainly, in such a case as this, the international law of Europe has no application, against historical facts and actual constitutional enactments. The sophism of this plea in the mouths of anti-slavery men, the uniform assertors of consolidation doctrines, would make the States, in the same breath, independent nations, in order that the international law of a different hemisphere may be applied against them, and also subject provinces of an anti-slavery nation, in order that they may be stripped of that equality of rights, belonging to sovereign constituent parties in a confederation.

CHAPTER IV.
HISTORY OF EMANCIPATION.

The motive for introducing the historical facts contained in this chapter is the following: That the credit of Virginia as a slaveholding State is relatively illustrated by the conduct of her partners in the confederation touching the same matter. Virginia never passed a general act of emancipation; on the contrary, she forbade masters to free their slaves within her borders, unless they also provided for their removal to new homes. But what was it which the Northern States actually did? The general answer to this question cannot be better given than in the words of the Hon. A. H. H. Stuart of Virginia, in his Report to the General Assembly, as chairman of its joint committee on the Harper's Ferry outrages. He says:

"At the date of the declaration of our national independence, slavery existed in every colony of the Confederation....

"Shortly after the Declaration of Independence, the Northern States adopted prospective measures to relieve themselves of the African population. But it is a great mistake to suppose that their policy in this particular was prompted by any spirit of philanthropy or tender regard for the welfare of the negro race. On the contrary, it was dictated by an enlightened self-interest, yielding obedience to overruling laws of social economy. Experience had shown that the African race were not adapted to high northern latitudes, and that slave labour could not compete successfully with free white labour in those pursuits to which the industry of the North was directed. This discovery having been made, the people of the North, at an early day, began to dispose of their slaves by sale to citizens of the Southern States, whose soil, climate, and productions were better adapted to their habits and capacities; and the legislation of the Northern States, following the course of publick opinion, was directed, not to emancipation, but to the removal of the slave population beyond their limits. To effect this object, they adopted a system of laws which provided, prospectively, that all slaves born of female slaves, within their jurisdiction, after certain specified dates, should be held free when they attained a given age. No law can be found on the statute-book of any Northern State, which conferred the boon of freedom on a single slave in being. All who were slaves remained slaves. Freedom was secured only to the children of slaves, born after the days designated in the laws; and it was secured to them only in the contingency that the owner of the female slave should retain her within the jurisdiction of the State until after the child was born. To secure freedom to the afterborn child, therefore, it was necessary that the consent of the master, indicated by his permitting the mother to remain in the State, should be superadded to the provisions of the law. Without such consent, the law would have been inoperative, because the mother, before the birth of the child, might, at the will of the master, be removed beyond the jurisdiction of the law. There was no legal prohibition of such removal, for such a prohibition would have been at war with the policy of the law, which was obviously removal, and not emancipation. The effect of this legislation was, as might have readily been foreseen, to induce the owners of female slaves to sell them to the planters of the South, before the time arrived when the forfeiture of the offspring would accrue. By these laws, a wholesale slave trade was inaugurated, under which a large proportion of the slaves of the Northern States were sold to persons residing south of Pennsylvania; and it is an unquestionable fact that a large number of the slaves of the Southern States are the descendants of those sold by Northern men to citizens of the South, with covenants of general warranty of title to them and to their increase."

Thus wrote Mr. Stuart, after thorough research. A brief recital of the enactments of the Northern slaveholding States will show that his general representation is correct. We begin with Massachusetts. No law against slavery, (which had been long legally established in the colony,) was ever passed by her legislature; and in that sense, the right to hold slaves may be said to have formally existed, until it was extinguished by her adoption of the "constitutional amendment," in 1866! Practically, slavery was gradually removed after 1780, by the current of the legal decisions against it, grounded upon a clause in the new bill of rights, adopted by the State in that year. This clause asserted, nearly in the words of the Declaration of Independence, the native equality and liberty of men. In 1781 a slave of N. Jennison, of Worcester County, recovered damages of his master for beating. This decision, if sustained, of course implied the cessation of slavery. Although the Legislature of the State was moved in 1783, by this Jennison and others, to declare that slavery did not exist legally, so that the doubt might be ended, that body refused to act; nor did it ever after abolish slavery. But judicial decisions after the example of the Jennison case were made from time to time, until, in 1796, the Supreme Court of Massachusetts, in the case of Littleton v. Tuttle, gave its countenance to the doctrine, that the bill of rights virtually made slavery illegal. That all this was a glaring instance of the judicial abuse, *ampliandi jurisdictionem*, is manifest from many facts: That the Massachusetts statesmen who adopted the same proposition in the Declaration of Independence, never dreamed of its possessing any force to abolish slavery in the United States which set it forth: That the convention which drew up the bill of rights for Massachusetts did not think of such an application; That this document declared "no part of any citizen's property could be taken from him without his own consent:" That slaves continued to be bought and sold, and advertised as before; And that the abolitionists, still in the minority, continued after 1780 to remonstrate against slavery as a sin still legalized. But such a mode of determining the question was well adapted to the meddlesome and crooked temper of that people. By this judicial trick the envious non-slaveholders were enabled to attack their richer slaveholding neighbours, and render them so uneasy as to insure their disposing of their slaves; while still there was neither law nor publick opinion prevalent enough to procure a legal act of emancipation.

New Hampshire and Vermont embodied the principle of prospective emancipation in their new constitutions. In 1790 there were 158 slaves in New Hampshire. In 1840 there was still *one*! Rhode Island passed a law in 1784, that no person born after that year should continue a slave. Connecticut embodied in the revision of her laws, in 1784, a law providing that all children born of slave parents after March 1st of that year, should be free at twenty-five years of age. In 1797 the term of servitude was reduced to twenty-one years for all born after August 1st of that year. Slavery was not actually abolished by law until June 12th, 1848; when the census shows there were no fewer than seventeen slaves in the State; and how old and worthless they must have been, appears from the fact that the youngest of them must have been born before March 1st, 1784.

In New York, the laws for slaves were more severe than in the Southern States, and the African slave trade was zealously encouraged during the whole colonial period. The slave could not testify, even to exculpate a slave. Three justices, with a sort of jury of five freeholders, could try capitally, and inflict any sentence, *inclusive of burning alive*. It was not until 1799 that the State commenced a system of laws for the gradual abolition of slavery. Every slave child born after July 4th of that year was to be free, the males after twenty-eight, and the females after twenty-five years. In 1810, the benefit of freedom was also extended to those born before July 4th, 1799, to take effect July 4th, 1827, the date at which the earliest born of those freed by previous law reached their majority of twenty-eight years. Still the census of 1830 found 75 slaves! The Revised Statutes of New York, after 1817, provided a penalty for those carrying them out of the State for sale; showing that the tendency to do so existed.

In New Jersey, the first act looking towards prospective emancipation was adopted in 1784. By it all born after 1804 were to be free in 1820. It was not until 1820 that action was taken to give effect to this promise; and then the nature of the law was such as to postpone the hopes of the slaves. The first section of the law of February 24th, 1820, says: "Every child born of a slave within this State since the 4th day of July 1804, or which shall hereafter be born as aforesaid, shall be free; but shall remain the servant of the owner of his or her mother, and the executors, administrators and assigns of such owners, in the same manner as if such child had been bound to service by the Trustees or Overseers of the poor, and shall continue in such service, if a male until the age of twenty-five years, and if a female until the age of twenty-one years." It was within the scope of possibility that slave women whom this law left slaves for life might bear children as late as the year 1848: whence bondage would not have been terminated wholly by it until 1873. New Jersey had 236 slaves for life in 1850. It is stated by one of the best informed of her old citizens, that the prospective effect of these enactments was to cause a considerable *exodus* to Southern markets; and that when a boy, he heard much talk of the sale of negroes, and the sending of them to "the Natchez," and was cognizant of the continual apprehension of the negroes concerning the danger.

In Pennsylvania, emancipation was also prospective and gradual. Her first act was passed March 1st, 1780. The rate at which it operated may be seen from these figures: In 1776 she had about 10,000 slaves; in 1790, (ten years after her first act,) she had 3,737; in 1800, 1,706; in 1810, 795; in 1820, 211; in 1830, 403; and in 1840, 64 slaves.

Thus, the emancipation legislation of the Northern States has been reviewed, and the assertions of the Hon. Mr. Stuart substantially sustained. That Northern emancipation was prompted by no consideration for the supposed rights of Africans, but by regard to their own interests, is evinced by many facts. Of these, perhaps the most general and striking is the persistent neglect of the welfare of their emancipated slaves; the refusal to give them equal civic rights, until they found a motive for doing so in malice against the South; and the shocking decadence, vice and misery to which a nominal liberty, according to the testimony of Northern writers, has consigned their wretched free blacks. Another proof is found in the current language of the men of the generation which effected the change. That language, as is well remembered by elderly persons still living, was usually such as this: that now that the population had filled up the country, the question of emancipation was simply one of choice between their own children and the negro—whether their sons should emigrate, or the negro be gotten rid of, as there was no longer room for both. Another conclusive proof is in the fact that while these States were getting rid of their own negroes, they were deliberately voting (Massachusetts, New Hampshire, Connecticut, in the Convention of 1787,) to prolong the introduction of slaves into the Carolinas nineteen years more. Still another evidence is found in the repugnance of those States to the influx of free blacks, and the stringent laws of some of them to prevent it. Thus, Massachusetts, in March, 1788, (eight years after the pretended extinction of human bondage,) passed a law ordering every black, mulatto or Indian who came into the State and remained two months to be publickly whipped; and this punishment was to be repeated "if he or she shall not depart *toties quoties.*" *This law remained in force until 1834!* as is shown by its appearance in the Revised Laws of Massachusetts, 1823. It is also to be noted that the scheme of gradual emancipation, upon which the whole North acted, obviously recognizes the property of the master in his slave as legitimate in itself. It only touches it, (because private rights are here required to give place to publick interest,) in the case of those born after a certain day. The slavery of the others is left as perpetual and legal as ever. And even as to the later born, the right of the master receives a certain recognition, in that he is allowed twenty-five years' service as a partial compensation for the surrender of the remainder.

But how different is the summary abolition forced upon Virginia and the South! Here, the general legislation of the State was steadily multiplying, elevating and blessing the black race, which in the North was so rapidly dying out under its pretended liberty. And private beneficence of Virginians, without any legal compulsion, had actually given the boon of freedom to at least one hundred thousand blacks; which is more than all the citizens of the New England States, New York, New Jersey, and Pennsylvania together, ever did, under the force of all their laws. In this wise and beneficent career Virginia has been violently interrupted, against her recognized and guaranteed rights, by instant and violent abolition. The motive of the North, as a whole, has manifestly been, not love for the negro, but hatred of the white man, and lust of domination. This abolition is purely the result of a supposed military necessity, because the North believed that otherwise she could not overthrow the South in an unjust war. But for this single fact, the Africans would still be in bondage, so far as the Yankee was concerned. The proof is, that the Chicago platform of the Black Republican party in 1860, expressly repudiated the purpose ever to meddle with slavery in the States. Mr. Lincoln, the chosen man of the North, solemnly asserted the same thing in his letter to A. H. Stephens of Georgia, in his publick inaugural, and in his messages. The Congress, after the beginning of the war, solemnly declared to the world by a joint resolution, that the purpose of the war was only to restore the Union, and not to restrict or change State institutions. Mr. Lincoln constantly declared to the Abolitionists, that if the perpetuation of slavery tended to restore the Union, it should be perpetuated. His standing invitation to the States in arms against him was: "If you wish to keep your slaves, come back into the Union." Can the North be believed in her own declarations? Then, the charge made is true—that abolition in the South was prompted by ambition and hatred, not by philanthropy.

Nor has this act been less wicked in its effects than in its motive. To the white race it was the most violent, convulsive, reckless and mischievous act ever perpetrated by a civilized government. As a war measure, it was calculated and expected to evoke all the savage horrors of servile war, neighbourhood massacre and butchery of non-combatants. Only the kindly relations which the benevolence and justice of the people of Virginia had established between themselves and their slaves, and the good character which we had given to these former savages, disappointed this desired result. As an economic measure, it was the most violent ever attempted in modern history; being a sudden confiscation of half, (and in some of the counties two-thirds) the existing property of the country; and a dislocation of its whole labour system, just when the people were bowed under the burden of a gigantic war, and a collapsed currency. That it did not then again result in a total paralysis of industry, in famine and anarchy, (which was probably intended), is only to be explained by the exercise of an energy, versatility, good sense, and industry in the Southern people, which are almost miraculous. By annihilating at one blow so much of the property on which the indebtedness of the country was based, it insured a financial confusion and general bankruptcy which are destined to plunge hundreds of thousands of innocent persons (innocent even from Yankee points of view) into destitution and domestic distress, which three generations will not heal. It confiscated the property of "loyal Union men," of helpless minors and lunatics, of venerable and infirm widows, without compensation, just as it did the possessions of the Confederate leader most obnoxious to the Yankee wrath. And what was the species of possession? Was it some foul lucre, like the spoils of an Achan, so unrighteous that it must be instantly plucked away, regardless of consequences? No; it was a species of property legalized by Moses and Christ, owned for ages by the boasted ancestors of the despoilers, now owned by themselves in the form of its fruits and increase, guaranteed by the Constitution which alone gave them any right to govern us, legalized by all our State laws, which were of earlier and superior authority to that Constitution, and recognized by the sacred pledges of the North itself, even so late as the beginning of this war.

But the step has been far more mischievous and unjust to the poor blacks, its pretended beneficiaries. It did not tarry to inquire whether they were fit for the change. It has resulted in the outbreak of a flood of vice, before repressed; of drunkenness, of illicit lust, of infanticide, of theft; and above all, of idleness, the least flagrant, but most truly mischievous fault of the African. It has suddenly and greatly diminished their share of the material goods they before enjoyed. The supplies of clothing and shoes now acquired by them do not reach a third of what they received before the war. Immediately on their emancipation, all the rural mill-owners testified that their grists *fell off one-half*, and have remained at that grade since. In those neighbourhoods where the blacks did not emigrate, (which was true of many neighbourhoods,) this showed that the consumption of bread was reduced one-half; for although the large proprietors now had no occasion to send their large grists, yet, unless there were less consumed, the aggregate of the little grists of the freedmen's families should have made good that decrease. Every statesman knows that any burden or disaster imposed upon the industrial pursuits of a country, is transmitted down by the property classes to the destitute class, and presses there with its whole force; just as inevitably as the weight of a statue placed upon the top of a column, is ultimately delivered upon the lowest *stratum* of foundation-stones. For the great law of self-preservation prompts each man, who has any property, to employ it in evading that pressure for himself and his family. Thus the actual *onus* is handed down, until it reaches that class who have no property, and must therefore bear it, because they have nothing wherewith to pay for the shifting of it. Thus, all the malice of the conqueror, aimed at the hated white man, while it crowds us down, also crowds down equally the labourer beneath us; and the blow alights ultimately on him.

The famine which is now preying upon some parts of the South illustrates the mischief done by the disorganization of labour, and the comparative excellence of the old system. Such was its beneficence, that it carried the Southern country through all the exhausting trials of the war, without actual dearth in any part of the Confederacy. Hundreds of thousands of our most vigorous men were wholly withdrawn from productive pursuits; our own armies were to be sustained; great hosts of enemies were continually tearing the vitals of the country; the year 1864 brought a drought so severe that in some parts of the country the crops of grain were reduced to one-tenth of the usual harvests; and yet, such was the happiness of our system, that it endured all these enormous trials, and met the wants of all. But after the new *régime* was well established, there came in 1866 such a drought as the South had several times experienced before, without inconvenience; and although all was peace, there were no armies to support, and no labouring man was called from the farm to the unproductive toils of the camp and the intrenchment, famine immediately resulted. Here is a fair comparison of the system of free African labour, with the old one. Indolence is the parent of crime. While the smaller misdemeanours are more frequent, there has been an alarming increase of felonies. In the orderly little county of Prince Edward, the criminal convictions of black persons averaged only one per year before the war. The last year they numbered twelve! An inquiry into the statistics of crime in our cities would reveal a yet larger increase.

Last, facts already evince, that the doom of ultimate extermination which Southern philanthropists have ever predicted as the result of premature emancipation, is already overtaking the negro with giant strides. About the end of 1866 the officers of the State revenue made their returns, which showed that there were then about 275,650 negro males over 21 years within the present limits of Virginia. Repeated calculations made from previous returns show that there are usually four and a half times as many souls among the blacks of Virginia as there are males over 21 years. The entire black population of the State then, at the end of the last year, was 340,500. The census of 1860 returned 531,000 blacks within the present limits of the State. The diminution is therefore 190,500; or nearly two-fifths, in less than two years. Some may suppose that more negro men have left the State since the war than women and children. If this is true, the number of males is now relatively smaller, and should be multiplied by a larger ratio than 4-1/2 to find the correct total. But, on the other hand, it is certain that the neglect and mortality have been much larger among the aged and little children than among the robust men. This fact, therefore, reduces the ratio of the total to the males over 21 years, and renders it certain that 340,500 is a large estimate. The same officers brought in returns which show that the white population of Virginia, although decimated by a terrible war, has actually increased since 1860. But we exposed no negro to the dangers of the battle. Thus it is made manifest that the philanthropy of Yankees has been to the poor negro an infinitely more desolating scourge than a tremendous war has been to the race against which the sword was openly wielded. And it requires little arithmetic to discover how long it will be, at this rate, before the monstrous consummation will be reached of the extinction of a whole nation of people by their professed friends.

CHAPTER V.
THE OLD TESTAMENT ARGUMENT.

§ 1. Let us appeal, then, to the Bible, to learn the moral character of Domestic Slavery. It will be well for both writer and readers, if they recall the reverence and honesty with which such a book should be approached; if the one is cautious to permit no party zeal, pride of opinion, or love of hypothesis, to tempt him to warp the sacred text to any thing inconsistent with its own truth and purity; and if the others are equally careful to receive its teachings with impartiality and docility. That no misunderstanding may attend the discussion, we must define at the outset, what we mean by that domestic slavery which we defend. By this relation we understand *the obligations of the slave to labour for life, without his own consent, for the master.* The thing, therefore, in which the master has property or ownership, is the involuntary labour of the slave, and not his personality, or his soul. A certain right of control over the person of the slave is incidentally given to the master by his property in the bondsman's labour; that is, so much control as is necessary to enable him to secure the labour which belongs to him. But we repeat, it is not the person, but the labour of the slave, which is the master's property. This is substantially the definition of Paley, an enemy of slavery; and it is obviously correct; it expresses the general result of the laws of all modern nations which have had slaves, touching that relation.

The abolitionists clamorously insist upon a different definition, which makes the master claim property in the very personality of the slave, in his soul, in the highest capacities which connect him with his God, and in his very being. According to this description, slavery converts the responsible, rational being, into a mere thing, a chattel, a commodity, by converting him into mere property of another man. The motive of this preposterous definition is obvious enough. One of the most astute of American Abolitionists has been candid enough to avow it, saying that if our definition be adopted, there is an end of the discussion; for every logician must see that it is absurd to declare the mere ownership of one man's labour by another, an essential and necessary moral wrong; which is the character it suits them to ascribe to slavery. Their object is so to represent it, that it shall appear a self-evident injustice, and the apologist shall be overwhelmed and silenced by a foregone prejudice. For, if it gave a literal ownership in the person and being of the slave, which can belong to none but the Creator; if it made not only his labour, but his conscience, the property of the master, destroying his moral responsibility, it would indeed dehumanize him, and would be an iniquity indefensible by any fair mind. The trick of securing the victory before the contest begins, by raising a false issue, is not very novel. The utter absurdity of applying such a definition to African slavery in America, appears from this: that it is contrary to the whole tenour of the legislation which establishes and regulates the institution among us. These laws, first, legislate for the slave, as to his own conduct, as a responsible human being, govern him by precepts sanctioned by rewards and punishments, and require of him intelligent obedience to the same moral rules which are enforced on his master. Second, the laws assign to the master precisely that amount of control over his slave's person which they suppose (whether correctly or not is no concern to us in this argument) to be incidental to his property in the servant's labour; and no more. Third, they protect the person, being, and moral responsibility of the slave against his own master. If the master kills him, it is murder, by the law. The slave's Sabbath is secured to him by the law. If the master force him to commit a crime, the former is held by the law guilty therefor, as accessory before the fact: and the latter is also held to his personal responsibility for it. And last, the law treats the slave so fully as a rational and responsible human, that it even bestows on him the right of litigation against his own master, in one case. Any African setting up a plea of unlawful detention in bondage, against his master, is allowed to sue *in forma pauperis*, in the courts of law. How could the fact be more clearly defined, that the institution of slavery treats the slave as a rational human being, and gives the master property in nothing but his labour?

Yet Senator Sumner points triumphantly to the words of the South Carolina statute as proving that slavery makes the servant a mere thing; and all smaller Abolitionists have caught up his special pleading. The cane of Mr. Brooks having given him, as it seems, a special taste for things South Carolinian, he hunted up a clause where the law of that State declares, that slaves and their children shall be held in every respect as "chattels personal." This proves beyond a peradventure, he says, that the law reduces the slave to a mere thing, as though he were an *ox* or *bureau*. Yet, a hundred other laws of South Carolina treat him as a responsible man! Any honest mind will perceive the explanation, at once; which is, that the lawyers of South Carolina were not aiming, in this law, to settle the question of the moral nature of slavery; but to decide whether property in a slave should be regarded as pertaining to the *real*, or to the *personal* estate of a citizen; and in deciding it, they very properly had more regard to legal perspicuity than to ethical accuracy of definition. Let us suppose that among the statutes of the British Parliament, there should be one (as there very probably is) declaring that when a master mechanic dies, having an indentured apprentice, the unfinished term of service of this apprentice should be held as belonging to his personal effects, and should be so used for the benefit of his heirs or creditors. And let us suppose, farther, that in defining this fact, some such words as these should be used: that said apprentice should be held in every respect, as pertaining unto the personal estate of the deceased. Then, the same logic would prove that the British laws reduce an apprentice to a mere chattel! But we have a better illustration of its folly. God says, Genesis xxvi. 14: "Isaac had *possessions* of flocks, and herds, and servants." Leviticus, xxv. 45: "Of the children of strangers that do sojourn among you, of them shall you buy: ... and they shall be your *possession*." Exodus, xxi. 20, 21: "And if a man smite his servant or his maid with a rod, and he die under his hand: he shall be surely punished. Notwithstanding, if he continue a day or two, he shall not be punished: *for he is his money*." Does God's law dehumanize the slave, and reduce him to a mere chattel? We repeat, then, that, according to the slave institutions of the Southern States, it is only the labour of the servant which belongs to the master, and is treated as property.

Let it be understood, then, from the beginning, that we are not inquiring into the moral character of that thing which Abolitionists paint as domestic slavery; a something horrid with the groans of oppressed innocence and the clang of unrighteous stripes; a something which aims to reduce a man to a brute, and denies him his natural right to serve his Creator and save his soul. We begin by asserting that these things, if they ever exist in fact, are not domestic slavery, but the abuses of it. We are not the apologists of them: we no more defend them than do the Abolitionists. In this discussion we have nothing more to do with them, except to express, once for all, our strong abhorrence and reprobation of all such unlawful abuses of a lawful institution. It has been a favourite trick of our opponents, to represent the abuses of the relation so prominently and odiously, that the defender of slavery shall be held up to the abhorrence of the publick as the defender of the abuses. Especially if he is a clergyman, (and necessity has thrown our side of this discussion very much into the hands of Southern clergymen,) do they raise a holy clamour, representing the unnatural wickedness of a desecrating of the sacred office to apologize for such iniquities. Their object is to raise a prejudice against us in advance, which will deprive us of a dispassionate and just hearing. With all dispassionate and just readers, for whom alone we write, it should be enough for us to repeat emphatically, that it is only the relation of domestic slavery as authorized by God, that we defend; and not the abuses it has received at the hands of wicked men. The parental authority, and civil government, and the operations of God's own church, are often abused also. The intelligent reader, and especially the intelligent Englishman, will remember how triumphantly this shallow sophism of arguing against a thing from its abuses, is exposed by Burke, in his reply to Bolingbroke's posthumous assault on Christianity, the ironical "Defence of Natural Society." Such argument from abuses can only be just when it is shown that the wrongs pointed out are not incidental abuses, but legitimate, and necessary, and uniform consequences of the institution itself. But that the incidental evils of African slavery among us are not such, is abundantly proved by the simple fact, that thousands of masters held slaves among us, and yet perpetrated none of these abuses. About the relative frequency of such abuses, we shall have something to say at a subsequent place. Enough now to point to the fact, that by the vast majority of our servants they were unfelt, so that they cannot be necessary parts of the system.

We conclude these preliminary definitions by requesting the reader to note well what is the moral character which we understand the Bible to assign to slavery. We do not admit that it is a thing in itself evil, but yet attended with such circumstances, in the eyes of many merciful and humane masters who have found themselves by inheritance unwilling slaveholders, that a change would be attended with still greater mischiefs: so that they are excusable for its continuance for a time. This is the view of many moderate and kind anti-slavery men; it is not ours. We do not hold that slaveholding is only justified as belonging to that class of wrongs, to which the laws of Moses assigned polygamy, which ought not to have been done, but which, when done, cannot be undone, except by the perpetrating of a greater wrong. We assert that *the Bible teaches that the relation of master and slave is perfectly lawful and right, provided only its duties be lawfully fulfilled*. When we say this, we shall not be understood as saying that all men ought to live in this relation, notwithstanding the wide diversities of their condition and characters, or that it would be politic, or even right, for all. But we say that the relation is not sin in itself; but may be perfectly righteous and innocent, and not merely excusable. And we are free to confess that unless the Bible taught us this truth, we should be obliged to hold with the decided Abolitionists. We could never be of the number of those, who attempt to transmute the essential traits of moral right and wrong, at the demand of expediency, and to excuse the continuance of a radical injustice, by the inconvenience of repairing it. Duty belongs to man; consequences to God.

§ 2. THE CURSE UPON CANAAN.

The student of history perceives that, whatever may be the moral character of domestic slavery, it is one of the most hoary institutions of the human race. It has prevailed in every age and continent, and under patriarchal, monarchical, despotic, aristocratic, republican and democratic governments; while secular history gives us no account of its origin. But Sacred Writ informs us, and traces it to the earlier generations of the human family as refounded after the flood. In Genesis, ix. 20 to 27, we have the following brief narrative: "And Noah began to be an husbandman, and he planted a vineyard: and he drank of the wine and was drunken: and he was uncovered within his tent. And Ham, the father of Canaan, saw the nakedness of his father, and told his two brethren without. And Shem and Japhet took a garment, and laid it upon both their shoulders, and went backward and covered the nakedness of their father; and their faces were backward, and they saw not their father's nakedness. And Noah awoke from his wine, and knew what his younger son had done unto him; and he said, Cursed be Canaan; a servant of servants shall he be unto his brethren. And he said, Blessed be the Lord God of Shem; and Canaan shall be his servant. God shall enlarge Japhet and he shall dwell in the tents of Shem; and Canaan shall be his servant."

In explanation of it, the following remarks may be made; on which the majority of sound expositors are agreed. In this transaction, Noah acts as an inspired prophet, and also as the divinely chosen, patriarchal head of church and state, which were then confined to his one family. God's approbation attended his verdict, as is proved by the fact that the divine Providence has been executing it for many ages since Noah's death. Canaan probably concurred in the indecent and unnatural sin of Ham.

As these early men were extremely ambitious of a numerous and prosperous posterity, Ham's punishment, and Canaan's, consisted in the mortification of hearing their descendants doomed to a degraded lot. These descendants were included in the punishment of their wicked progenitors on that well-known principle of God's providence, which "visits the sin of the fathers upon the children," and this again is explained by the fact, that depraved parents will naturally rear depraved children, unless God interfere by a grace to which they have no claim; so that not only punishment, but the sinfulness, becomes hereditary. Doubtless God's sentence, here pronounced by Noah, was based on his foresight of the fact, that Ham's posterity, like their father, would be peculiarly degraded in morals; as actual history testifies of them, so far as its voice extends.

Some have been weak enough to draw a justification of slavery from the fact, that the bondage of Canaan's posterity is predicted. This logic the Abolitionists have, of course, delighted to expose; it was easy to show, by sundry biblical instances, like that of the Assyrian employed to chastise Israel, and then punished by God for his own rapacity, that it is no justification of one's acts to find that God, in his inscrutable and holy workings, has overruled them to the effectuation of his own righteous, secret purposes. And our opponents, with a treachery fully equal to the folly of our unwise advocates, usually represent this as nearly the whole amount, and the fair exemplar, of our biblical argument. Such is not the use we design to make of this important piece of history.

It does in the first place, what all secular history and speculations fail to do: it gives us the origin of domestic slavery. And we find that it was appointed by God as the punishment of, and remedy for (nearly all God's providential chastisements are also remedial) the peculiar moral degradation of a part of the race. God here ordains that this depravity shall find its necessary restraints, and the welfare of the more virtuous its safeguard against the depraved, by the bondage of the latter. He introduces that feature of political society, for the justice of which we shall have occasion to contend; that although men have all this trait of natural equality that they are children of a common father, and sharers of a common humanity, and subjects of the same law of love; yet, in practice, they shall be subject to social inequalities determined by their own characters, and their fitness or unfitness to use privileges for their own and their neighbours' good.

But second: this narrative gives us more than a prediction. The words of Noah are not a mere prophecy; they are a verdict, a moral sentence pronounced upon conduct, by competent authority; that verdict sanctioned by God. Now if the verdict is righteous, and the execution blessed by God, it can hardly be, that the executioners of it are guilty for putting it in effect. Can one believe that the descendants of Shem and Japhet, with this sentence in their hands, and the divine commendation just bestowed on them for acting unlike Ham, could have reasonably felt guilty for accepting that control over their guilty fellow-men which God himself had assigned? For the vital difference between the case of the Assyrians, when their guilty ambition was permissively employed by God to punish the back-slidings of his own people, and the case of Shem and Japhet, is this: The Assyrians were cursed by God for doing their predicted work, in the very sentence; Shem and Japhet were blessed by Him in the very verdict which assigns Canaan as their servant.

It may be that we should find little difficulty in tracing the lineage of the present Africans to Ham. But this inquiry is not essential to our argument. If one case is found where God has authorized domestic slavery, the principle is settled, that it cannot necessarily be sin in itself. It is proper that we should say, in conclusion, that this passage of Scripture is not regarded, nor advanced, as of prime force and importance in this argument. Others more decisive will follow.

§ 3. ABRAHAM A SLAVEHOLDER.

The references to the bondsmen of Abraham and his son Isaac are the following: Genesis xiv., 14, "And when Abram heard that his brother," (or relative, viz.: Lot,) "was taken captive, he armed his trained servants, born in his own house, three hundred and eighteen, and pursued them unto Dan. And he divided himself against them, he and his servants, by night," etc. Genesis xvii., 10, etc., "This is my covenant which ye shall keep, between me and you, and thy seed after thee; every man-child among you shall be circumcised," ... v. 12, "And he that is eight days old shall be circumcised among you, every man-child in your generations; he that is born in the house, or bought with money of any stranger, which is not of thy seed. He that is born in thy house and he that is bought with thy money must needs be circumcised," and v. 26, 27, "In the self-same day was Abraham circumcised, and Ishmael his son; and all the men of his house, born in the house and bought with money of the stranger, were circumcised with him." Genesis xviii. 17 to 19, "And the *Lord* said, Shall I hide from Abraham that thing which I do: seeing that Abraham shall surely become a great and mighty nation, and all the nations of the earth shall be blessed in him? For I know him, that he will command his children and his household after him, and they shall keep the way of the *Lord,* to do justice and judgment: that the Lord may bring upon Abraham that which he hath spoken of him." Genesis xx. 14, "And Abimelech" (seeking reconciliation with Abraham for the wrong intended to Sarah his wife, at God's command,) "took sheep and oxen, and men-servants and women-servants, and gave them unto Abraham, and restored him Sarah his wife." Genesis xxiv. 35, Eliezer, when seeking a wife for Isaac, says: "And the Lord hath blessed my master greatly, and he is become great; and he hath given him flocks, and herds, and silver, and gold, and men-servants, and maid-servants, and camels and asses." And Genesis, xxvi. 12, 14, it is said of Isaac: "And the LORD blessed him. And the man waxed great and went forward and grew until he became very great. For he had possession of flocks, and possession of herds, and great store of servants."

It appears then, that Abraham, "the friend of God," and Isaac, the most holy and spotless of the Patriarchs, were great slaveholders. But before pursuing the argument farther, it may be prudent to remove the quibble that these servants were not slaves, in the sense of our African slaves, but only humble clansmen, retainers, or hirelings. At least one writer would prove this by the fact that Abraham did not fear to arm three hundred and eighteen of them. For had they been real slaves, says he, they would not have continued so one day after getting arms in their hands. The retort most appropriate would be, that Abraham was not afraid to arm his slaves, though actual slaves, because there were no saucy, meddling, Yankee Abolitionists in those days to preach insubordination and make ill blood between masters and servants. But, more seriously, what shall we say of the professed reasoning which assumes the very point in debate? viz.: that slavery is an evil; and thence infers the conclusion that these could not be slaves, because they did not seize the power to burst the bonds of such an evil when placed in their reach? If their bondage was not evil, which is the question *sub judice* in this debate, then they would not necessarily desire to burst from it. And that these were actual slaves is clear, because the words for bondsman and bondsmaid here used are, in every case, *ebed* and *shippheh*, which are defined by every honest lexicon to mean actual slaves, which are used in that sense alone everywhere else in the Hebrew Scriptures, which are contrasted in the book of Leviticus with the "hired servant," or *sasir*. A part of these servants were bought from foreigners with Abraham's money. They are represented along with his very sheep and oxen as his property.

Abraham and Isaac then, were all their lives literal slaveholders, on a large scale. Now we do not argue that this fact alone, coupled with the other, that they were good men, proves that slaveholding is innocent. The Abolitionists, fond of an easy victory on a false issue, always hasten to represent this as the amount of the argument; and then, their reply is obvious—that the example of truly good men is no rule of ethics for us, unless supported by the expressed or implied approval of God; for good men are imperfect, and many of their errors are recorded, by the honesty of the sacred writers, for our warning—that Abraham himself was guilty of falsehood to Abimelech, King of Gerar, and especially that he was betrayed into the gross sin of concubinage. Hence they say, Abraham's example no more proves slaveholding innocent than concubinage. We reply, that all these remarks, except the last, are perfectly just; but they have no application to the case, because God's sanction of Abraham's example as a slaveholder is expressly found in the narrative. The cases of slaveholding and concubinage are totally different. First, because the origin of the latter sin in the accursed lineage of Cain, and the act of the murderer Lamech, is impliedly stamped with God's condemnation, (Genesis iv. 19,) whereas the origin of domestic slavery is given us in the righteous sentence of God for depraved conduct. Second, Abraham fell into the sins of falsehood and concubinage but once, under violent temptation. There is no evidence that either he or Isaac ever practised them again, but both lived and died without one recorded qualm of conscience, in the practice of slaveholding, and made it one of their last acts, before passing to the judgment-seat of God, to bequeath their slaves, as property, to their heirs. Third, in Genesis xxiv. 35, and xxvi. 12, 14, it is represented that the bestowal of a multitude of slaves on Abraham and Isaac was a mark of the divine favour. In the first passage, it is indeed only the pious Eliezer who states this; but in the second, it is stated of Isaac by the sacred narrative itself. Now to represent God as blessing a favoured saint by bestowing providentially gifts which it is a sin to have, implicates God in the sin. Fourth, in Genesis xviii. 17 to 19, Jehovah expresses his love for Abraham, approbation for his character, and purpose to exalt him as a blessing to all nations, because "He knew him that he would command his children and his household after him, that they shall keep the way of the *Lord* to do justice and judgment." What was this "household," distinct from his children? Hebrew usage and the context answer with one voice, his slaves. Then, God's high favour to Abraham was explained by the fact that he foresaw the patriarch would govern his children and slaves religiously and righteously. Now we ask emphatically, does a holy God bless a misguided and sinning man for the manner in which he perseveres in the sinful practice, be that manner what it may? If the relation of master and slave were sinful, would not the virtue of terminating the relation at once, so far transcend the questionable credit of using it to make the wronged and oppressed victim live piously, that it would be impossible for God to bestow his peculiar praise on the latter, where the former was lacking? There is no righteous way to perpetuate an unrighteous relation. Therefore God's blessing Abraham for his good government of his slaves, is proof that it is not a sin to have slaves to govern.

But, last and chiefly, we have a still stronger fact to present. When Abraham was directed in Genesis xvii., 10, etc., to circumcise himself as a sign of the covenant between God and him, he was also directed to circumcise all his male children. The parental relationship was made the ground of their inclusion in the same covenant. And God directed his slaves also, "born in his house, or bought with his money of any foreigner," to be circumcised along with him. The parental tie brought his children under the religious rite of circumcision; the bond of master and servant brought his servants under it. Here then, we have the relationship of domestic slavery sanctioned, along with the parental and filial, by God's own injunction, by a participation in the holiest sacrament of the ancient church. Would a holy God thus baptize an unholy relation? Would he make it the ground of admission to a religious ordinance? To see a feeble illustration of the absurdity of such a conclusion, consider what would be thought of a minister of the New Testament, in which our Saviour has forbidden a plurality of wives, if that minister should desecrate the marriage ceremonial of his church, knowingly, to sanctify the union of the felon in the act of bigamy? Such a desecration would surely be not less shocking in the Author, than in a minister of religion.

And here, the favourite plea of the anti-slavery men fails entirely—that Abraham lived in the dawn of religious light; that the revelation given him was only partial, and that while he possessed the rectitude of conscience which would have made him relinquish all sinful relations, if enlightened as to their true character, the customs of his age misled him to commit things which Christians afterwards taught to be sinful, and that therefore, these things, excusable in him because of his ignorance, would be wickedness in us. There is some truth in these statements, but they have nothing on earth to do with this example; because the circumcision of the slaves was God's act, and not Abraham's. God knows all things. He is perfectly holy and unchangeable. If he had seen that slavery is intrinsically wrong, and had intended at some future day to declare it so, would he at this time have sanctioned it by making it the ground of a solemn ordinance of religion? As we shall see, this cry of the imperfection of the Old Testament revelation is of Socinian origin, and is essentially false, in the sense in which it is uttered. But be it as just as any statement could be, it has no application here; because our whole inference is drawn from the acts of God himself, and not of an Old Testament Saint.

§ 4. HAGAR REMANDED TO SLAVERY BY GOD.

Sarah, in a season of desperation at her childless condition, seems to have been tempted to imitate the corrupt expedient which was prevalent among the Canaanites around her, and which still prevails in the East. According to this usage, the chief wife, or wife proper, gives to her husband a concubine from among her slaves, as a sort of substitute for herself; and the offspring of the connexion is regarded as her own child. Abram, misled by evil example, and by the solicitations of his wife—the person who would have had the best right to complain of his act—concurred temporarily in the arrangement, and received his Egyptian slave Hagar as an inferior wife. The favour of her master, and the prospective honour of being the mother of offspring, which has always been exceedingly prized by Oriental women, so inflated the servant with impudence, that she no longer treated her mistress with decent respect. When Sarah bitterly complained of this, Abram replied by reminding her that Hagar was still her slave; and that she was entitled, as a mistress, to compel her to observe a suitable demeanour. When Sarah proceeded to exert this authority, probably administering corporal punishment to Hagar for some instance of impertinence, the latter ran away, and pursued the direction which led to her native country, Egypt. It was then that the angel of the LORD found her "by the fountain in the way to Shur. And he said, Hagar, Sarai's maid, whence camest thou? and whither wilt thou go? And she said, I flee from the face of my mistress Sarai. And the angel of the LORD said unto her, Return to thy mistress, and submit thyself under her hands." Genesis xvi., 7 to 9. He then proceeded to unfold the future of her unborn son, and Hagar obeyed his commands. From verses 10th and 13th, we learn certainly that this angel was a Divine Person. For, in the first place, he promises Hagar, "I will multiply thy seed exceedingly;" but none but the Almighty could truthfully make such a promise in his own name, as it is here made. In the latter place we are informed that it was the LORD (in Hebrew, *Jehovah*; the most characteristic and incommendable name of God) that spake unto her; and Hagar called his name: "Thou God, seest me." We remark again, that Hagar was certainly in the relation of domestic slavery, and not of a hired servant, to Abraham and Sarai. She is called *Shiphheh*, which is the regular word for female slave in the Old Testament. Had she not been an actual slave, Sarai would never have presumed, according to Oriental usage, to dispose of her person in the manner related. Here, then, we have God, himself, the Angel Jehovah, who can be no other than the Second Person of the Trinity, Christ, commanding this fugitive to return into the relation of domestic slavery, and submit to it. Can that relation be in itself sinful? To assert this, would make our adorable Saviour *particeps criminis*. He cannot have required a soul to return into a sinful state. He never requires of his servants more than their duty; so that if Sarai had possessed no real and just title to Hagar's services as a slave—if the claim had been a mere imposition and injustice, she would not have been required to submit to it. Abolitionists attempt to evade this by saying that Hagar was instructed to return and submit to bondage on the same principle on which Christ instructs us, when wrongfully smitten on one cheek to turn the other likewise. This, say they, by no means implies that the smiting was just. We reply, that the parallel cannot be drawn. Had Hagar been in the hand of an unjust mistress, it would have been her duty in Christian forbearance to "take it patiently, though buffeted wrongfully." But she was not now in Sarai's hand. She had successfully escaped it, and was far advanced in her' journey to her native Egypt, where she evidently expected to find friends and shelter. Under these circumstances, it is preposterous to say that the grace of Christian forbearance required of her to return voluntarily whither no claim of right drew her, and subject herself to unjust and unauthorized persecution again. We ask, Does Christ so press the duty of peaceableness, as to sacrifice to it the whole personal well-being and rightful interests of the innocent victim of unjust aggression? Is his chief object, in these lessons of forbearance, to gratify and pamper the lust of persecution in the aggressor? Is there no right of just self-defence left? Surely he teaches us that we owe a duty to our own life and well-being, as well as to our fellow-men's. When we are wronged, we are to defend this right only in such ways as become a son of peace—a man of forgiveness. But the same Saviour who taught his disciples to render good for evil when injured, also commanded them: "When they persecute you in one city, flee ye into another." When a peaceable escape can be secured from injustice, it is both the privilege and duty of the most forgiving Christian on earth to use it. Now Hagar was in such a condition; had her subjection to Sarai been, as the Abolitionists say slavery is, a condition of unjust persecution, the Saviour's instructions to her would doubtless have been: "Now that you have escaped the injustice of her that wronged you, flee to another city." His remanding her to Sarai shows that the subjection was lawful and right.

It has been objected again, that we cannot argue this, unless we are willing to argue the lawfulness of concubinage; because to send Hagar back to her bondage was to resign her again to this relation. We utterly deny it. The LORD only says to her: "Return to thy mistress and submit thyself under her hands;" not "Return to thy master's bed." There is not one particle of proof that Abram continued his improper connexion with her after these transactions. Nor is there more worth in the remark, that subsequently, the same divine Being met Hagar wandering in the same wilderness, and did not require her to return, but assisted her journey. The answer is, that she was then under no obligation to return; because her master had fully manumitted her, and bestowed her freedom on her.

§ 5. SLAVERY IN THE LAWS OF MOSES.

God, in accordance with his covenant with Abraham, set apart Israel, through the ministry of Moses, to be his peculiar and holy people, his witness in the midst of an apostate world, to keep alive the services and precepts of true morality and true religion, till, in the fulness of time, Jesus Christ should come in the flesh, and begin the Christianizing of all nations. To effect these objects, He renewed his revelation of the eternal and unchangeable moral law, from Sinai, in the Decalogue; and he also gave, by the intervention of Moses, various religious and civil laws, which were peculiar to the Jews, and were never intended to be observed after the resurrection of Jesus Christ. The great object of all this legislation, was to set apart the Jewish nation as a holy people, peculiarly dedicated to purity of moral life, and the maintenance of true religion, amidst corrupt and idolatrous generations. To effect this, God found it necessary to raise a barrier to familiar social intercourse between the Israelites and their corrupting heathen neighbours; and sundry of the expedients by which this barrier was raised, were prohibitions of usages which would have been, in themselves, neither right nor wrong, but morally indifferent, as the eating of pork. Some of those laws having the same object in view, required acts in their original nature indifferent; such as circumcision and eating the Passover. But it is totally inconsistent with the holiness of God, and with his purpose of setting Israel apart to a holy life, that any of those peculiar laws should require acts in themselves wicked, or forbid things in themselves morally binding. It would be impiety to represent God as capable of commanding what is wrong; and to enjoin sin in order to make people holy, would be a folly and a contradiction. God's revealed will, so far as it is revealed for a rule of life, either permanent or temporary, can contain nothing but what is right, and pure, and just. If it had been a positive moral duty to eat pork, this holy God would never have made the prohibition to eat it a part even of the temporary, ceremonial laws of his servants. Had it been morally wrong to kill, roast, and eat a lamb, God would never have enjoined on them the institution of the Passover. These conclusions are as plain as the alphabet.

Now then, if we find any particular thing either sanctioned or enjoined, in the peculiar ceremonial or civil institutions of Moses, it does not prove that thing to be morally binding on us, in this century, or necessarily politic and proper for us; but it does prove it to be, in its essential moral character, innocent. That thing cannot be sin in itself. So, Jno. David Michaelis, in his *Commentaries on the Laws of Moses*, Book 1, Art. 1. This is the important and just distinction. The fact that animal sacrifices were required in the ceremonial laws of Moses, does not prove that it is our duty, under the Christian dispensation, to offer sacrifices, or that it is appropriate for us to do so; but it does prove that the act would be in itself innocent (though useless) for us, and for every one, if it had not been forbidden in subsequent revelation. Otherwise, a holy God would never have enjoined or sanctioned it at all.

Therefore, the fact that God expressly authorized domestic slavery, among the peculiar and temporary civil laws of the Jews, while it does not prove that it is our positive duty to hold slaves, does prove that it is innocent to hold them, unless it has been subsequently forbidden by God. Now then, let us see what God authorized by Moses. Exodus xxi. 2 to 6: "If thou buy an Hebrew servant, (Ebed,) six years he shall serve; and in the seventh he shall go out free for nothing. If he came in by himself he shall go out by himself: if he were married, then his wife shall go out with him. If his master have given him a wife, and she have borne him sons or daughters, the wife and her children shall be her master's, and he shall go out by himself. And if the servant shall plainly say, I love my master, my wife, and my children; I will not go out free: then his master shall bring him unto the judges; he shall also bring him unto the door, or unto the door-post; and his master shall bore his ear through with an awl; and he shall serve him forever," (that is, probably, until the year of Jubilee, which came once in fifty years. See Leviticus xxv. 41.)

This, cries the anti-slavery man, was only temporary servitude. We reply: but it was involuntary servitude, though temporary. It gave to the master the right to compel the labour of the servant without his consent; and this is a sanction of the principle of our institution. What will be said then to the following? Leviticus xxv. 44 to 46: "Both thy bondmen and thy bondmaids which thou shalt have, shall be of the heathen that are round about you; of them shall ye buy bondmen and bondmaids. Moreover, of the children of the strangers that do sojourn among you, of them shall ye buy and of their families that are with you, which they begat in your land; and they shall be your possession," (your property.) "And ye shall take them as an inheritance for your children after you, to inherit them for a possession; they shall be your bondmen forever; but over your brethren, the children of Israel, ye shall not rule over one another with rigour."

The antithesis in the position of the two laws shows that these heathen slaves were not to go free at the year of Jubilee, like Hebrew slaves. They are to be bondmen forever. They and their children, slaves by birth, are to descend from father to son, as heritable property. There was to be "no seventh year freedom here; there is no Jubilee liberation." So says the learned divine, Moses Stuart, of Andover, himself an anti-slavery man. And so say all respectable Hebrew antiquaries. Indeed it would be hard to construct language defining more strongly and fully all those features of domestic slavery most contradictory to the theory of Abolitionists. They were to be bought and sold. They were heritable property: (Mr. Sumner would prove hence, "mere chattels.") Here is involuntary slavery for life, expressly authorized to God's own peculiar and holy people, in the strongest and most careful terms. The relation, then, must be innocent in itself. With what show of candour can men say, in the face of a sanction so full, so emphatic, so hearty, that Moses, finding the hoary institution of domestic slavery so deeply rooted that it would be impossible then to abolish it, *tolerated* it, and limited it by all the restrictions which he could apply, calculated to cut off its worst horrors? We ask, was Moses the author of these laws, or God? Does the Almighty, the Unchangeable, the Holy, connive at moral abuses, like a puny human magistrate, and content himself, where he dare not denounce a sin, with pruning its growth a little? We ask again: Is this gloss borne out by the facts? Was Moses, in fact, timid in assailing old and deeply-rooted vices, and in demanding that they should be eradicated wholly? Let his uncompromising legislation against Idolatry and Adultery answer. The truth is, such writers as use the above language know nothing about the true nature of domestic slavery, and draw their inferences only from their prejudices. God and Moses knew it well. They knew that it was an institution which, when not abused, was suitable to the character of the depraved persons for whom it was designed, and wholesome and benign. Hence, they prohibit all inhuman abuses of it; and then they do not tolerate it merely as an unavoidable wrong; but they expressly legalize it, as right. An honest mind can make nothing less of their words. But in Numbers xxxi. 25 to 30, and Joshua ix. 20 to 27, we have instances which are, if possible, still stronger. In the former passage the people of Midian had been conquered by God's command, and the captives and spoils brought home; the captives to be slaves for life according to the law of Leviticus, ch. xxv. The book of Numbers then proceeds: "And the Lord spake unto Moses saying, Take the sum of prey that was taken both of man and of beast, thou and Eleazer the priest and the chief fathers of the congregation; and divide the prey into two parts; between them that took the war upon them who went out to battle, and between all the congregation. And levy a tribute unto the Lord of the men of war which went out to battle: one soul of five hundred, both of the persons, and of the beeves, and of the asses and of the sheep: Take it of their half, and give it unto Eleazer the priest, for an heave-offering of the *Lord.* And of the children of Israel's half thou shalt take one portion of fifty, of the persons, of the beeves, of the asses and of the flocks, of all manner of beasts, and give them unto the Levites which keep the charge of the tabernacle of the Lord." In verses 40th and 46th, we read farther that the "*Lord's* tribute of the persons" of the first half, "was thirty and two persons," and of the second half, "three hundred and twenty." Here God commands a portion of these slaves to be set apart to a sacred use, and dedicated to himself, that they might become the property of the ministers of religion. The second instance is not contained in the books of Moses, but in the history of his successor Joshua: we group it with the former, for its similarity. In Joshua, ch. ix., we are told that while he was triumphantly engaged in the destruction of the condemned heathen tribes of Palestine, according to God's command, the people of Gibeon, a part of the doomed race, despairing of a successful defence, adopted this stratagem to save themselves. Under pretence that they were not of Palestine at all, but from a very distant place, their ambassadors obtained from the leaders of the Israelites a very stringent oath of amity. This pledge the elders incautiously gave, without seeking the divine direction. In a very few days they learned to their astonishment, that these Gibeonites lived in the very heart of Palestine, close to the spot where they were encamped, and that they were of the very race which they were appointed to destroy. But they had sworn in the name of Jehovah not to destroy them. In this state of things, the princes and Joshua determined to punish them for their falsehood, and at the same time substantially observe their oath, by leaving them unhurt, but reducing them to slavery as the serfs of the Tabernacle and its ministers. In verses 23d and 27th, Joshua told them: "Now, therefore, ye are cursed, and there shall none of you be freed from being bondmen," (Ebed, i. e., slaves,) "and hewers of wood and drawers of water for the house of my God." "And Joshua made them that day hewers of wood and drawers of water for the congregation and for the altar of the *Lord*, even unto this day, in that place which he should choose." This compact the Gibeonites seem gladly to have accepted. In 2d Samuel, ch. xxi., we find this same race of serfs still living among the Israelites, under the same compact. King Saul, David's predecessor, having broken it by killing many of them, God himself interposed, and required a satisfaction for the breach. Here we have evidence that the slaves of heathen origin were not freed by the Jubilee, for centuries had now elapsed and they were still slaves. We also see evidence that the contract made by Joshua was not regarded by God as unlawful. In this case, also, we find God accepting a religious offering of slaves for the service of his sanctuary. And these, while real slaves, did not belong each to an individual master, but were slaves to an institution and a caste, a form of bondage always justly regarded as less benevolent than the former.

Yet men say slavery is a wicked relation, which God only tolerated and curbed in the Old Testament. The *Lord's* claiming his tythe of slaves (as of cattle and wheat) seems to the candid man a strange way of expressing bare tolerance! Was it not enough to leave the laity of the "holy people" polluted with the sin of slaveholding, without proceeding by his own express injunction to introduce the "taint" into the still more sacred caste of the priesthood? Did the God of all holiness direct a part of the wages of iniquity to be set apart for his holy uses? Perhaps it may be said that He regarded the holy use as sanctifying the unholy source of the offering. The surmise is blasphemous. But see Deuteronomy xxiii. 18: "Thou shalt not bring the hire of a whore or the price of a dog into the house of the *Lord* thy God for any vow: for even both these are abomination to the *Lord* thy God." To set apart to God's use property wickedly acquired was an insult to his holiness: and to offer Him even what was acquired by the sale of an animal ceremonially unclean, was resented as a type of the same sin. The consecration of these slaves to sacred uses is therefore the strongest possible proof that slaves are lawful property. To sum up: The divine permission and sanction of slavery to the very people whom God was setting apart to a holy life, the consecration of slaves as property to a sacred purpose, the regulating by law of the duties flowing from the relation, all prove that it was then a lawful and innocent one. Otherwise, we should have the holy God teaching sin. If it was innocent once in its intrinsic nature, it is innocent now, unless it has been subsequently prohibited by God. But no such prohibition can be shown.

§ 6. SLAVERY IN THE DECALOGUE.

Although the Ten Commandments were given along with the civil and ceremonial laws of the Hebrews, we do not include them along with the latter, because the Decalogue was, unlike them, given for all men and all dispensations. It is a solemn repetition of the sum of those duties founded on the natures of man and of God, and on their relations, enjoined on all ages alike. It contains nothing ceremonial, or of merely temporary obligation; (which is binding merely because it is commanded;) but all is of perpetual, moral obligation. It claims to be, rightly explained, a perfect and complete rule. Our Saviour repeatedly adopts it as the eternal sum of all duty, on which hang all the law and the prophets, that is, all Scripture. Accordingly, we find that the mode of its republication gave to this Decalogue a grandeur and weight shared by no secular or ceremonial precepts. Deuteronomy v. informs us that it was delivered first, thus receiving the precedence, that it was spoken by God himself in articulate words, heard by all the quaking multitude, in tones of thunder, from the smoking summit of Sinai, with the terrible concomitants of angelic hosts, devouring fire, lightnings and earthquakes; that God added no more, thus refusing to all the subsequent precepts the honour of such a publication, and that He himself then engraved it on stone, signifying by the imperishable material, the perpetuity of this law.

Hence, all the principles of right stated or implied in this Decalogue, are valid, not for Hebrews only, but for all men and ages. They rise wholly above the temporary and positive precepts, which were only binding while they were expressly enjoined. They have not been, because they cannot be, repealed or modified; they are as immutable as God's perfections. In our Saviour's words, "Till heaven and earth pass, one jot or one tittle of this law shall not pass away."

Now, our argument is, that in this short summary, the relation of master and slave is mentioned twice; and that in modes which are a recognition of its lawfulness. It is introduced as a basis of duties and rights founded upon it, and those rights are defended, and those duties enjoined. But if it were an unlawful relation, what rights could grow out of it except the slave's right to have it broken? And what duties of the master could be founded on it, except the duties of discontinuing, repenting of, and repairing its wrongs? In the 4th Commandment, Exod. xx. 10, it is made the master's duty to cause the slave to observe the Sabbath day. After the 8th Commandment had forbidden injury to our fellow-man's property in act, by overt theft, the 10th, (v. 17,) prohibits its injury even in thought by corrupt coveting. And in the enumeration of possessions thus carefully covered from assault, are men-servants (*ebed*) and maid-servants, along with real estate and cattle. If the reader would feel the strength of the argument implied in these facts, let him ask himself what would have been his amazement, if, after the description which God's word gives of the authority, righteousness, purity, and perpetuity of this Decalogue, he had read in it, that highwaymen and pirates are commanded to enforce Sabbath observance on their injured victims, and that we must not covet our neighbour's concubine, or the stolen goods in his possession? And this, without hint of the guilt of violence, concubinage, and theft. It would be impossible for either understanding or conscience to reconcile itself to the anomaly; he would feel, inevitably, that God was incapable of such implied sanction of sin.

§ 7. OBJECTIONS TO THE OLD TESTAMENT ARGUMENT.

To state the arguments from the laws of Moses and the Decalogue has not required a large space, because those conclusions are so plain and sound, that many words were not needed. But the cavils, objections and special pleadings of the Abolitionists teem like the frogs of Egypt, engendered in the mire of ignorance and prejudice, so numerous because so worthless. And when it is seen that we perhaps expend more space in their refutation than we did in the direct argument, the heedless reader may possibly be inclined to say to himself, that there must be something wrong in an argument to which so much can be objected. We beg him to observe then, that we pause to explode these objections, not because they are of any weight, but because we purpose to make thorough work with our opponents. When we have finished these rejoinders, we shall take the impartial reader to witness, that not only the weight, but the least appearance of plausibility in these cavils has been blown into thin air. And then we shall have the right to infer that their number indicates, not the questionable character of our positions, but only a fixed and blind prejudice against the truth in our adversaries.

It is objected that domestic slavery among the Hebrews was a much milder institution than in Virginia, and that, therefore, we have no right to argue from the one to the other. If it were true that Hebrew slavery was milder, it might show that we were wrong in the way in which we treated our slaves; but it could not prove that slaveholding was wrong. The principle would still be established, for the lawfulness of the relation. But let it be noted that the peculiar mitigations of slavery affected only slaves of Hebrew blood, not Gentiles. Whatever may have been the leniency of the system, the state of the Gentile slaves showed the essential features of slavery among us, the right to the slave's labour for life without his consent, property in that labour, the right to buy, sell and bequeath it; the right to enforce it on the slave by corporal punishments, which might have any degree of severity short of death. (See Exod. xxi. 20, 21.) Virginians had no interest to contend for any stricter form of slavery than this.

Second. It is said that the permission to buy, possess, and bequeath slaves of heathen origin, which we have cited, related only to the seven condemned tribes of Canaan, and was part of the divinely appointed penalty for their wickedness. Even such a man as Dr. Wayland, of Brown University, Rhode Island, has adopted this plea, thus justifying in a prominent instance the assertion that Abolitionism is grounded in a shameful ignorance of facts. The answer to the plea is, that it is expressly contrary to fact. The Hebrews were positively prohibited to reserve any of the seven condemned nations for slaves, and were enjoined to exterminate them all, lest the contagion of their vile morals should corrupt Israel. On the other hand, they were told that they might buy them slaves of any of the other Gentile nations around them, with whom they were to live on terms of national amity. (See Deuteronomy, xx. 10 to 18.) After directing the policy of the Hebrews towards conquered enemies from these nations, and permitting the enslaving of the captives, Moses proceeds: (v. 15.) "Thus shalt thou do unto all the cities which are very far off from thee, which are not of the cities of these nations. But of the cities of these people which the Lord thy God doth give thee for an inheritance, thou shalt save nothing alive that breatheth; but thou shalt utterly destroy them, namely, the Hittites and the Amorites, the Canaanites and the Perizzites, the Hivites and the Jebusites, as the Lord thy God hath commanded thee; that they teach you not to do after all their abominations," etc. (See also, Josh. vi. 17 to 21; viii. 26; x. 28 to 32, etc., etc.)

Third. It is objected from these very injunctions, that the examples of the commands given to the Israelites are no rules for us; that God commanded them to exterminate the seven nations of Canaan; but if we should therefore proceed to attack and destroy a neighbouring nation which had not assailed us, it would be a horrible wickedness. It is asked: Were the fanatics of the English Commonwealth in the 17th century correct when they justified their barbarities upon royalists by the examples of Joshua's slaughter of the Amorites, and Samuel's of Amalek? And we are told that our argument from Hebrew slavery is of the same absurd kind.

We reply: We willingly accept the instances. God's command to Joshua and Samuel to exterminate the Canaanites and Amalek, does prove that killing is not necessarily murder. This very instance gives us an unanswerable argument against those who oppose all capital punishments as wrong. And just so we employ the other instance, which our assailants say is parallel—Hebrew slavery—to prove that slaveholding is not necessarily sinful. But the instances are not parallel. The sanction of domestic slavery was a statute law for all generations of Hebrews; the command to exterminate the seven tribes imposed a specific task on certain individuals. It is absurd to confound an executive command, given to particular men for the once, under particular circumstances, with the sanctions of a permanent institution, designed to descend from generation to generation. The command to exterminate the seven guilty tribes was the former, the permission to hold slaves the latter. True, the example of Joshua in blotting these tribes from existence, is no authority for us to do likewise, unless we also can show a direct divine commission authorizing us for a special case. But neither was that example authority to any subsequent generation of Hebrews, after Joshua, to exterminate any other pagan tribe. Will any one say that the authority given by Moses to his fellow-citizens to hold slaves was not just as good to enable subsequent generations of Hebrews to hold slaves? Prejudice cannot carry sophistry so far. There is, therefore, no analogy between the two cases, in the point necessary for grounding the objection to our argument.

Fourth. It is said that Moses himself commanded that a runaway slave should not be surrendered to his master; thereby plainly teaching that slaves had a right to their liberty, if they could escape. This, it is urged, proves that there must be some mistake in our conclusions. Of course, this passage is quoted triumphantly as settling the question against the fugitive slave-law, required by the late Constitution of the United States. It is found in Deuteronomy xxiii. 15, 16: "Thou shalt not deliver unto his master the servant which is escaped from his master unto thee: he shall dwell with thee, even among you, in that place which he shall choose in one of thy gates, where it liketh him best; thou shalt not oppress him."

We need no better answer to this citation, than that given by a Northern divine already named, who is no friend to slavery, Rev. Moses Stuart. He says: "The first inquiry of course is: Where does his master live? Among the Hebrews or among foreigners? The language of the passage fully developes this, and answers the question. He has 'escaped from his master unto the Hebrews.' (The text says, unto *thee*, i. e., Israel.) 'He shall dwell with thee, even among you, in one of thy gates.'

Of course then, he is an immigrant, and did not dwell among them before his flight. If he had been a Hebrew servant, belonging to a Hebrew, the whole face of the thing would be changed. Restoration or restitution, if we may judge by the tenour of other property laws among the Hebrews, would have surely been enjoined. But, be that as it may, the language of the text puts it beyond a doubt, that the servant is a foreigner and has fled from a heathen master." Mr. Stuart then proceeds to assign obvious reasons why a foreign servant escaping from a heathen master was not to be restored: that the bondage from which he escaped was inordinately cruel, including the power of murder for any caprice; and that to force him back was to remand him to the darkness of heathenism, and to rob him of the light of true religion, which shone in the land of the Hebrews alone. He adds: "But if we put now the other case, viz.: that of escape from a Hebrew master, who claimed and enjoyed Hebrew rights, is not the case greatly changed? Who could take from him the property which the Mosaic law gave him a right to hold? Neither the bondsman himself, nor the neighbours of the master to whom the fugitive might come. Reclamation of him could be lawfully made, and therefore must be enforced." This explanation forces itself upon our common sense. To suppose that Moses could so formally authorize and define slavery among the Hebrews, and then enact that every slave might gain his liberty by merely stepping over the brook or imaginary line which separated the little cantons of the tribes from each other, or even by going to the next house of his master's neighbours, and claiming protection, whenever petulance, or caprice, or laziness should move him thereto; this is absurd; it is trivial child's play. It takes away with one hand what it professed to give with the other. The fact that slavery continued to exist from age to age, is proof enough that the Hebrews did not put the Abolitionist construction on the law. To this agree the respectable Hebrew antiquarians, as Horne, etc.

Fifth. It is urged that Revelation was in its plan progressive, like the morning twilight; that the Mosaic code was the early dawn; that God, for wise reasons, left many points in darkness, which the full daylight of the Gospel has since shown to be sin. And, therefore, several practices, which we are now taught to be sinful, may have been ignorantly followed by good men, and tolerated by this imperfect legislation of God's law. Yet if we, who enjoy a fuller revelation, should indulge in these practices, we should be guilty and disobedient.

Grant this, for the present. Grant, for argument's sake, that it may have been consistent with the plan of revelation to make known at first only a partial rule of duty, leaving some sins unmentioned. Yet surely it was not consistent with the truth and holiness of God, to throw a false light in that partial revelation, on those parts of man's duty which he professed to reveal! So far as any revelation from God goes, it must be a true and righteous one. If it undertook to fix a point of duty, it must fix it correctly, whatever else it might omit. Otherwise; we should have a holy, true, and good Creator, while professing to guide man to duty and life, misleading him to sin and death. Let now the reader note that the lawfulness of slavery was not one of the points omitted. God spake expressly upon it; and what he said was to authorize it.

But we do not admit that Moses' was an incomplete revelation in the sense of the Abolitionists. They are fond of representing the New Testament revelation as completing, amending, and correcting that of the Old. Its details the New Testament does complete; but if it were amended or corrected by any subsequent standard of infallible truth, this would prove it not truly inspired. Indeed, the history of theological opinion shows plainly enough that this anti-slavery view of Old Testament revelation is Socinian and Rationalistic. Modern Abolitionism in America had, in fact, a Socinian birth, in the great apostasy of the Puritans of New England to that benumbing heresy, and in the pharisaism, shallow scholarship, affectation, conceit and infidelity of the Unitarian clique in the self-styled American Athens, Boston. It is lamentable to see how men professing to be evangelical are driven by blind prejudices against Southern men and things, to adopt this skeptical tone towards God's own word. The ruinous issue has been seen in the case of a minister of the Gospel, who, after floundering through a volume of confused and impotent sophisms, roundly declares that if compelled to admit that the Bible treated slavery as not a sin in itself, he would repudiate the Bible rather than his opinions.

But we point these objectors to that Saviour who said, in the full meridian of revealed light of this Old Testament law: "Whosoever shall keep these commandments shall enter into eternal life;" and to the fact that the Decalogue itself twice recognizes the right of the master. Will they say that this too was an old, partial, and imperfect revelation? Not so says the sweet Psalmist of Israel: "The law of the Lord is perfect." Psalms, xix. 7. Whatever Abolitionists may cavil, Jesus Christ acknowledged no more perfect rule of morals than the Ten Commandments, as expounded by the "law and the prophets."

Sixth. An objection has been raised against the Old Testament argument, from the supposed permission of, or connivance at, polygamy and causeless divorce in the laws of Moses. This objection has been urged by Dr. Channing, the celebrated Unitarian, and since, in a more exact form, by Dr. Wayland. In substance it is this: That polygamy was allowed by the Old Testament law, and divorce for a less cause than conjugal infidelity was expressly permitted by Moses. But both these are as expressly forbidden as sinful by our Saviour. Matthew xix. 3 to 9. Therefore the main assertion in defence of slavery, on which the argument rested, does not hold: for these two instances show that a thing is not intrinsically innocent because it was permitted for a time to the Jews.

Our reply is, that both the premises of the objection are absolutely false. Polygamy and capricious divorce never were authorized by Old Testament law, in the sense in which domestic slavery was; and, second, the latter was never prohibited in the New Testament, as polygamy and such divorces expressly are. Either of these facts, without the other, makes the objection invalid, as we shall show; but we shall establish both. Before doing this, however, we would ask: Suppose these assertions of Drs. Wayland and Channing proved that God expressly permitted polygamy and causeless divorce to his own chosen and holy people, and that Jesus Christ yet denounced these things as sins; what is gained? Not only is this part of our defence of slavery overthrown, but the holiness of God is also overthrown; or else the inspiration of the Scriptures. (The latter would be a result evidently not very repugnant to Socinians and their sympathizers.) For then these Scriptures would make Him the teacher of sin to the very persons whom he was setting apart to peculiar holiness. If God did indeed authorize polygamy and causeless divorce in the Old Testament law, then the only inference for the devout mind is, that those things were then innocent, and would still be so, had not Christ afterwards forbidden them. Now, when we pass into the New Testament, and find that domestic slavery (which these objectors would make the parallel of polygamy and divorce without just cause) is not forbidden there, as the latter two were, but is again permitted, authorized and regulated, we must conclude that it is still innocent, as it must have been when a holy God allowed it to his holy people.

But the first part of the objectors' premise is also false; polygamy and causeless divorce never were sanctioned by Moses as domestic slavery was. Even admitting the more ignorant rendering of the matter, how wide is the difference in God's treatment of the two subjects! Slaves are mentioned as lawful property, not only in the biographies of God's erring and fallible servants, but in his own legislation; the acquisition of them is a blessing from him; their connexion with their masters is made the basis of religious sacraments; property in slaves is protected by laws of divine enactment; and the rights and duties of them and their masters defined. But when we pass to the subjects of plurality and change of wives, while we see the lives of imperfect, though good men, candidly disclosing these abuses, no legislative act recognizes them, except in the single case of divorce. In all God's laws and precepts, He always says *wife*, not *wives*, so carefully does He avoid a seeming allowance of a plurality. The Decalogue throws no protection around concubines, against the coveting of others. The rights and duties of polygamists are never defined by divine law, save in seeming exceptions which will be explained. How unlike is all this to the legislation upon slavery!

What has been already said leaves our argument impregnable. But so much misapprehension exists about the two cases, that the general interests of truth prompt a little farther separate discussion of each. The two enactments touching divorce which present the supposed contradiction in the strongest form, are those of Moses in Deuteronomy xxiv. 1 to 4, and Matthew xix. 3 to 9. These the reader is requested to have under his eye. The form of the Pharisees' question to Christ, ("Is it lawful for a man to put away his wife *for every cause?*") concurs with the testimony of Josephus, in teaching us that a monstrous perversion of Moses' statute then prevailed. The licentious, and yet self-righteous Pharisee claimed, as one of his most unquestioned privileges, the right to repudiate a wife, after the lapse of years, and birth of children, for any caprice whatsoever. The trap which they now laid for Christ was designed to compel him either to incur the *odium* of attacking this usage, guarded by a jealous anger, or to connive at their interpretation of the statute. Manifestly Christ does not concede that they interpreted Moses rightly; but indignantly clears the legislation of that holy man from their licentious perversions, and then, because of their abuse of it, repeals it by his plenary authority. He refers to that constitution of the marriage tie which was original, which preceded Moses, and was therefore binding when Moses wrote, to show that it was impossible he could have enacted what they claimed. What then did Moses enact? Let us explain it. In the ancient society of the East, females being reared in comparative seclusion, and marriages negotiated by intermediaries, the bridegroom had little opportunity for a familiar acquaintance even with the person of the bride. When she was brought to him at the nuptials, if he found her disfigured with some personal deformity or disease, (the undoubted meaning of the phrase "some uncleanness,") which effectually changed desire into disgust, he was likely to regard himself as swindled in the treaty, and to send the rejected bride back with indignity to her father's house. There she was reluctantly received, and in the anomalous position of one in name a wife, yet without a husband, she dragged out a wretched existence, incapable of marriage, and regarded by her parents and brothers as a disgraceful incumbrance. It was to relieve the wretched fate of such a woman, that Moses' law was framed. She was empowered to exact of her proposed husband a formal annulment of the unconsummated contract, and to resume the *status* of a single woman, eligible for another marriage. It is plain that Moses' law contemplates the case, only, in which no consummation of marriage takes place. She finds *no favour* in the eyes "of the bridegroom." He is so indignant and disgusted, that desire is put to flight by repugnance. The same fact appears from the condition of the law, that she shall in no case return to this man, "after she is defiled," i. e., after actual cohabitation with another man had made her unapproachable (without moral defilement) by the first. Such was the narrow extent of this law. The act for which it provided was divorce only in name, where that *consensus, qui matrimonium facit,* (in the words of the law maxim,) had never been perfected. The state of social usages among the Hebrews, with parental and fraternal severity towards the unfortunate daughter and sister, rendered the legislation of Moses necessary, and righteous at the time; but "a greater than Moses" was now here; and he, after defending the inspired law-giver from their vile misrepresentation, proceeded to repeal the law, because it had been so perverted, and because the social changes of the age had removed its righteous grounds. Let the Abolitionists show us a similar change in the law of domestic slavery, made by Christ, and we will admit that the moral conditions of the relation have changed since Moses' day.

The case of the polygamist is still clearer; for we assert that the whole legislation of the Pentateuch and of all the Old Testament is only adverse to polygamy. As some Christian divines have taught otherwise, we must ask the reader's attention and patience for a brief statement. Polygamy is recorded of Abraham, Jacob, Gideon, Elkanah, David, Solomon; but so are other sins of several of these; and, as every intelligent reader knows, the truthful narrative of holy writ as often discloses the sins of good men—for our warning, as their virtues for our imitation. And he who notes how, in every Bible instance, polygamy appears as the cause of domestic feuds, sin, and disaster, will have little doubt that the Holy Spirit tacitly holds all these cases up for our caution, and not our approval. But, then, God made Adam one wife only, and taught him the great law of the perpetual unity of the twain, just as it is now expounded by Jesus Christ. (Genesis ii. 23, 24, with Matthew xix. 4 to 6.) God preserved but one wife each to Noah and his sons. In every statute and preceptive word of the Holy Spirit, it is always *wife*, and not *wives*. The prophets everywhere teach how to treat a *wife*, and not *wives*. Moses, Leviticus xviii. 18, in the code regulating marriage, expressly prohibits the marriage of a second wife in the life of the first, thus enjoining monogamy in terms as clear as Christ's. Our English version hath it: "Neither shalt thou take a wife to her sister to vex her, to uncover her nakedness, besides the other, in her lifetime." Some have been preposterous enough to take the word *sister* here in its literal sense, and thus to force on the law the meaning that the man desiring to practise polygamy may do so provided he does not marry two daughters of the same parents; for if he did this, the two sisters sharing his bed would, like Rachel and Leah, quarrel more fiercely than two strangers. But the word "*sister*" must undoubtedly be taken in the sense of *mates, fellows*, (which it bears in a multitude of places,) and this for two controlling reasons. The other sense makes Moses talk nonsense and folly, in the supposed reason for his prohibition; in that it makes him argue that two sisters sharing one man's bed will quarrel, but two women having no kindred blood will not. It is false to fact and to nature. Did Leah and Rachel show more jealousy than Sarah and Hagar, Hannah and Peninnah? But when we understand the law in its obvious sense, that the husband shall not divide his bed with a second mate, the first still living, because such a wrong ever harrows and outrages the great instincts placed in woman's heart by her Creator, we make Moses talk truth and logick worthy of a profound legislator. The other reason for this construction is, that the other sense places the 18th verse in irreconcilable contradiction to the 16th verse. This forbids the marriage of a woman to the husband of her deceased sister; while the 18th verse, with this false reading, would authorize it.

Once more: Malachi, (chapter ii. 14, 15.) rebuking the various corruptions of the Jews, evidently includes polygamy; for he argues in favour of monogamy, (and also against causeless divorce,) from the fact that God, "who had the residue of the Spirit," and could as easily have created a thousand women for each man as a single one, made the numbers of the sexes equal from the beginning. He states this as the motive, "that he might seek a godly seed;" that is to say, that the object of God in the marriage relation was the right rearing of children, which polygamy notoriously hinders. Now the commission of an Old Testament prophet was not to legislate a new dispensation; for the laws of Moses were in full force; the prophets' business was to expound them. Hence, we infer that the laws of the Mosaic dispensation on the subject of polygamy had always been such as Malachi declared them. He was but applying Moses' principles.

To the assertion that the law of the Old Testament discountenanced polygamy as really as the New Testament, it has been objected that the practice was maintained by men too pious towards God to be capable of continuing in it against express precept; as, for instance, by the "king after God's own heart," David. Did not he also commit murder and adultery? Surely there is no question whether Moses forbids these! The history of good men, alas, shows us too plainly the power of general evil example, custom, temptation, and self-love, in blinding the honest conscience. It has been objected that polygamy was so universally practised, and so prized, that Moses would never have dared to attempt its extinction. When will men learn that the author of the Old Testament law was not Moses, but God? Is God timid? Does he fear to deal firmly with his creatures? But it is denied that there is any evidence that polygamy was greatly prevalent among the Hebrews. And nothing is easier than to show, that if it had been, Moses was a legislator bold enough to grapple with it. What more hardy than his dealing with the sabbatical year, with idolatry? It is objected that the marriage of the widow who was childless to the brother of the deceased, to raise up seed to the dead, presents a case of polygamy actually commanded. We reply, no one can show that the next of kin was permitted or required to form such marriage when he already had a wife. The celebrated J. D. Michaelis, a witness learned and not too favourable, says, in his Commentaries on the Laws of Moses, of this law, "Nor did it affect a brother having already a wife of his own." Book III., ch. vi., § 98. It is objected that polygamy is recognized as a permitted relation in Deuteronomy xxi. 15-17, where the husband of a polygamous marriage is forbidden to transfer the birthright from the eldest son to a younger, the child of a more favoured wife; and in Exodus xxi. 9, 10, where the husband is forbidden to deprive a less favoured wife of her marital rights and maintenance. Both these cases are explained by the admitted principle, that there may be relations which it was sin to form, and which yet it is sinful to break when formed. No one doubts whether the New Testament makes polygamy unlawful; yet it seems very clear that the apostles gave the same instructions to the husbands of a plurality of wives entering the Christian church. There appears, then, no evidence that polygamy was allowed in the laws of Moses.

We have thus shown that the objection of Dr. Channing to our Old Testament argument for the lawfulness of domestic slavery, is false in both its premises. First, it is not true that Moses sanctioned polygamy and causeless divorce in the sense in which he sanctioned slavery. And second, if he did, it would prove that those practices were lawful until they were prohibited by our Redeemer; but domestic slavery has met no such prohibition from him, and is therefore lawful still. If not, why did the divine Reformer strike down the two "sister sins," and leave the third, the giant evil, untouched? There is but one answer: He did not regard it as a sin.

If too much space has been devoted to this objection, the apology is, that it is a subject much misunderstood by Christian divines. The explanation is, that the study of Hebrew antiquities has, in our day, been left so much to German rationalists and secret Socinians; the late essays of British and Yankee scholars being to so great a degree servile imitations of theirs. But these skeptical *literati* of Germany, while wearing the clergyman's frock for the sake of the emoluments of an established church, have usually been unsanctified men, harbouring the most contemptuous views of Old Testament inspiration. The reader will bear in mind that, whether he is convinced, with us, that Moses actually prohibited polygamy, or not, the refutation of the Abolitionist objection is still perfectly valid.

The seventh and last objection against our Old Testament argument consists of various passages from the Hebrew prophets, which denounce the oppression of the poor, and the withholding of the labouring man's wages. Every phrase which sounds at all like their purpose is violently seized by the Abolitionists, and pressed incontinently into the service of condemning slavery, without regard to the sacred writer's intention or meaning. Were all the texts thus wrested discussed here, this section would be swelled into a book. A few passages which our opponents regard as their strongest will be cited, therefore; and the reply to these will be an answer to all. One such is Isaiah, lviii. 6: "Is not this the fast which I have chosen, to loose the bands of wickedness, to undo the heavy burdens, and to let the oppressed go free; and that ye break every yoke?" Another is found in Jeremiah xx. 13: "Woe unto him that buildeth his house by unrighteousness, and his chambers by wrong; that useth his neighbour's services without wages, and giveth him not for his work." Another is in Jeremiah xxxiv. 17: "Therefore, thus saith the Lord: Ye have not hearkened unto me in proclaiming liberty every man to his brother, and every man to his neighbour." And to find a scriptural stone to pelt the fugitive slave-law, they quote Isaiah xvi. 3: "Hide the outcasts; betray not him that wandereth."

Now, one would think that it should have given some pause to these perversions of Scripture, to remember that these same prophets were undoubtedly slaveholders. Witness, for instance, Elisha, who was so large a slaveholder as to have eleven ploughmen at once, and who, after he devoted himself exclusively to his prophetic ministry, still had his servants, Gehazi and others. (2 Kings, v. 20, and vi. 15.) How could they have aimed such denunciations at slave-owners, and escaped the sarcasm, "Physician, heal thyself?" It should have been remembered again, that Moses' laws, in which slaveholding was expressly sanctioned, were enacted by authority just as divine as that by which Isaiah and Jeremiah preached; that Moses was more a prophet than even they—"the greatest of the prophets;" that his laws were still in full force; that they bore to these prophets' instructions the relation of text to exposition; and that always the great burden of their accusations against their guilty countrymen was, that they had forsaken Moses' statutes. Were the guardians and expounders of the Constitution armed with power not only to repeal, but to vilify, the very law which they were appointed to expound? May the sermon contradict its own text? Before these rebukes of oppression can be applied, then, as God's condemnation of domestic slavery, it must be proved that in His view slavery is oppression. To take this for granted is a begging of the whole question in debate. But not only is it not proved by any such texts; it is obvious from the above remarks, that it cannot be proved by them, unless God can be made to contradict himself. But when we examine a little the connected words of these prophets themselves, we learn from them what they do mean; and we see an instance, ludicrous if it were not too painful, of the heedless folly with which the Word of God is abused. Thus, in Isaiah, lviii. 6, 7, we proceed to the very next words, and learn that the duty in hand consists in "bringing to their homes the poor that are cast out," and being charitable to "their own flesh." Were the Gentile slaves of the Hebrews "their own flesh" in the sense of the Old Testament, i. e., their kindred by blood? Manifestly, the phrase intends their fellow-citizens of Hebrew blood in distress. Are slaveholders in danger of sinning by driving away from their houses their domestic slaves; and do they need objurgation to make them receive them back? Such is the "infinite nonsense" forced upon Isaiah's words by Abolitionists. There is, then, no reference here to the emancipation of Gentile slaves; but to the duties of charity, justice and hospitality towards the oppressed of their fellow-citizens. And if the passage has any reference to servants, it is only to the sin of detaining Hebrew servants beyond the Sabbatical year's release.

When we turn to Jeremiah xxii. 13, a glance at the connexion shows us that the woe against using a neighbour's services without wages, is denounced against Shallum, the wicked king of Judah, who built his palaces, not by his domestic servants, but by unlawfully impressing his political subjects. Such is the marvellous accuracy of Abolitionist exposition! So in Jeremiah xxxiv. 17, which rebukes the Jews for not "proclaiming every man liberty to his brother," one little question should have staggered our zealous accusers: Were Gentile slaves "brethren" to Jews, in the sense of the prophet? And we have only to carry the eye back to verse 14, to see him explaining himself, that they did not comply with the Mosaic law, "at the end of seven years to let go every man his brother a Hebrew, which hath been sold unto thee." From the obligation of that law, the masters of Gentiles were expressly excepted.

But the illustration of crowning folly is Isaiah xvi. 3, which is so boldly wrested to countenance the harbouring of runaway slaves. The words are not the language of the prophet at all! The chapter is a dramatic picture of the distress of the pagan nations near Judea, and especially of Moab, one among them, in a time of invasion which Isaiah denounces upon them in punishment for their sin; and this verse represents the fugitive Moabites as entreating Jews for concealment and protection when pursued by their enemies. So that there is no slave nor slave-owner in the case at all; nor does the prophet's language contain any thing to imply whether it was righteous or not for the Jews to grant the request of these affrighted sinners in the hour of their retribution.

We have now reviewed, perhaps at too much length, the various impotent attempts made to escape from the meshes of our inexorable Old Testament argument. It is an argument short, plain, convincing. Although every thing enjoined on the Hebrews is not necessarily enjoined on us, (because it may have been of temporary obligation,) yet every such thing must be innocent in its nature, because a holy God would not sanction sin to his holy people, in the very act of separating them to holiness. But slaveholding was expressly sanctioned as a permanent institution; the duties of masters and slaves are defined; the rights of masters protected, not only in the civic but the eternal moral law of God; and He himself became a slave-owner, by claiming an oblation of slaves for his sanctuary and priests. Hence, while we do not say that modern Christian nations are bound to hold slaves, we do assert that no people sin by merely holding slaves, unless the place can be shown where God has uttered a subsequent prohibition. But there is no such place, as the next chapter will show. While we well know that to secret infidels and rationalists, as all Abolitionists are, this has no weight, to every mind which reverences the inspiration of the Old Testament it is conclusive. And let every Christian note, that with the inspiration of the Old Testament stands or falls that of Christ and the apostles, because they commit themselves irretrievably to the support of the former.

CHAPTER VI.
THE NEW TESTAMENT ARGUMENT.

Inspiration always represents the New Testament as its final teaching. Revelation is there completed; and all the instruction concerning right and wrong which man is ever to ask from God, must be sought in this book. We have done, then, with all sophistical pleas concerning the twilight of revelation: for we have come now to the meridian splendour. If slaveholding was allowed to the Old World for the hardness of its heart, here we may expect to see it repealed. Wherever the New Testament leaves the moral character of slavery, there it must stand. What, then, is its position here?

§ 1. *DEFINITION OF* ΔΟΥΛΟΣ.

The word commonly translated servant in the authorized version of the New Testament is Δουλος, (*doulos,*) which is most probably derived from the verb δεω, (*deo,*) 'I bind.' Hence the most direct meaning of the noun is 'bondsman.' Many Abolitionists, with a reckless violence of criticism which cannot be too sternly reprobated, have endeavoured to evade the crushing testimony of the New Testament against their dogma, by denying that this word there means slave. Some of them would make it mean son, some *hired servant,* and some *subject,* or dependent citizen. Even Mr. Albert Barnes, in his Commentaries on the Epistles, denies that the Word carries any evidence that a servile relation, proper, is intended by the sacred Writers. Every honest and well-informed biblical scholar feels that it would be an insult to his intelligence to suppose that a discussion of this preposterous assertion was needed for him: but as our aim is the general reader, we will briefly state the evidence that δουλος, when not metaphorical, means in the mouth of Christ and his apostles a literal, domestic slave.

Judea and the Roman Empire in their day were full of domestic slaves, so that in many places they were more numerous than the free citizens. Δουλος is confessedly the Word used for slave by secular writers of antiquity, in histories, statutes, works on political science, such as Aristotle's, in the allusions of Greeks to the Roman civil law, where they make it uniformly their translation for *Servus,* so clearly and harshly defined in that law as a literal slave. Did apostles and evangelists use the Greek language of their day correctly and honestly? And if δουλος in them does not mean slave, there is no stronger word within the lids of the New Testament that does; (nor in the Greek language;) so that there is in all the apostolic histories and epistles, no allusion to this world-wide institution which surrounded them! Who believes this? Again: The current Greek translation of the Old Testament, the Septuagint, whose idioms are more imitated in the New Testament than any other book, uses δουλος, as in Leviticus xxv. 44, for translation of the *Ebed*, bought with money from the Gentiles. The places where the New Testament writers use δουλος metaphorically imply the meaning of *slave* as the literal one, because the aptness of the trope depends on that sense. Thus, Acts iv. 29, xvi. 17, Romans i. 1, apostles are called God's δουλοι, servants, to express God's purchase, ownership and authority over them, and their strict obedience. Make the literal sense any thing less than slave proper, and the strength and beauty of the trope are gone. Again, the word is often used in contrast with *son*, and *political subject*, so as to prove a different meaning. Thus, John viii. 34, 35: "Whosoever committeth sin is the servant (δουλος) of sin. And the δουλος abideth not in the house forever: but the son abideth ever." Luke xix. 13, 14: "He called his ten δουλοι, and delivered them ten pounds, etc.; but his citizens (πολιται = political subjects) hated him," etc. Galatians iv. 1: "Now the heir, as long as he is a child, differeth nothing from a δουλος, though he be lord of all, but is under tutors and governors," etc. In conclusion: all well-informed and candid expositors tell us, that by δουλος, the New Testament means slave. We may mention Drs. Bloomfield, Hodge, and Trench. The classical authorities of the Greek language give this as the most proper meaning; and the biblical lexicons of the New Testament Greek testify the same. Of the latter, we may cite Dr. Edward Robinson, of New York, no friend to slavery. He says:

"Δουλος ου.δ = (subst. fr. δεω,) a bondsman, a slave, servant, properly by birth, diff. from ανδροποδον, 'one enslaved in war.' Compare Xen. Anab. iv. 1, 12, αιχμαλωτα αυδραποδα. Hell. i. 6, 15; Thuc. viii. 28, τα ανδραποδα παντα, και δουλα και ελευθερα. But such a captive is sometimes called δουλος, Xen. Cyr. 3, 1, 11, 19, ib., 4, 4, 12. Different also from ὁ διακονος, see that art. No. 1. In a family, the δουλος was one *bound to serve*, a slave, the property of his master, a 'living possession,' as Aristotle calls him, Pol. 1, 4. ὁ δουλος κτημα τι εμψυχον. Compare Gen. xvii. 12, 27; Exod. xii. 44. According to the same writer, a complete household consisted of slaves and freemen, Polit. 1, 3. οικια δε τελειος εκ δουλων και ελευθερον. The δουλος, therefore, was never a *hired* servant, the latter being called μισθιος, μισθωτος, q. v. Dr. Robinson then proceeds to define δουλος in detail as meaning, "1, Properly of involuntary service, a *slave*, servant, as opposed to ελευθερος. 2, Tropically, of voluntary service, a *servant*, implying obligation, obedience, devotedness. 3, Tropically, a *minister*, attendant, spoken of the officers and attendants of an Oriental court, who are often strictly slaves."

§ 2. SLAVERY OFTEN MENTIONED; YET NOT CONDEMNED.

The mere absence of a condemnation of slaveholding in the New Testament is proof that it is not unlawful. In showing that there is no such condemnation, we are doing more than we could be held bound to do by any logical obligation: we might very properly throw the burden of proof here upon our accusers, and claim to be held innocent until we can be proved to be guilty by some positive testimony of holy writ. But our cause is so strong, that we can afford to argue ex *abundantia*; to assert more than we are bound to show. We claim then the significant fact, that there is nowhere any rebuke of slaveholding, in express terms, in the New Testament. Of the truth of this assertion it is sufficient proof, that Abolitionists, with all their malignant zeal, have been unable to find a single instance, and are compelled to assail us only with inferences. The express permission to hold slaves given by Moses to God's people, is nowhere repealed by the 'greater than Moses,' the Divine Prophet of the new dispensation. Let the reader consider how this fact is strengthened by the attendant circumstances. Christ and his apostles preached in the midst of slaves and slaveholders. The institution was exceedingly prevalent in many parts of the world. Potter tells us that in Athens, (a place where Paul preached,) the freemen citizens, possessed of franchises, were twenty-one thousand, and the slaves four hundred thousand. The congregations to which Christ and his apostles preached, were composed of masters and their slaves. The slavery of that day, as defined by the Roman civil law, was harsh and oppressive, treating the slave as a legal nonentity, without property, rights, or legal remedy; without marriage, subject, even as to his life, to the caprice of his master, and in every respect a human beast of burden. Again: to this institution Christ and his apostles make many allusions, for illustration of other subjects; and upon the institution itself they often speak didactically. Yet, while often condemning the abuses and oppressions incident to it, they never condemn the relation.

Several times the apostles give formal enumerations of the prevalent sins of their times; as in Romans i. 29, 31; Galatians v. 19 to 21; Matthew xv. 19; Colossians iii. 8, 9; 2 Timothy iii. 2 to 4. These catalogues of sins are often full and minute; but the owning of slaves never appears among them.

Now, we are entitled to claim, that this silence of the later and final revelation leaves the lawfulness of slaveholding in full force, as expressly established in the earlier. On that allowance we plant ourselves, and defy our accusers to bring the evidence of its repeal. On them lies the burden of proof. And we have indicated by the circumstances detailed above, how crushing that burden will be to them.

This is the most appropriate place to notice the evasion attempted from the above demonstration. They plead that slavery is not specially forbidden in the New Testament, because the plan of the Bible is to give us a rule of morals, not by special enactments for every case, but by general principles of right, which we must apply to special cases as they arise. "Inspiration has not," say they, "specially condemned every possible sin which may occur in the boundless varieties of human affairs, because then the whole world would not contain the books that should be written; and the voluminous character of the rule of duty would disappoint its whole utility; and if any sin were omitted in order to abridge it, this would be taken as a sanction. Hence, God gives us a set of plain general principles, of obvious application under the law of love." Therefore, it is argued, we are not to expect that the sin of slaveholding should be singled out. Enough that general principles given exclude it.

There is a portion of truth in this statement of the matter, and in the grounds assigned for it. But waiving for the present the exposure of the groundless assertion that there are any general principles in the New Testament condemnatory of slaveholding, we deny that this book teaches morals only by general rules. It also does it, in a multitude of cases, by special precepts. A multitude of special sins prevalent in that and all ages are singled out. This being so—the lists of particular sins being so full and specific as they are—we assert it would have been an unaccountable anomaly to pass over a thing so important, open, prevalent, had it been intrinsically wrong. But why does Revelation omit a number of particulars, and state general principles? For the lack of room, it is said. The other plan would have made the Bible too large.

Now we ask, as the case actually stands in the New Testament, would not a good deal of room have been saved as to slavery, by simply specifying it as wrong? It is a queer way to economize space, thus to take up a subject, define it at large, limit, modify it, retrench its abuses, lay down in considerable detail a part of its duties and relations; and then provide by some general principle for its utter prohibition! Would not the obvious way have been, to say in three plain words, what was the only fundamental thing, after all, which, on this supposition, needed to be taught, "Slavery is sinful?" This would have settled the matter, and also have saved space and ambiguity, and made an end of definitions, limitations, abuses, inferences and all, in the only honest way. But farther, we admit that the Bible has left a multitude of new questions, emerging in novel cases, to be settled by the fair application of general principles, (which are usually illustrated in Scripture by application to some specific case.) Now must not an honest mind argue, that since the human understanding is so fallible in inferential reasonings, especially on social ethics, where the premises are so numerous and vague, and prejudices and interests so blinding, a special precept, where one is found applicable, is better than an inference probably doubtful? Will it not follow a 'thus saith the Lord,' if it has one, rather than its own deduction which may be a blunder? Well, then, if God intended us to understand that he had implicitly condemned slavery in some general principles given, it was most unlucky that He said any thing specific about it, which was not a specific condemnation. For what He has specifically said about it must lead His most honest servants to conclude that He did not intend to leave it to be settled by general inference, that He exempted it from that class of subjects. Had God not alluded to it by name, then we should have been more free to apply general principles to settle its moral character, as we do to the modern duel, not mentioned in Scripture, because it is wholly a modern usage. But since God has particularized so much about slaveholding, therefore, honesty, humility, piety, require us to study his specific teachings in preference to our supposed inferences, and even in opposition to them. Here, then, we stand: Inspiration has once expressly authorized slaveholding. Until a repeal is found equally express, it must be innocent.

§ 3. CHRIST APPLAUDS A SLAVEHOLDER.

Our Lord has thrown at least a probable light upon his estimation of slaveholders by his treatment of the Centurion of Capernaum, and his slave. The story may be found in Matthew viii. 5 to 13, and Luke vii. 2 to 10. This person, though a Gentile and an officer of the Roman army, was, according to the testimony of his Jewish neighbours, a sincere convert to the religion of the Old Testament, and a truly good man. He had a valued slave very sick, called in Matthew his "boy," (παις,) a common term for slave in New Testament times; but Luke calls him again and again his "slave," (δουλος.) Hearing of Christ's approach, he sent some of his Hebrew neighbours, (rulers of the synagogue,) to beseech our Lord to apply his miraculous power for the healing of his sick slave. A little later he appears himself, and explains to Jesus, that it was not arrogance, but humility, which prevented his meeting him at first, with his full confidence. For as he, though a poor mortal, was enabled, by the authority of an officer and master, to make others come and go at his bidding, so he knew that Christ could yet more easily bid away his servant's disease. And therefore he had not deemed it necessary to demand (what he was unworthy to receive) an actual visit to his house. Hereupon Christ declares with delight, that he "had not found so great faith, no, not in Israel." This was high praise indeed, after the faith of a Nathanael, a John, a James, a Mary Magdalene, a Martha, and a Lazarus. Yet this much-applauded man was a slaveholder! But our Lord comes yet nearer to the point in dispute. He speaks the word, and heals the slave, thus restoring him to the master's possession and use. Had the relation been wrong, here, now, was an excellent opportunity to set things right, when he had before him a subject so docile, so humble, so grateful and trustful. Should not Christ have said: "Honest Centurion, you owe one thing more to your sick fellow-creature: his liberty. You have humanely sought the preservation of his being, which I have now granted; but it therefore becomes my duty to tell you, lest silence in such a case should confirm a sinful error, that your possession of him as a slave outrages the laws of his being. I cannot become accomplice to wrong. The life which I have rescued, I claim for liberty, for righteousness. I expect it of your faith and gratitude, that instead of begrudging the surrender, you will thank me for enlightening you as to your error." But no; Christ says nothing like this, but goes his way and leaves the master and all the people blinded by his extraordinary commendation of the slave-owner, and his own act in restoring the slave to him, to blunder on in the belief that slavery was all right. Certain we are, that had Dr. Channing, or Dr. Wayland, or the most moderate Abolitionist, been the miracle-worker, he would have made a very different use of the occasion. However he might have hesitated as to immediate and universal emancipation, he would have felt that the opportunity was too fair to be lost, for setting up a good strong precedent against slavery. Hence we feel sure that Christ and they are not agreed in the moral estimate of the relation.

§ 4. THE APOSTLES SEPARATE SLAVERY AND ITS ABUSES.

We find the apostles everywhere treating slavery, in one particular, as the Abolitionists refuse to treat it; that is to say, distinguishing between the relation and its incidental abuses. Our accusers now claim a license from the well-known logical rule, that it is not fair to argue from the abuses of a thing to the thing itself. Hence they insist that in estimating slavery, we must take it in the concrete, as it is in these Southern States, with all that bad men or bad legislation may at any time have attached to it. And if any feature attaching to an aggravated case of oppression should be proved wrong, then the very relation of master and slave must be held wrong in itself. The bald and insolent sophistry of this claim has been already alluded to. By this way it could be proved that marriage, civil government and church government, as well as the parental relation, are intrinsically immoral; for all have been and are abused, not only by the illegal license of individual bad men, but by bad legislation. Just as reasonably might a monk say to all Mohammedans, that marriage is a sin, for the character of the institution must be tried in the concrete, with all the accessaries which usually attend it in Mohammedan lands, and most certainly with such as are established by law; and among these is polygamy, which is sinful; wherefore the marriage relation is wrong. And this preposterous logick has been urged, although it has been proved that, in the vast majority of cases in these States, masters did preserve the relation to their slaves, without connecting with it a single one of the incidents, whether allowed by law or not, which are indefensible in a moral view. To say that the relation was sinful, in all these virtuous citizens, because some of the occasional incidents were sinful, is just as outrageous as to tell the Christian mother that her authority over her child is a wicked tyranny, because some drunken wretch near by has been guilty of child-murder. But our chief purpose here is to show, that the apostles were never guilty of this absurdity; and that, on the contrary, they separated between the relation and its abuses, just as Christian masters now claim to do.

Let the reader note then, that the type of slavery prevailing where the apostles preached, was, compared with ours, barbarous, cruel, and wicked in many of its customary incidents, as established both by usage and law. Slaves were regarded as having neither rights nor legal remedies. No law protected their life itself against the master. There was no recognized marriage for them, and no established parental or filial relations. The chastity of the female slave was unprotected by law against her master. And the temper of society sanctioned the not infrequent use of these powers, in the ruthless separation of families, inhuman punishments, hard labour, coarse food, maiming, and even murder. Such were the iniquities which history assures us connected themselves only too often with this relation in the apostles' days, and were sanctioned by human laws.

But did they provoke these inspired law-givers to condemn the whole institution? By no means. As we have seen, they nowhere pronounce the relation of master and slave an inherent wrong. They everywhere act as though it might be, and when not abused, was, perfectly innocent. And that it might be innocent, they forbade to the members of the Christian church all these abuses of it. Thus they separated between the relation and its abuses. Doubtless, the standard which they had in view, in commanding masters to "render to their servants those things which are just and equal," *was the Mosaic law*. We have seen how far this was in advance of the brutalities permitted by pagan laws, and how it protected the life, limbs, and chastity of servants among the Hebrews. This law, being founded in righteousness, was in its general spirit the rule of the New Testament church also. When this separation is made by the apostles between the relation and its abuses, we find that the former includes, as its essentials, just these elements: a right to the slave's labour for life, coupled with the obligation on the master to use it with justice and clemency, and to recompense the slave with a suitable maintenance; and on the slave's part, the obligation to render this labour with all good fidelity, and with a respectful obedience. Is not this just the definition of slavery with which we set out?

§ 5. SLAVERY NO ESSENTIAL RELIGIOUS EVIL.

The Apostle Paul teaches that the condition of a slave, although not desirable for its own sake, has no essential bearing on the Christian life and progress; and therefore, when speaking as a Christian minister, and with exclusive reference to man's religious interests, he treats it as unimportant. The proof of this statement may be found in such passages as the following: 1 Cor. xii. 13, "For by one Spirit we are all baptized into one body, whether we be Jews or Gentiles, whether we be bond or free: and have all been made to drink into one Spirit." Galat. iii. 28, "There is neither Jew nor Greek; there is neither bond nor free; there is neither male nor female; for we are all one in Jesus Christ." So, substantially, says Colos. iii. 11. But the most decisive passage is 1 Cor. vii. 20, 21: "Let every man abide in the same calling wherein he was called. Art thou called being a servant? care not for it; but if thou mayest be made free, use it rather." (Paul had just defined his meaning in the phrase "calling in which he was called," as being circumcised or uncircumcised, bond or free.)

The drift of all these passages is to teach that a man's reception by Christ and by the Church does not depend in any manner on his class or condition in secular life; because Christianity places all classes on the same footing as to the things of the soul, and offers to all the same salvation. When, therefore, men come to the throne of grace, the baptismal water, the communion table, distinctions of class are left behind them for the time. Hence, these distinctions are not essential, as to the soul's salvation. The last passage quoted brings out the latter truth more distinctly. Is any Christian, at his conversion, a Jew? That circumstance is unimportant to his religious life. Was he a Gentile? That also is unimportant. Was he a slave when converted to Christ? Let not this concern him, for it cannot essentially affect his religious welfare: the road to heaven is as open to him as to the freeman. But if a convenient and lawful opportunity to acquire his freedom, with the consent of his master, occurs, then freedom is to be preferred. Such is the meaning found in the words by all sober expositors, including those of countries where slavery does not exist. Who can believe that the apostle would have taught thus, if slavery had been an iniquitous relation?

But when he tells the Christian servant that freedom is to be preferred by him to bondage, if it may be rightfully acquired, we must remember the circumstances of the age, in order to do justice to his meaning. The same apostle, speaking of marriage, says, "Art thou loosed from a wife? seek not to be bound." Does he mean to set himself against the holy estate of matrimony, and to contradict the divine wisdom which said that "it is not good for man to be alone?" By no means. He explains himself as advising thus "because of the present distress." Exposure to persecution, banishment, death, made it a step of questionable prudence at that time, to assume the responsibilities of a husband and father. Now the laws and usages of the age as to slaves were, as we have seen, harsh and oppressive. But worse than this, many masters among the heathen were accustomed to require of their slaves offices vile, and even guilty; and scruples of conscience on the slave's part were treated as an absurdity or rebellion. In such a state of society, although the relation of servitude was not in itself adverse to a holy life, the prudent man would prefer to be secured against the possibility of such a wrong, by securing his liberty if he lawfully could. Moreover, society offered a grade, and a career of advancement, to the "freedman" and his children. Master and slave were of the same colour; and a generation or two would obliterate by its unions the memory of the servile condition. But in these States, where the servant's rights were so much better protected by law and usage, and where the freed servant, being a black, finds himself only deprived of his master's patronage, and still debarred as much as ever from social equality by his colour and caste, the case may be very different. Freedom to the Christian slave here, may prove a loss.

Now who can believe that the Apostle Paul would have spoken thus of slavery, if he had thought it an injurious and iniquitous relation, as hostile to religion, as degrading to the victim's immortal nature, and as converting him from a rational person into a chattel, a human brute? He treats the condition of bondage, in its religious aspects, precisely as he does accidents of birth, being born circumcised or uncircumcised, a citizen of the Empire or a subject foreigner, male or female. We have a practical evidence how incompatible such language is with the Abolitionist first principle, in their very different conduct. Do they ever say to the Christian slave: "Art thou called being a servant? care not for it." We trow not. They glory in teaching every slave they can to break away from his bondage, even at the cost of robbery and murder. And Mr. Albert Barnes informs his readers, that in his interviews with runaway slaves, he long ago ceased to instruct them that it was their duty to return to their masters. It is evident, therefore, that this abolitionist and St. Paul were not agreed.

§ 6. SLAVEHOLDERS FULLY ADMITTED TO CHURCH-MEMBERSHIP.

We now proceed, in the sixth place, to a fact of still greater force: that slaveholders were admitted by Christ to full communion and good standing in the Christian church. Let us first establish the fact. In Acts X. 5-17, we learn that the pious Cornelius had at least two household servants, (οικετων, one of the Septuagint words for domestic slave.) There is no hint of his liberating them; but the Apostle Peter tells his brethren, Acts xi. 15-17, that he was obliged to admit him by baptism to the church, by the act of God himself. Says he: "Forasmuch then as God gave them the like gift as he did unto us," (power of miracles,) "who believed on the Lord Jesus Christ, what was I, that I could withstand God?" So he baptized him and his servants together. Again we find the Epistle to the Ephesians addressed in the first verse, "to the saints which are at Ephesus, and to the faithful brethren in Christ Jesus," with a blessing in the second verse appropriate to none but God's children. When, therefore, in subsequent parts of the Epistle, we find any persons addressed in detail with apostolic precepts, we conclude of course that they are included in "the saints and faithful." But all expositors say these terms mean church members in good standing. If we find here any persons commanded to any duty, we know that they are church members. This thought confirms it, that St. Paul knew well that his office gave him no jurisdiction over the external world. He had himself said to the church authorities at Corinth, "What have I to do, to judge them that are without?" 1 Cor. v. 12. Now, in the sixth chapter and ninth verse of Ephesians, we find him, after commanding Christian husbands, Christian wives, Christian parents, Christian children, and Christian slaves, how to demean themselves, addressing Christian masters: "And ye, masters, do the same things unto them, forbearing threatening, knowing that your Master also is in heaven," &c. Here, therefore, must have been slaveholders in good standing in this favourite church, which was organized under St. Paul's own eye. The Epistle to the Colossians is also addressed "to the saints and faithful brethren in Christ which are at Colosse:" and in ch. iv. 1, Christian slaveholders are addressed: "Masters, give unto your servants that which is just and equal," &c. There were, therefore, slaveholders in full communion at Colosse. Again: Mr. Albert Barnes (whom we cite here for a particular reason which will appear in the sequel) says correctly, that Timothy received his first Epistle from St. Paul at Ephesus, three or four years after that church was planted, having been left in charge there. But in Ephes. vi. 2, St. Paul Writes: "And they" (i. e. these Christian slaves) "that have believing masters, let them not despise them because they are brethren, but rather do them service because they are faithful and beloved, partakers of the benefit," (i. e. of the blessings of redemption.) "These things teach and exhort." There were still slaveholders then, in this church, three or four years after its organization; and Timothy is commanded to have them treated as brethren faithful and beloved, partakers of the favour of God. The Epistle to the Ephesians, according to the same Mr. Barnes, was written from four to seven years after the founding of the church, and that to the Colossians from ten to thirteen. So that this membership of slaveholders had continued for these periods.

But we have a stronger case still. St. Paul, during his imprisonment at Rome, addresses Philemon of Colosse thus: "Paul, a prisoner of Jesus Christ, and Timothy our brother, unto our dearly beloved and fellow-labourer, (συνεργος) and to our beloved Apphia and Archippus, our fellow-soldier, and to the church in thy house." Philemon, then, was a church member; his house was a place of meeting for the church; he was beloved of Paul; and last, he was himself a Christian minister. (Such is the only meaning of συνεργος here, according to the agreement of all expositors, of whom may be mentioned Bloomfield, Doddridge, and Dr. Edward Robinson of New York.) But Philemon was a slaveholder: the very purpose of this affectionate epistle was to send back to him a runaway slave. Here, then, we have a slaveholder, not only in the membership, but ministry of the Church.

Now when we consider how jealously the apostles guarded the purity of the church, it will appear to be incredible that they should receive slaveholders thus, if the relation were unrighteous. The terms of admission (for adults) were the renunciation of all known sin, and a credible repentance leading to reparation, where ever practicable. Even the Baptist, who was unworthy to loose the shoe-latchet of Christ, could say: "Bring forth therefore the fruits meet for repentance." From all the prevalent and popular sins of Pagan society, the church members were inexorably required to turn away; else excommunication soon rid the church of their scandal. Thus, 1 Cor. v. 11, says: "But now I have written unto you not to keep company, if any man that is called a brother be a fornicator, or covetous, or an idolater, or a railer, or a drunkard, or an extortioner; with such an one no not to eat." Christ separated his church out of the world, to secure sanctity and holy living. To suppose that he, or his apostles, could avowedly admit and tolerate the membership of men who persisted in criminal conduct, betrays the very purpose of the church, and impugns the purity of the Saviour himself. And here, all the evasions of Abolitionists are worthless; as when they say that Christ's mission was not to meddle with secular relations, or to interfere in politics; for the communion of the church was his own peculiar domain; and to meddle with every form of sin there was precisely his mission. Entrance to the church was voluntary. The terms of membership were candidly published; the penalty for violating them was purely spiritual, (mere exclusion from the society,) and interfered with no man's political rights or franchises. So that within this spiritual society, Christ had things his own way; there was no difficulty from without that could possibly restrain his action; and if he tolerated deliberate sin here, his own character is tarnished.

So cogent is this, that Mr. Albert Barnes, in his 'Notes' on 1 Tim. vi. 2, seeks to evade it thus: "Nor is it fairly to be inferred from this passage that he (Paul) meant to teach that they (masters) might continue this (i. e. slaveholding) and be entitled to all the respect and confidence due to the Christian name, or be regarded as maintaining a good standing in the church. Whatever may be true on these points, the passage before us only proves, that Paul considered that a man who was a slaveholder *might* be converted, and be spoken of as a 'believer' or a Christian. Many have been converted in similar circumstances, as many have in the practice of all other kinds of iniquity. What was their duty *after* their conversion was another question."

That is, as a murderer or adulterer *might* become a subject of Almighty grace, so might a slaveholder; but all three alike must cease these crimes, when converted, in order to continue credible church members! To him who has weighed the Scripture facts, this statement will appear (as we shall find sundry others of this writer) so obviously uncandid, that it is mere affectation to refrain from calling it by its proper name, dishonesty. The simple refutation is in the fact, by which Mr. Barnes has convicted himself, that the slaveholders were still in the churches from three to thirteen years after they were organized, with no hint from the apostle that they were living in a criminal relation; that they were still beloved, approved, yea applauded, by Paul; and that one of them was even promoted to the ministry. The last case is particularly ruinous to Mr. Barnes. For when did Philemon first acquire his slave Onesimus? Before the former first joined the Church? Then Paul permitted him to remain all these years a member, and promoted him to the ministry, with the 'sin of slavery' unforsaken! Was it after he joined the church? Then a thing occurred which, on Mr. Barnes' theory, is impossible: because buying a slave, being criminal, must have terminated his church membership.

We thank God that it is true that some sinners of every class are converted. But their conversion must be followed by a prompt repentance and forsaking of their sins. Thus, it is said to the Corinthians, 1 Cor. vi. 9 to 11: "Be not deceived; neither fornicators, nor idolaters, nor adulterers, nor effeminate, nor abusers of themselves with mankind, nor thieves, nor covetous, nor drunkards, nor revilers, nor extortioners, shall inherit the kingdom of God. And such were some of you; but ye are washed, but ye are sanctified, but ye are justified in the name of the Lord Jesus, and by the Spirit of our God." According to the Abolitionists, another class of criminals fully deserving to be ranked in the above black list—slaveholders—enter the church under Paul's administration, without being washed or sanctified. If slaveholding is wrong, it was their duty on entering the Church to repent of, forsake and repair this wrong; to liberate their slaves, and to repay them for past exactions so far as possible. If this was their duty, it was the duty of the apostle to teach it to them. But he has not taught it: he has taken up the subject, and merely taught these masters that they would discharge their whole duty by treating their slaves, as slaves, with clemency and equity; and then he has continued them in the Church. It remains true, therefore, that this allowed membership of slaveholders in the apostolic churches, proves it no sin to own slaves.

§ 7. Relative Duties of Masters and Slaves Recognized.

Another fact equally decisive is, that the apostles frequently enjoin on masters and slaves their relative duties, just as they do upon husbands and wives, parents and children. And these duties they enforce, both on master and servant, by Christian motives. Pursuing the same method as under the last head, we will first establish the fact, and then indicate the use to be made of it.

In Ephesians vi. 5 to 9, having addressed the other classes, the Apostle Paul says: "Servants, be obedient to them that are your masters according to the flesh, with fear and trembling, in singleness of your heart as unto Christ; not with eye-service, as men-pleasers; but as the servants of Christ, doing the will of God from the heart; with good-will doing service as to the Lord and not unto men; knowing that whatsoever good thing any man doeth, the same shall he receive of the Lord, whether he be bond or free. And ye masters, do the same things unto them, forbearing threatening: knowing that your Master also is in heaven; neither is there respect of persons with him."

In Colos. iii. 22 to iv. 1, inclusive, almost the same precepts occur in the same words, with small exceptions, and standing in the same connexion with recognized relations. Let the reader compare for himself. In 1 Tim. vi, 1, 2, we read: "Let as many servants as are under the yoke count their own masters worthy of all honour, that the name of God and his doctrine be not blasphemed. And they that have believing masters, let them not despise them because they are brethren; but rather do them service, because they are faithful and beloved, partakers of the benefit. These things teach and exhort." So, in the Epistle to Titus, having directed him how to instruct sundry other classes in their relative duties, he says, ch. ii. 9 to 12: "Exhort servants to be obedient unto their own masters, and to please them well in all things: not answering again; not purloining, but showing all good fidelity; that they may adorn the doctrine of God our Saviour in all things. For the grace of God that bringeth salvation hath appeared unto all men, teaching us that, denying ungodliness and worldly lusts, we should live soberly, righteously and godly in this present world," etc. So, the Apostle Peter, 1 Ep. ii. 18, 19: "Servants, be subject to your masters with all fear; not only to the good and gentle, but also to the froward. For this is thankworthy, if a man for conscience towards God endure grief, suffering wrongfully."

The word for *servant* in all these passages is δουλος, except the last, where the Apostle Peter uses οικετια. But this is also proved to mean here, domestic slaves proper, by the current Septuagint and New Testament usage, by its relation to δεσποταις, (masters,) which always means in this connexion the proprietor of a slave, and by the reference in the subsequent verse to being buffeted for a fault; an incident of the slave's condition, rather than of the hired freeman's. Now the drift of all these precepts is too plain to be mistaken. Slaves who are church-members are here instructed that it is their religious duty to obey their masters, to treat them with deferential respect, and with Christian love where the masters are Christian, and to render the service due from a servant with fidelity and integrity, without requiring to be watched or threatened. The motives urged for all this are not carnal, but evangelical, a sense of duty, love for Christ and his doctrine, the credit of which was implicated in their Christian conduct here, and the expectation of a rich reward from Jesus Christ hereafter.

But the apostles are not partial. In like manner they positively enjoin on masters who are church-members, the faithful performance of their reciprocal duties to their slaves. They must avoid a harsh and minatory government: they must allot to the slave an equitable maintenance and humane treatment, and in every respect must act towards him so as to be able to meet that judgment, where master and slave will stand as equals before the bar of Jesus Christ, at which social rank has no weight. These precepts imply, of course, that both master and servant are church-members; otherwise they would not have been under the ecclesiastical authority of the apostles. They imply with equal clearness, that the continuance of the relation was contemplated as legitimate: for if this is terminated as sinful, the duties of the relation are at an end, and such precepts are so much breath thrown away. Does any sophist insist that the "rendering of that which is just and equal" must not be less than emancipation? The very words refute him; for then he would no longer be his servant, and the master no longer master; so that he could owe no duties as such. Further, the same passage proceeds to enjoin on the slave the duties of a continued state of servitude. We repeat: all these passages contemplate the continuance of the relation among church-members, as legitimate. What would men say of the Christian minister who should instruct the penitent gambler how to continue the stated practice of his nefarious art in a Christian manner: and the penitent adulterer how to continue his guilty connexion exemplarily? When such a law-giver as Christ legislates concerning such a thing, there is but one thing he can consistently enjoin: and that is its instant termination. If slaveholding is a moral wrong, the chief guilt, of course, attaches to the master, because on his side is the power. When the apostles pass, then, from the duties of servants to those of masters, it is unavoidable that they must declare the imperative duty of emancipation. But they say not one word about it: they seek to continue the relation rightfully. Therefore, either slaveholding is not wrong, or the apostles were unfaithful. The explanation of these passages, which we have given, is that of all respectable expositors, especially the British, no friends of slavery.

The attempt is made to argue, that if this were correct, then the holy apostles would be implicated in a connivance at the excesses and barbarities which, the history of the times tells us, often attached to the servile condition. The answer is: that they condemn and prohibit all the wrongs, as criminal, and leave the relation itself as lawful. No other defence can be set up for their treatment of the conjugal and parental relations. Antiquarians tell us they also were then deformed by great abuses. The wife and child were no better than slaves. Over the latter the father had the power of life and death, and of selling into bondage. From the former he divorced himself at pleasure, and often visited her with corporal punishment. How do the apostles treat these facts? They recognize the relation and forbid its abuses. Shall any one say that because these abuses were current, therefore they should have denounced the domestic relations, and invented some new-fangled communism? Or shall it be said that, because they have not done this, they wink at the wife-beatings, the child-murders, and the other barbarities so common in Greek and Oriental families? We trow not. Why then should these absurd inferences be attached to their treatment of domestic slavery?

But the favourite evasion of these Scriptures is that of Dr. Wayland: "The scope of these instructions to servants is only to teach patience, fidelity, meekness, and charity, duties which Christians owe to all men, even their enemies." In like strain, Mr. Albert Barnes, in his 'Notes on Ephesians,' vi. 7, writes: "But let not a master think, because a pious slave shows this spirit, that therefore the slave feels the master is right in withholding his freedom; nor let him suppose, because religion requires the slave to be submissive and obedient, that therefore it approves of what the master does. It does this no more than it sanctions the conduct of Mary and Nero, because religion required the martyrs to be unresisting, and to allow themselves to be led to the stake. A conscientious slave may find happiness in submitting to God, and doing His will, just as a conscientious martyr may. But this does not sanction the wrong, either of the slave-owner or of the persecutor." It is difficult to restrain the expression of natural indignation at so shameless a sophism as this, which outrages at once the understanding of the reader and the honour of Christ. It represents the pure and benign genius of Christianity as walking abroad, and finding oppressor and oppressed together, the oppressor avowedly within her reach, as well as his victim, as a subject of her spiritual jurisdiction and instruction. To the one she is represented as saying: "Oh, injured slave! glorify thy meek and lowly Saviour under this unrighteous oppression, by imitating His patience." Turning then to the other, who is present, and equally subject to her authority, must she not, of course, give the correlative injunction: "Oh, master! since thy yoke is wicked, cease instantly to persecute Christ in the person of his follower." But no:

abolitionism represents her as saying nothing at all on this point; but merely dismissing his side of the case with the injunction to oppress equitably! The honest mind meets such a statement, not only with the '*Incredulus sum*,' but with the '*Incredulus odi*,' of the Latin satirist. And the suffering victim of oppression could not but feel, while he recognized the duty of patience, that the counterpart treatment of his oppressor by Christianity was a foul injustice. The fact that Christ and apostles admitted these masters, with these slaves, to the same communion, proves that the comment of Mr. Barnes is preposterous. The fact that these Christian slaves are commanded to treat these pretended oppressors as "brethren, faithful and beloved, partakers of the benefit," proves it. Do the apostles, while enjoining patience under the persecutions of a bloody Nero, admit that Nero, with his brutality, to the same Christian communion with the peaceful and holy victims, address him as "saint and faithful in Christ Jesus," and instruct him to burn and tear the Christians for their faith, in a godly manner? The comment is disproved by Peter, when he says that there were slave-owners who were "good and gentle," as well as others who were "froward." Does truth or common sense distinguish "good and gentle" persecutors? It is disproved farther, by the fact that the apostles do not enjoin patience only, on these servants, as on Christians forbearing under an injury; but they enjoin duty, obedience, and fidelity also, as upon Christians paying reciprocal obligations. It is not patience under ruthless force, which they require, as a tribute to Christ's honour; but it is obedience due to the master's legitimate authority, and that, a tribute due to the master also. Servants must "show all good fidelity." This implies an obligation to which to be faithful. Fidelity does not exist where there is no debt. To unrighteous exaction we may be submissive; but fidelity has no place. But the crowning refutation is, that St. Paul sent back an escaped slave to his master Philemon, from Rome to Colosse, hundreds of miles away. Will any one say that the duty of Christian submission and patience under wrongs extends so far as to require an injured Christian to go back several hundred miles, and hunt up his oppressor in order to be maltreated again, after Providence had enabled him to escape from his injuries? If Mr. Barnes is correct, Onesimus should have claimed that he had now availed himself of Christ's own command: "When they persecute you in one city, flee ye into another;" and was rightfully concealed in the midst of the vast metropolis. This was requiring him to "turn the other cheek" with a vengeance: to waive the right of peaceable escape which his Divine Lord had given him, and go all the way to Asia to be unjustly smitten again! There is this farther absurdity: the pious servant is required to stretch his forbearance to so Quixotic a degree, as to waive, not only the claim of forcible self-defence, but that of legal protection. (Oh that the holy Abolitionists had practised towards the injured South a little tythe of this forbearance which their learned scribe so consistently inculcates!) Is it Christ's requirement, that the Christian under oppression must refuse the shield of legal protection? Did Paul think thus, when, prosecuted at the bar of Porcius Festus by unscrupulous enemies, he claimed the rights of his citizenship with so admirable a union of forbearance and courage? Now, if Messrs. Wayland and Barnes are right, these oppressed slaves possessed a tribunal in common with their oppressors, to which they could lawfully, peaceably, forgivingly, yet righteously summon them: *the church court.* They could have demanded of these authorities, with the strictest Christian propriety, to use all their spiritual powers, so far as they went, to induce the masters, their fellow-members, to give them that liberty which was their due. But, so exceedingly forbearing are they, that they not only forego forcible resistance, but the peaceable claim of their ecclesiastical right, for fear they might be thought to act in an impatient manner! A highwayman meets me in a wood, and begins to beat me and rob me: I have a weapon, but I forbear to use violence against him. Meantime, the legal authorities pass by, and I also forbear to claim their protection under the law, lest it should scandalize the amiable highwayman, and make him think less favourably of my religion!

It may be well, in concluding this point, to notice the plea that Christians were required by the apostles to render not only patience and submission to the Emperor Nero, but also allegiance and hearty obedience. Yet none will say that Nero was a righteous ruler. We reply, the case is precisely in our favour: for it proves the proposition exactly parallel to ours, that civil government is a lawful institution, notwithstanding it is abused. The government of the Cæsars was providentially the *de facto* one, and Nero, bad as he was, its recognized head. As such, all his magisterial acts which were not specifically contrary to God's law, were legitimate, and were the proper objects of the civic obedience of the Christian subject. Otherwise, the apostles would never have exacted it for him. The instance does imply, therefore, that civil government is a lawful relation; and this is precisely what we infer from the parallel instances of obedience enjoined on servants to masters. If Abolitionists are not willing to argue that the relation of ruler and subject is sin *per se*, notwithstanding the obedience required to Nero, they cannot argue from their proposed analogy between Nero's cruelties and slaveholding. But an equally conclusive reply is, that apostles never admitted a Nero, with his barbarities in full sway, to the same communion-table with his patient Christian victims, commanding the latter to forbear as towards a wrongdoer, and yet failing to give him the correlative command, to cease the wrong-doing.

§ 8. PHILEMON AND ONESIMUS.

The Epistle to Philemon is peculiarly instructive and convincing as to the moral character of slavery. This Abolitionists betray, by the distressing wrigglings and contortions of logic, to which they resort, in the vain attempt to evade its inferences. The whole Epistle need not be recited. The apostle, after saluting Philemon as a brother and fellow-minister, and commending him in terms of peculiar beauty, warmth, and affection, for his eminent piety, and his hospitalities and charities to Christians, proceeds thus, v. 8 to 19: "Though I might be much bold in Christ to enjoin thee that which is convenient, yet, for love's sake, I rather beseech thee, being such an one as Paul the aged, and now also a prisoner of Jesus Christ. I beseech thee for my son Onesimus, whom I have begotten in my bonds; which in time past was to thee unprofitable, but now profitable to thee and to me; whom I have sent again: thou, therefore, receive him, that is, mine own bowels: Whom I would have retained with me, that in thy stead he might have ministered unto me in the bonds of the Gospel. But without thy mind would I do nothing: that thy benefit should not be as it were of necessity, but willingly. For perhaps he therefore departed for a season, that thou shouldst receive him forever; not now as a servant, but above a servant, a brother beloved, especially to me, but how much more unto thee, both in the flesh, and in the Lord. If thou count me therefore, a partner, receive him as myself. If he hath wronged thee, or oweth thee aught, put that on mine account; I Paul have written it with mine own hand, I will repay it," &c. That it may not be supposed we give an explanation of these words warped to suit our own views, we will copy the very words of the judicious Dr. Thomas Scott, one of the most fair and reasonable of expositors, and a declared enemy of slavery. In his introduction to the Epistle, he says: "Philemon seems to have been a Christian of some eminence, residing at Colosse, (Col. iv. 9, or 17,) who had been converted under St. Paul's ministry, (19,) perhaps during his abode at Ephesus, (Acts xix. 10.) When the apostle was imprisoned at Rome, Onesimus, a slave of Philemon, having, as it is generally thought, been guilty of some dishonesty, left his master and fled to that city, though at the distance of several hundred miles. When he came thither, curiosity or some such motive induced him to attend on St. Paul's ministry, which it pleased God to bless for his conversion. After he had given satisfactory proof of a real change, and manifested an excellent disposition, by suitable behaviour, which had greatly endeared him to Paul, he judged it proper to send him back to his master, to whom he wrote this epistle, that he might procure Onesimus a more favourable reception than he could otherwise have expected." Notes on v. 12 to 16: "Onesimus was Philemon's legal property, and St. Paul had required, and prevailed with him, to return to him, having made sufficient trial of his sincerity: and he requested Philemon to receive him with the same kindness as he would the aged apostle's own son according to the flesh, being equally dear to him, as his spiritual child. He would gladly have kept him at Rome, to minister to him in his confinement, which Onesimus would willingly have done in the bonds of the Gospel, being attached to him from Christian love and gratitude; and as he knew that Philemon would gladly have done him any service in person, if he had been at Rome, so he would have considered Onesimus as ministering to him in his master's stead. But he would not do any thing of this kind without his consent, lest he should seem to extort the benefit, and Philemon should appear to act from necessity, rather than from a willing mind. And though he had hopes of deriving benefit from Onesimus' faithful service, at some future period, by Philemon's free consent, yet he was not sure that this was the Lord's purpose concerning him; for perhaps he permitted him to leave his master for a season in so improper a manner, in order that, being converted, he might be received on his return with such affection, and might abide with Philemon with such faithfulness and diligence, that they should choose to live together the rest of their lives as fellow-heirs of eternal felicity. In this case he knew that Philemon would no longer consider Onesimus merely as a slave, but view him as 'above a slave, even a brother beloved.' This he was become to Paul in an especial manner, who had before been entirely a stranger to him; how much more, then, might it be supposed that he would be endeared to Philemon, when he became well acquainted with his excellency! seeing he would be near to him both in the flesh as one of his domestics, and in the Lord, as one with him in Christ by faith."

Thus far Dr. Scott. These are substantially the views given of this epistle by Calvin, Whitby, Henry, Doddridge, McKnight, Hodge, and others: none of whom were slaveholders, or friends of the institution. Now, our purpose is not to vindicate the intrinsic innocence of slaveholding here, by dwelling again upon the just arguments, which have been already stated: that a slaveholder here receives from an inspired apostle the highest Christian commendations; and that he is addressed as a brother minister in the church. The Epistle presents still more emphatic evidence: First, if the relation is unrighteous, and the master's authority unfounded, then the only ground upon which the duty of the slave's submission rests, is that of Christian forbearance. When the wicked bonds were once happily evaded, and the oppressed person in safety, that ground of obligation was wholly at an end. A captive has been unlawfully detained by a gang of highwaymen, for the purpose of exacting ransom. He has given them the slip, and is secure. Is there any obligation to go back, because, while there, there was an obligation to refrain from useless violence and bloodshed? Let us even suppose that the means of the captive's escape were in some point immoral: does this fact make it his duty to go back and submit himself to the freebooters? By no means. To God he ought to repent of whatever was immoral in the manner of his escape: but he is bound to make no reparation for it to the robbers, because they had no right to detain him at all. But we see St. Paul here enjoining on the newly-awakened conscience of Onesimus, the duty of returning to his master. That the apostle sent him, and that he went back under a sense of moral obligation, is proved by two facts: St. Paul had a strong desire to retain him, being greatly in need of an affectionate domestic, in his infirm, aged, and imprisoned condition, but he felt that he must not. (Verse 13.) Paul had no power, except moral power, to make Onesimus go back, being himself a helpless captive; so that the latter must have been carried back by a sense of duty. Hence this instance proves, beyond a cavil, that the relation of master and servant was moral; it lies above the level of all those quibbles which we have been compelled to rebut. Second: the transaction clearly implies a moral propriety or ownership in Onesimus' labour, as pertaining to Philemon; of which the latter could not be rightfully deprived without his consent. For proof, see the fact that Paul says, (v. 14,) "Without thy mind I would do nothing, that thy benefit should not be as it were of necessity, but willingly." The attendance of Onesimus on Paul, *i. e.*, the bestowal of his labour, would have been, if given, Philemon's "benefit" to Paul. If, as Abolitionists say, Onesimus belonged to himself, how could it be Philemon's benefit, or benefaction? See also the fact that St. Paul (v. 18) explicitly recognizes the justice of Philemon's claim to indemnity for Onesimus' bad conduct. In order to smoothe the way for his pardon by his justly offended master, he proposes to pay this himself, whatever it may be, and (v. 19) gives the force of a pecuniary bond to his promise, by writing and signing it with his own hand: (the rest of the Epistle, as the most of Paul's, being evidently written by an amanuensis.) Some expositors, indeed, explain the 18th verse by supposing that Onesimus, when running away, had stolen something from Philemon. There is not a particle of evidence for this in the narrative; and it is a most unsafe method of explaining the Scriptures, to do it by bringing in gratuitous surmises. But be this as it may, Paul's language covers both suppositions, of debt for his delinquent services, and retention of his master's property: ("If he hath wronged thee, or oweth thee any thing.") Is it objected that St. Paul suggests, v. 19th, that gratitude ought to cause Philemon to forego the exaction of such a vicarious payment from him? The reply is, that the very nature of this plea implies most strongly the legal completeness of Philemon's title to the compensation. A poor man is sued for a debt. His only answer is, that he thinks the suitor ought to be *generous* enough to remit this debt to him, inasmuch as he had once saved that suitor's life. Surely this plea is itself an admission that the debt is legal; and if the claimant chooses to be ungracious enough to press it under the circumstances, it must be paid. Moreover, Philemon's debt of gratitude was, thus far, to Paul, and not to Onesimus. Paul's stepping under the burden of his debt was an act of voluntary generosity only. The apostle makes no claim of any obligation, even of courtesy, from Philemon to his delinquent slave.

But if Onesimus' labour was Philemon's property, of which he could not be rightfully deprived without his own consent, and for the loss of which he was entitled to an equivalent, slaveholding cannot be in itself unlawful. We have here a recognition of the very essence of the relation.

This case is so fatal to the theory of all Abolitionists who admit the canonical authority of the Epistle, that desperate efforts are made to pervert its meaning. Mr. Albert Barnes, Coryphæus of these expository sophists, says in one of his comments, that it does not appear from the

Epistle that Paul really sent Onesimus back to his master at all! "There is not the slightest evidence that he *compelled*, or even urged him to go. The language is just such as would have been used on the supposition, either that he *suggested* to him to go and bear a letter to Colosse, or that Onesimus desired to go, and that Paul sent him agreeably to his request. Compare Philip. ii. 25, Col. iv. 7, 8. But Epaphroditus and Tychicus were not sent against their own will; nor is there any more reason to think that Onesimus was." Mr. Barnes then adds the notable reason, that Paul had no sheriff or constable to send Onesimus by; so that if he did not choose to return, he could not compel him. But the stubborn fact is, that Onesimus went; and it must be accounted for. This author's account is, that he probably found he had not mended his condition by running away, and so, desired to return to regain his comfortable home; whereupon Paul availed himself of the occasion to write to his friend. This solution is not particularly honourable to the religious character of either party: we shall neither insult the apostle by adopting, nor the understanding of readers by refuting it. As to Paul's 'sending' of Epaphroditus to Phillippi, and Tychicus to Colosse, we note that the word is not the same with the one used of Onesimus. This is ανεπεμψα; and it is expressly defined by Robinson's Lexicon as an authoritative sending up, or remitting to a higher tribunal, such as the sending of Paul by Festus to Cæsar, Acts xxv. 21. Further, Paul did 'send' these two brethren, not indeed as slaves are sent, but by his apostolic authority, to which they doubtless cheerfully responded. Paul had no physical force by which to drive Onesimus all the way from Rome to Colosse; but there is such a thing as moral power, and the fact that the conscience of the sent freely seconds the righteous authority of the sender, surely does not prove this authority to be naught. How perverse must he be, who can see in the words, "whom I (Paul) have sent," nothing but that Onesimus sent himself! Is not this the state of facts, plain to any honest mind: that Paul instructed him it was his duty to return to his lawful master, and as his spiritual teacher told him to do so? And this injunction the converted Onesimus cheerfully obeyed.

Mr. Barnes also says, it is not proved that Onesimus was a literal slave at all; he may have been a hired servant or apprentice. Here, as will appear more fully, he expressly contradicts himself. But as to the assumption, we reply, that Onesimus is called, v. 16, δουλος, a name never given to the hired servant: that he is sent back to his rightful owner, a thing which necessarily implies his slavery: that St. Paul intercedes for him; and that he recognizes his master's property in his labour. The whole company of expositors, ancient and modern, until Mr. Barnes, have declared that Onesimus was Philemon's slave.

But others again, following the same notable guide, learn that he was manumitted by the letter of Paul; so that they find here, not a justification of the slaveholder, but an implied rebuke of slavery. Thus contradictory is error! Just now he was not a slave at all: now he is a slave manumitted; and that by one who had no power to do it. The ground claimed for the latter position is, v. 16, "Not now as a servant, but above a servant, a brother beloved." Now, the obvious sense of these words is, that Philemon should now receive Onesimus back, not as a slave only, but as both a slave and Christian brother. For proof: By what law could Paul manumit another man's servant? And he had admitted Philemon's rightful authority, v. 10, by saying: "I beseech thee for my son Onesimus." Why beseech, if he might have commanded? If Paul had a right to emancipate, why did he send him back at all, when every other motive prompted to keep him? He again disclaims such right, v. 14, "But without thy mind I would do nothing." Still another proof appears, v. 18, 19, where St. Paul fully recognizes Onesimus' continued servitude by undertaking to pay for his delinquencies. The Epistle then adds, that Philemon was "to receive him back forever," v. 15, *i. e.*, for life. The residence of a free denizen or dependent could not be defined as for life; because he would go away whenever he pleased. And last, St. Paul expressly declares that this life-long relation was to be political as well as spiritual, both that of a servant and fellow-Christian—"How much more (beloved) now unto thee both in the flesh and in the Lord."

Such are the wretched quibblings by which abolitionism seeks to pervert the plain meaning of God's Word, as clearly apprehended by the great current of Christian expositors, both ancient and modern, Greek, Latin, and English. We almost feel that an apology is due to the enlightened reader, for detaining him with the formal exposure of these miserable follies; but our promise was to display the thorough emptiness of our opponents.

§ 8. St. Paul reprobates Abolitionists.

One passage of the New Testament remains to be noticed. It is that which commands the exclusion of Abolitionist teachers from church communion, 1 Tim. vi. 3-5. St. Paul had just enjoined on this young minister the giving of proper moral instruction to servants. The pulpit was to teach them the duty of subordination to masters, as to rightful authority; and if those masters were also Christians, then the obligation was only the stronger. See v. 1, 2. The apostle then proceeds, v. 3, "If any man teach otherwise, and consent not to wholesome words, even the words of our Lord Jesus Christ, and to the doctrine which is according to godliness," (the opposite teaching of abolitionism contradicts Christ's own word,) "he is proud, knowing nothing, but doting about questions and strifes of words, whereof cometh envy, strife, railings, evil surmisings, perverse disputings of men of corrupt minds, and destitute of the truth, supposing that gain is godliness: from such withdraw thyself."

The more carefully these words of the Holy Ghost are considered, the more exceedingly remarkable will they appear. Doubtless, every reader of previous ages has felt a slight trace of wonder, that the apostle should have left on record a rebuke of such particularity, sternness, and emphasis, when there appeared nothing in the opinions or abuses of the Christian world, of sufficient importance quite to justify it. We have no evidence that, either in the primitive or mediæval church, any marked disposition prevailed to assail the rights of masters over their slaves, to such extent as to threaten the disorganization of civil society or the dishonouring of Christianity thereby. This denunciation of the apostle seems to have been sufficient to give the *quietus* to the spirit of abolition, so long as any reverence for inspiration remained. Even while the policy of the Roman Church and clergy was steadily directed to the extinction of feudal slavery in Western Europe, it does not appear that the doctors of that church assailed the master's rights or preached insubordination to the slaves. Why then did St. Paul judge it necessary to leave on record so startling a denunciation? The question is answered by the events of our age: these words were written for us on whom these ends of the world have come. And we have here a striking proof that his pen was guided by omniscient foreknowledge. The God who told Paul what to write, foresaw that though the primitive church stood in comparatively slight need of such admonitions, the century would come, after the lapse of eighteen ages, when the church would be invaded and defiled by the deadly spirit of modern abolitionism, a spirit perverse, blind, divisive and disorganizing, which would become the giant scourge and opprobrium of Christianity. Therefore has this stern warning been recorded here, and left standing until events should make men understand both its wisdom and the lineaments of the monster which it foreshadowed. The learned Calvin, and the amiable Henry, in explaining the Epistle to Philemon, allude to the question: Why should this short letter, which directly touches no publick concernment of the churches, written on a personal topick from Paul to his friend, be preserved among the canonical Scriptures by God's Spirit and providence? They answer, that it was placed there because, although short and of private concernment, it teaches us many pleasing lessons of Paul's condescension and courtesy, and above all, of the adaptation of Christianity to visit, purify, and elevate the lowest and vilest of the ranks of men. This is true, so far as it goes; but another part of God's purpose is now developed. He left this little Epistle among his authoritative words, because he foresaw that the day would come when the Church would need just the instructions against insubordination, which are here presented in a concrete case.

Those who have seen and suffered by modern abolitionism best know, how astonishingly true is the picture here drawn of it by the Divine limner. God here declares that the principles of the lawfulness of slavery, the rights of masters, and the duty of obedience in slaves, are wholesome, and according to godliness. In addition, the sacred authority of our Lord Jesus Christ is claimed for them. The Abolitionist who assails these teachings is described as a man proud, yet ignorant. This combined arrogance and vindictiveness, with ignorance of the true facts and merits of the case upon which they presume to dictate, are proverbial in modern abolitionism, according to the testimony of neutral parties, and even of some of their own clique. With a stupid superciliousness, equally ludicrous and offensive, they revile men wiser and better than themselves, and pass an oracular verdict upon questions of which they know nothing. They are doting about questions and strifes of words: that is, as the original word means, their minds are morbid with logomachies, and idle debates, and corrupted by prejudice and the spirit of disputation. ("Perverse disputings of men of corrupt minds.") Those who have read thus far in this discussion have seen, in the prejudiced sophisms which we have been compelled to quote for refutation, sufficient evidence of the perverse, erroneous, and disputatious spirit of abolitionism. Their dogmas are not supported by the testimony of Scripture, nor the lights of practical experience, nor sound political philosophy; but by vain and Utopian theories of human rights, and philosophy falsely so called. The fruit of their discussions has been naught but "envy, strife, railings, and evil surmisings." The fact betrays itself in a thousand ways, that envy of the slaveholder and his supposed advantages and power, is the root of much of their zeal. Hence the epithets of "aristocrat," "lordly slaveholder," "Southern nabob," as ridiculously false to fact as envious, which form so large a part of the staple of their abuse. They hate us because they suppose we possessed a privilege of which they were deprived. The angry and divisive tendencies of abolitionism have manifested themselves but too familiarly in the rending of churches, in the awakening of fierce contention wherever it has appeared, in the destruction of the union both of law and of love between the American States, and in a gigantic war which has filled a continent with woe and crime. And the remaining trait of "railings" is verified by the fact that these professed friends of humanity have exhausted the most inhuman stores of vituperation upon a class of Christian people whom none can know without loving for their purity and benevolence. There is no sect that knows how to scold so virulently as the Abolitionists. The apostle adds that they are "men of corrupt minds, and destitute of the truth." Now it is notoriously the fact that this sect, although claiming to be the special advocates of righteousness, have ever prosecuted their ends by unprincipled and false means. Their party action has been hypocritical and unscrupulous. Their main weapons have been slanders. And the tendency to mendacity has since been illustrated on a scale so grand in the recent War, by falsifications of fact, diplomatic treacheries, and wholesale breaches of covenant, that the accuracy of the apostle's description becomes startling. It would seem that when once a man is swayed by this spirit fully, he is under a fatality to speak untruth, whether he be prime-minister, historian, official of government, or divine.

The last trait of abolitionism which the apostle draws, is one which, at the first glance, strikes the observer with surprise, but which is fully verified by the reality. This is the intensely mercenary spirit of the sect. "Supposing that gain is godliness." Without due reflection, one would suppose that a party animated as much as this is by an intense and sincere fanaticism, and that, a fanaticism of pretended humanity, whatever violences it might commit, would at least be free from the vice of a calculated avarice. But the suppleness of fanaticism in affiliating with every other vice, is not duly appreciated; it is a fact, true, if unexpected, that genuine fanaticism can tolerate any thing except the peculiar object of its hate, and that it is compatible with supreme selfishness. For what is fanaticism but selfishness acting under the forms of pride with its offspring censoriousness, the lust of power, envy, and dogmatism? Modern events verify the apostle's picture: the religion and humanitarianism of abolition are only a covert avarice. The people of the American States are notorious for their worship of wealth, just in proportion as they are swayed by the anti-slavery furor. No party has ever appeared on the stage of Federal politics, whose ends were so avowedly selfish and mercenary. The wrongs of the slave have been the pretext, sectional and personal aggrandizement the true ends. That party, under the phase of "free-soil," has thrown off the mask, and avowed the declaration that the true meaning of their opposition to the rights of Southern masters in the territories is, that "the soil of America belongs to the white man;" and the poor negro, though now a native of it, is begrudged a home and a living upon it. There is no class of people in America which has expended so little of its money for the actual advantage of the black race, as the abolitionists. Usually, the history of the case has been, that they would give of their money, neither to ransom a slave from bondage, nor to aid the cause of African colonization, nor to assist a distressed free negro of their own section: the only use to which they can be induced to apply it is the printing of vituperations against the masters. It was the testimony of the fugitive slaves themselves, that the philanthropy of the Abolitionists extended only to seducing them from their homes; thenceforth their whole thought was to make gain of their godliness. The crowning evidence, however, of the mercenary spirit of this party is in this fact, that their advent to power in the Federal government of the United States has been, according to the testimony of their mutual recriminations, the epoch of an unprecedented reign of peculation and official corruption. Such is the picture of abolitionism as drawn by the Apostle Paul, and verified in America in our day. It is our privilege and our wisdom to obey his closing injunction, "From such withdraw thyself," that we may not become partakers of their sins. From this stern and just denunciation, it may be learned how utterly the New Testament is opposed to the whole doctrine and spirit of the party.

We have now passed in review every passage in the New Testament, in which domestic slavery is directly treated, and we have seen that they every one imply the innocency of the institution. We have discussed many of the evasions by which Abolitionists attempt to escape these testimonies, and have found them utterly unsound. There remain two pleas, of more general application to the New Testament argument, to which the ablest of their advocates seem to attach prime importance. To these we will now attend.

§ 9. THE GOLDEN RULE COMPATIBLE WITH SLAVERY.

One of these general objections to our New Testament argument is the following. They say, Christ could not have intended to authorize slavery, because the tenour and spirit of His moral teachings are opposed to it. The temper He currently enjoins is one of fraternity, equality, love, and disinterestedness. But holding a fellow-being in bondage is inconsistent with all these. Especially is the great "Golden Rule" incompatible with slavery. This enjoins us to do unto our neighbour as we would that he should do unto us. Now, as no slaveholder would like to be himself enslaved, this is a clear proof that we should not hold others in slavery. Hence, the interpretations which seem to find authority for slavery in certain passages of the New Testament, must be erroneous, and we are entitled to reject them without examination. Abolitionists usually advance this with a disdainful confidence, as though he who does not admit its justice were profoundly stupid. But it is exceedingly easy to show that it is a bald instance of *petitio principii*, and it is founded on a preposterous interpretation of the Golden Rule, which every sensible Sabbath-school boy knows how to explode. Its whole plausibility rests on the *à priori* assumption of prejudice, that slaveholding cannot but be wicked, and on a determination not to see it otherwise. Our refutation, which is demonstrative, reveals the Socinian origin and Rationalistic character of these opinions. Socinianism harbours loose views of the authority of inspiration, and especially of that of the Old Testament. It scruples not to declare, that these venerable documents contain many admixtures of human error, and wherever it finds in them any thing it does not like, it boldly rejects and repudiates it. Moreover, Socinianism having denied the divinity of our Redeemer Christ, finds itself compelled to attempt an answer to the hard question: Wherein, then, is He greater than Moses, David, or Isaiah? And in what respect does He fulfil those transcendent representations which the Scriptures correctly give of His superiority of person and mission? The answer which orthodoxy makes is plain and good: That it is because He is God as well as man, while they were but sinful men, redeemed and inspired; and that His mission is to regenerate and atone, while theirs was only to teach. But the answer which Socinianism has devised is in part this:

Christ was commissioned to reform the moral system of the Old Testament, and to teach a new law of far superior beauty, purity, and benevolence. Thus, they have a corrupt polemical motive to misrepresent and degrade the Old Testament law, in order to make a *Nodus vindice dignus*, for their imaginary Christ, who does nothing but teach. To effect this, they seize on all such passages as those in the "Sermon on the Mount," which refute Pharisaic glosses, and evolve the true law of love. This is the mint from which abolitionists have borrowed their objections against our Old Testament defence of slaveholding; such as this, that however it may have been allowed to the Hebrews, by their older and ruder law, "because of the hardness of their hearts," it is condemned by the new law of love, taught by Jesus. Now, our refutation (and it is perfect) is, that this law of love was just as fully announced by slaveholding Moses as it is by Jesus; in terms just as full of sweetness, benevolence, and universal fraternity. Yea more, the very words of Jesus cited by them and their Socinian allies, as the most striking instances of the superior mildness and love of His teachings, are in most cases quoted from Moses himself! The authority by which Christ enforced them upon His Jewish auditors was Moses' own! Such is the shameful ignorance of these fanatics concerning the real contents of that Old Testament which they depreciate. Thus, Christ's epitome of the whole law into the two commands to love God and our neighbour, is *avowedly quoted* from "the law," *i. e.*, the Pentateuch. See Matthew xxii. 36 to 39, and Mark xii. 28 to 33. It may be found in Deut. vi. 4 and 5, and in Levit. xix. 18. Even the scribe of Mark, xii. 32, Pharisee as he was, understood better than these modern Pharisees of abolitionism, that Christ's ethics were but a reproduction of Moses'. He avows the correctness of Christ's rendering of the Pentateuch law, and very intelligently adduces additional evidence of it by evident allusion to 1 Samuel xv. 22, and Hosea vi. 6. Again: does Christ inculcate forgiveness of injuries, benefactions towards enemies, and the embracing of aliens in our philanthropy as well as kindred and fellow-citizens? He does but cite them to the authority of Moses in Levit. xix. 18, Exod. xxiii. 4, 5, Levit. xxiv. 22, Exod. xxii. 21, xxxiii. 9. For here their great prophet himself had taught them that revenge must be left to God, that an embarrassed or distressed enemy must be kindly assisted, and that the alien must be treated in all humane respects as a fellow-citizen, under a lively and sympathetic sense of their own sufferings when they were oppressed aliens in Egypt. The Golden Rule, as stated by our Saviour, is but a practical application of the Mosaic precept "to love our neighbours as ourselves," borrowed from Moses. In Matt. vii. 12, Christ, after giving the Golden Rule, adds, "for this is the law and the prophets." That is, the Golden Rule is the summary of the morality of the Pentateuch and Old Testament prophets. We repeat that there is not one trait of love, of benevolence, of sweet expansive fraternity, of amiable equity, contained in any of Christ's precepts or parables, that is not also found in the Laws of Moses. Their moral teachings are absolutely at one, in principle; and so they must be, if both are from the unchangeable God. To say otherwise is a denial of inspiration; it is infidelity; and indeed abolitionism is infidelity. Our reply, then, is, *that Christ's giving the law of love cannot be inconsistent with his authorizing slaveholding; because Moses gave the same law of love, and yet indisputably authorized slaveholding.* We defy all the sophisms of the whole crew of the perverse and destitute of the truth, to obscure, much less to rebut this answer, without denying the inspiration and even the common truthfulness of Moses. But that they will not stickle to do: for what do they care for Moses, or Christ either, in comparison of their fanatical idol?

But a more special word should be devoted to the argument from the Golden Rule. The sophism is so bald, and the clear evolution of it has been given so often, even in the humblest manuals of ethics prepared for school-boys, that it is tiresome to repeat its exposure. But as leading Abolitionists continue to advance the oft-torn and tattered folly, the friends of truth must continue to tear it to shreds. The whole reasoning of the Abolitionists proceeds on the absurd idea, that any caprice or vain desire we might entertain towards our fellow-man, if we were in his place, and he in ours, must be the rule of our conduct towards him, whether the desire would be in itself right or not. This absurdity has been illustrated by a thousand instances. On this rule, a parent who, were he a child again, would be wayward and self-indulgent, commits a clear sin in restraining or punishing the waywardness of his child, for this is doing the opposite of what he would wish were he again the child. Judge and sheriff commit a criminal murder in condemning and executing the most atrocious felon; for were they on the gallows themselves, the overmastering love of life would very surely prompt them to desire release. In a word, whatever ill-regulated desire we are conscious of having, or of being likely to have, in reversed circumstances, that desire we are bound to make the rule of our action in granting the parallel caprice of any other man, be he bore, beggar, highwayman, or what not. On this understanding, the Golden Rule would become any thing but golden; it would be a rule of iniquity; for instead of making impartial equity our regulating principle, it would make the accidents of man's criminal caprice the law of his acts. It would become every man's duty to enable all other men to do whatever his own sinful heart, *mutatis mutandis*, might prompt.

The absurdity of the abolitionist argument may be shown, again, by "carrying the war into Africa." We prove from it, by a process precisely as logical as theirs, that emancipation is a sin. Surely the principle of the Golden Rule binds the slave just as much as the master. If the desire which one would feel (*mutatis mutandis*) must govern each man's conduct, then the slave may be very sure that, were he the master, he would naturally desire to retain the services of the slaves who were his lawful property. Therefore, according to this abolition rule, he is morally bound to decline his own liberty; *i. e.*, to act towards his master as he, were he the master, would desire his slave to act.

It is clear, then, that our Saviour, by His Golden Rule, never intended to establish so absurd a law. The rule of our conduct to our neighbour is not any desire which we might have, were we to change places; but it is *that desire which we should, in that case, be morally entitled to have.* To whatsoever treatment we should conscientiously think ourselves morally entitled, were we slaves instead of masters, all that treatment we as masters are morally bound to give our servants, so far as ability and a just regard for other duties enables us. Whether that treatment should include emancipation, depends on another question, whether the desire which we, if slaves, should very naturally feel to be emancipated, is a righteous desire or not; or, in other words, whether the obligation to service is rightful. Hence, before the Golden Rule can be cited as enjoining emancipation, it must first be settled whether the master's title is unrighteous. The Apostle Paul gives precisely the true application of this rule when he says: "Masters, give unto your servants that which is just and equal." And this means, not emancipation from servitude, but good treatment as servants; which is proven by the fact that the precept contemplates the relation of masters and servants as still subsisting. All this is so clear, that it would be an insult to the intelligence of the reader to tarry longer upon the sophism. We only add, that the obvious meaning above put upon the Golden Rule is that given to it by all sensible expositors, such as Whitby, Scott, Henry, before it received an application to this controversy. Yet, though this obvious answer has been a hundred times offered, abolitionists still obtrude the miserable cheat, in speeches, in pamphlets, in tracts, as though it were the all-sufficient demonstration of the anti-Christian character of slavery. They will doubtless continue a hundred times more to offer it, to gull none, however, except the wilfully blind.

§ 10. WAS CHRIST AFRAID TO CONDEMN SLAVERY?

The other general evasion of the New Testament argument for the lawfulness of slavery, is to say: That Jesus Christ and his apostles did not indeed explicitly condemn slavery; but that they forbore from doing so for prudential reasons. They saw, say these abolitionists, that it was a sin universally prevalent, entwined with the whole fabrick of human society, and sustained by a tremendous weight of sinful prejudice and self-interest. To denounce it categorically would have been to plunge the infant church, at its feeble beginning, into all the oppositions, slanders, and strifes of a great social revolution, thus jeopardizing all its usefulness to the souls of men. For this reason, Christ and his apostles wisely refrained from direct attack, and contented themselves with spreading through the world principles of love and equity, before which slavery would surely melt away in due time. So say all the abolitionists. So says Dr. Wayland, in substance, not only in his discussion of slavery, but in his more responsible and deliberate work, the "Moral Science." In that essay, Bk. II., Pt. II., Chap. I., § 1, he says: "The Gospel was designed, not for one race, or for one time, but for all races, and for all times. It looked not at the abolition of this form of evil for that age alone, but for its universal abolition. Hence the important object of its author was to gain it a lodgement in every part of the known world: so that by its universal diffusion among all classes of society, it might quietly and peacefully modify and subdue the evil passions of men; and thus, without violence, work a revolution in the whole mass of mankind. In this manner alone could its object, a universal moral revolution, have been accomplished. For if it had forbidden the evil instead of subverting the principle—if it had proclaimed the unlawfulness of slavery, and taught slaves to *resist* the oppression of their masters, it would instantly have arrayed the two parties in deadly hostility throughout the civilized world; its announcement would have been the signal of servile war, and the very name of the Christian religion would have been forgotten amidst the agitations of universal bloodshed. The fact that, under these circumstances, the Gospel does not forbid slavery, affords no reason to suppose that it does not mean to prohibit it; much less does it afford ground for belief that Jesus Christ intended to authorize it."

Such is the Jesuitry which is gravely charged, by a professed minister of the Christian religion, and prominent instructor of youth, upon our Lord Jesus Christ and his apostles! Such is the cowardly prudence which it imputes to men who, every one, died martyrs for their moral courage and unvarying fidelity to truth. And thus is the divine origin and agency by which, the Bible declares, and by which alone Christianity is to succeed in a hostile world, quietly left out of view; and American youth are taught to apprehend it as a creed which has no Divine king ruling the universe for its propagation, no Almighty providence engaged for its protection, no Holy Ghost working irresistibly in the hearts of such as God shall call, to subdue their enmity to the obedience of Christ: but Christianity is merely a human system of moral reform, liable to total extinction, unless it is a little sly in keeping back its unpopular points, until an adroit occasion offers, (such, for instance, as the power and support of a resistless Yankee majority in some confederation of slaveholders,) to make the unpopular doctrine go down, or at least, to choke off those who dare to make wry faces! Christ and the twelve went out, forsooth, into a sinful and perishing world, professing to teach men the way of salvation; and yet, although they knew that any sin persevered in must damn the soul, they were totally silent as to one great and universal crime! They came avowedly to "reprove the world of sin, of righteousness, and of judgment;" and yet uttered no rebuke for this "sum of all villainies." They went preaching the Gospel of repentance from all known sin, as the sole condition of eternal life: and yet never notified their hearers of the sin of one universal practice prevalent among them, lest, forsooth, they should raise a storm of prejudice against their system! Nay, far worse than this: they are not satisfied with a *suppressio veri*, but as though to insure the fatal misleading of the consciences which they undertook to guide to life, their policy of pusillanimity leads them to a positive *suggestio falsi*. Had they been simply and wholly silent about the great sin, this had been bad enough. But this is not what they did. It is a glozing deceit to attempt to cover up the case under the pretended admission that "the Gospel does not forbid slavery," as though this were the whole of it. Christ and his apostles allude to slavery: they say a multitude of things about it: they travel all around it: they limit its rights and define its duties: they retrench its abuses: they admit the perpetrators of its wrong, (if it be a wrong,) unrepenting, into the bosom of the church, and to its highest offices. They do almost every thing which is calculated to justify in masters the inference that it is lawful. And then they finally dismiss the whole matter, without one explicit warning of its sinfulness and danger. According to this theory, the apostles find their trusting pupils on the brink of the precipice, surrounded with much darkness; and having added almost every circumstance adapted farther to obfuscate their consciences, they coolly leave them there, with no other guidance than a reference to those general principles of equity which, beautifully taught by Moses, had already signally failed to enlighten them.

Dr. Wayland's hypothesis is also deceitful and erroneous, in representing Christ as having no alternatives save the one which he imputes to him, or else of so denouncing slavery as to "teach slaves to *resist* the oppression of their masters," and thus lighting the flames of servile war. Is this so? When a given claim is condemned by the Bible as not grounded in right, does it necessarily follow on Gospel principles that those on whom it is made must resist it by force? Surely not. The uniform teaching of our Saviour to the wronged individual is, "that he resist not evil." Christ, if he had regarded slaveholding as sinful, would not indeed have incited slaves to resistance, any more than he did the victims of polygamy which he condemned. But he would have taught his disciples the sinfulness of the relation, and within the pale of his own spiritual commonwealth, the Church, he would have enforced reformation by refusing to admit or retain any who persevered in the wrong. Less than this he could not have done.

The hypothesis is also false to facts and to the actual method of his mission towards deeply rooted sins, as declared both by his words and conduct. He expressly repudiates this very theory of action. He declares that he came "not to send peace on earth, but a sword:" and announces himself as the grand incendiary of the world. How degrading to the almighty king of Zion is this imputation of politic cowardice! And how different from the real picture where we see him boldly exposing the hypocrisy of the Jewish rulers, and assailing their most cherished deceptions, though he knew that the price of his truthfulness would be his blood! And can this paltry theory be true of that Paul, who took his hearers to record, in full view of his dread account, that he was "clear from the blood of all men, because he had not shunned to declare to them all the counsel of God?" (Acts, xx. 27.) This of the man who everywhere assailed and explicitly denounced the idolatry of Greece and Rome, established by law, entwined with every feeling, and defended by imperial might? This of men who, sternly reprobating the universal libertinism of the heathen world, attacked what every one, countenanced by sages and statesmen, regarded as a lawful indulgence? This of men who boldly roused every prejudice of the Jewish heart, by declaring their darling system of rites and types effete, their ceremonial righteousness a cheat, and the middle wall of partition between them and the Gentiles, the bulwark of their proud spiritual aristocracy, broken down? It is slander.

Finally, this hypothesis represents that Saviour who claimed omniscience, as adopting a policy which was as futile as dishonest. He forbore the utterance of any express testimony against the sin of slaveholding, say they, leaving the church to find it out by deduction from general principles of equity. But in point of fact, the church never began to make such deduction, until near the close of the 18th century. Neither primitive, nor reformed, nor Romanist, nor modern divines taught the doctrine of the intrinsic sinfulness of slaveholding. The church as a body never dreamed it. Slavery remained almost universal. It remained for the political agitators of atheistic, Jacobin France, almost eighteen hundred years after Christ's birth, to give active currency to this new doctrine, and thus to infuse energy into the fanaticism of the few erratic Christian teachers, such as Wesley, who had hitherto asserted this novelty. Now, did Christ foresee this? If he did not, he is not divine. If he did, then Dr. Wayland believes that he deliberately chose a plan which consigned seventeen centuries of Christians to a sin, and as many of slaves to a wrong, which he all along abhorred. *Credat Judæus Apella!*

The book from which we have extracted these words of Dr. Wayland, was put forth by him as a text-book for the instruction of young persons in academies and colleges, in the *science of morals*. We are informed that it is extensively used for this purpose. What can be expected of that people which suffers the very springs of its morality to be thus corrupted, by inculcating these ethics of expediency? Not satisfied with teaching to mortals that species of morality, so called, which makes convenience the measure of obligation, this scribe of their Israel imputes the same degrading principle to the Redeemer of men, and Author of religion, in thus suppressing the truth, and intimating error to whole generations of his own followers, in order to avoid the inconveniences of candour. So that unsuspecting youth are thus taught to approve and imitate this corrupt expediency, in the very person of the Redeemer God, whom they are commanded to adore. Will the Yankee give an actual *apotheosis* to his crooked principles, in the person of an imaginary New England Christ? We thank God that this is not the Christ of the Bible, nor our Redeemer, but only the hideous invention of "men of perverse minds and destitute of the truth." But since we are taught (Psalm cxv. 8) that they who worship false Gods are like unto them, that is to say, that idolaters always reproduce in themselves all the abominations which they adore in their idols, we need no longer wonder at any thing which the Yankee people may do. Hence that state of publick morals blazoned to the world by the effrontery of their own corrupt press, charged upon each other in their mutual recriminations, and betrayed in their crimes against the general weal.

In concluding the biblical part of this discussion, it may be expected that we should indicate more exactly the influence which we suppose Christianity ought to have exerted upon slavery, and its ultimate destiny under pure Bible teachings. It may be asked: "When you claim that slavery is literally and simply a righteous relation, in itself, if it be not perverted and abused; do you mean that this is the normal and perfect relation for the labouring man; that this is to be the fullest and most blessed social development of Christianity: that it ought to subsist in the best states of Christian society, and will endure even in the millennium?" We reply, that one uniform effect of Christianity on slavery, has been to ameliorate it, to remove its perversions and abuses, just as it does those of the other lawful relations among men; to make better masters and better servants, and thus to promote the welfare of both. Domestic slavery has been violently and mischievously ended in the South; and it is doubtless ended here in this form, finally. And it has long been manifest that the radical and anti-Christian tendency of the age is likely speedily to break up this form of servitude in other places where it still prevails. But true slavery, that is, the involuntary subjection of one man to the will of another, is not thereby any more abolished than sin and death are abolished. And least of all will real bondage of man to man be abolished in countries governed by radical democracy. The Scriptural, the milder and more benign form of servitude is swept away, in the arrogance of false political philosophy, to be replaced by more pretentious but more grinding forms of society. But, it may be asked: Will not the diffusion of the pure and blessed

principles of the Gospel ultimately extinguish all forms of slavery? We
answer: Yes, we devoutly trust it will, not by making masters too
righteous to hold slaves, but by so correcting the ignorance,
thriftlessness, indolence, and vice of labouring people, that the
institution of slavery will be no longer needed. Just so, we hope that
the spread of Christianity will some day abolish penitentiaries and jails:
but this does not imply that to put rogues into penitentiaries is not now,
and will not continue, so long as rogues shall continue to deserve
imprisonment, an act which an angel might perform without sullying
his morality. So likewise, we hope that our ransomed world will see the
day when defensive war and military establishments will be superseded:
superseded not because defensive war and the calling of the Christian
soldier are immoral when one's country is wrongfully invaded; but
because there will be none immoral enough to commit the aggressions
which now justify these costly, though righteous expedients of defence.
There appears, in many minds, a strange impotency to comprehend the
truth, that the strict righteousness of the relation maintained, and the
treatment observed towards a person, may depend on that person's
character. They will not see that, as it may be strictly moral to punish
one who is guilty because of his guilt, and yet suffering is not intrinsic
good in itself; so it may be perfectly righteous to hold a class in
bondage, which is incapable of freedom, and yet it may be true still that
bondage is not a good in itself. Because they cannot accept the extreme
dogma, that domestic slavery is the *beau ideal* of the proper relation of
labour to capital, they seem to imagine that they are bound in
consistency to hold that it is somehow an evil. Yet they have too much
reverence for God's word to assert, with the abolitionists, in the teeth
of its fair meaning, that slavery is sin *per se*. So, they attempt to stand
on an intermediate ground of invisible and infinitesimal breadth. The
plain solution of the matter is, that slavery may not be the *beau ideal* of
the social organization; that there is a true evil in the necessity for it,
but that this evil is not slavery, but the ignorance and vice in the
labouring classes, of which slavery is the useful and righteous remedy;
righteous so long as the condition of its utility exists. Others pass to
another extreme, and seeing that the Bible undoubtedly teaches that
slaveholding is righteous, they liken the relation to those of the
husband and father. There is, however, this obvious difference: These
relations were established in paradise before man fell. Their
righteousness and usefulness are not dependent on the fact that man is
a sinner, and they would be appropriately continued as long as men are

in the body, though all were perfectly wise and holy. But the propriety of slavery, like that of the restraints and punishments of civil government, rests on the fact that man is depraved and fallen. Such is his character, that the rights of the whole, and the greatest welfare of the whole, may, in many cases, demand the subjection of one part of society to another, even as man's sinfulness demands the subjection of all to civil government. Slavery is, indeed, but one form of the institution, *government*. Government is controul. Some controul over all is necessary, righteous, and beneficent: the degree of it depends on the character of those to be controuled. As that character rises in the scale of true virtue, and self-command, the degree of outward controul may be properly made lighter. If the lack of those properties in any class is so great as to demand, for the good and safety of the whole, that extensive controul which amounts to slavery, then slavery is righteous, righteous by precisely the same reason that other government is righteous. And this is the Scriptural account of the origin of slavery, as justly incurred by the sin and depravity of man.

CHAPTER VII.
THE ETHICAL ARGUMENT.

§ 1. The flimsy character of the arguments based by the abolitionists on the Scriptures, betrays another than a biblical origin for their doctrines. They come primarily not from God's word, but from "philosophy falsely so called;" the abolitionists, having determined on them in advance, are only concerned with the sacred records, to thrust them aside by quibbles and evasions. But the only sure and perfect rule of right is the Bible. This, we have seen, condemns domestic slavery neither expressly nor by implication. It shows us the institution in the family of the "Father of the faithful," the "friend of God," and there recognized by God himself in the solemn sacrament of the Old Testament circumcision: We have found it expressly authorized to God's chosen people, Israel, and defended in the Decalogue itself: We see it existing throughout the ages of that dispensation, while inspired men, so far from condemning, practised it: We see that it is not removed by the fuller light of the New Testament; but on the contrary, its duties are defined, and slaveholders admitted to all the privileges of the Church: We learn, in a word, that domestic slavery existed throughout the ages of revelation, was practised continually by multitudes of God's own people, was never once rebuked, but often recognized and authorized. We assert then, that, according to that infallible standard, it is lawful.

Yet, it is condemned in unmeasured terms by most of the people of Christendom, is said to be abhorrent to the political ethicks of the age, and has been reprobated by some of the fathers of our own commonwealth. What then? In the emphatic language of the book whose protection we claim: "Let God be true, but every man a liar." Nor are we much concerned to explain away this collision between human speculation and God's word. When we consider the weakness of human reason, and the mortifying history of its vagaries; when we remember how many dogmas once held for axioms are now exploded, and what monstrous crimes and follies have been upheld by the unanimous consent of philosophers, we are not afraid to adopt the teachings of the All-Wise, in preference to the deductions of blundering and purblind mortals. When the political experience of the world shall have matured and corrected the opinions of men, we have no fear but that all the truly wise, and good, and philosophical, will justify us, and will acknowledge that this simple, this decried, this abhorred expedient of inspired law-givers was, after all, best conformed to the true wants and welfare of those to whom it was applied, and wiser than any of the conceited *nostrums* of political quackery; that, in short, "the foolishness of God was wiser than men." Here, then, we place our feet; and our answer to reviling abolitionists and a frowning world is: Your reproach is not against us, but God. Go and convict the All-Wise of folly, the Infinite Holiness of injustice. Amidst the cruel sufferings of the war which was thrust upon us for this institution, and of the violent and disastrous overthrow of our liberties; amidst the floods of obloquy which our interested persecutors have belched forth upon us, and the contemptuous neglect of the nations, our confidence is in God's countenance. He permits us to be sorely chastened for our sins; but he will not finally suffer his own honour to be reproached. He will surely rebuke in the end, the folly and impiety of our slanderers, and "bring forth our righteousness as the noonday."

The Socinian and skeptical type of all the evasions of our Scriptural argument has been already intimated. If the most profane and reckless wresting of God's word will not serve their turn, to make it speak abolitionism, then they not seldom repudiate its authority. One of their leaders, long a professed minister of the Gospel, declares, at the close of a train of tortuous sophisms, that if he were compelled to believe the Bible countenances slavery, he should be compelled to give up the Bible: thereby virtually confessing that he had never been convinced of the infallibility of that which, for thirty years, he had been pretending to preach to men as infallible. Others, more blatant and blasphemous, when compelled to admit that both the Bible and the American constitution recognized slavery, exclaimed: "Give me, then, an anti-slavery constitution, an anti-slavery Bible, and an anti-slavery God!"

Orthodox Christians have always held it as a rule perfectly settled, that a revelation which was made to yield to any and every supposed deduction of reason, would be no authoritative rule of faith at all. It is only when the express word of Scripture clearly contradicts a proposition which appears to be a primary intuition of the reason, that it constitutes any difficulty in the reception of God's word. But can this prejudice against slavery claim to be such? The tests of such truths are, that they shall be seen in their own light to be true; that they shall be necessary; and that all sane human beings shall inevitably believe them, if they comprehend the terms of the statements. Obviously, abolitionism can claim none of these traits. Instead of being self-evident, we shall show that it is a mere deduction from a deceitful and baseless theory. To the mind of all former ages, it has failed to commend itself as true. All ancient nations, and most moderns, have believed the contrary. All ancient philosophers, and all Bible saints, the latter at least as conscientious and clear-headed as modern fanatics, believed slavery to be lawful. The great philosophers of the middle ages, surpassed by none in acumen, and guided by the uninspired lights of a Plato, Aristotle and Cicero, thought and wrote without suspecting the sinfulness of slavery. Thousands of Christians in the Southern States, of as enlightened and honest consciences as any in the world, lived and died masters, with no other self-reproach than that they did not more faithfully fulfil the master's duties. Since it is not a self-evident, not a necessary, not a universally received truth, that slavery is sinful, we therefore claim the authority of the Scriptures as conclusive, and boldly repudiate all logical obligation to reconcile them with the vain conclusions of human speculation. "He that reproveth God, let him answer it."

Yet we acknowledge the obligation of those who undertake to expound God's word, "to commend it to every man's conscience in the sight of God," so far as the self-confidence and petulance of the depraved reason will permit. To show, therefore, that we have no fear of any legitimate human speculation, and to do what in us lies "to justify the ways of God to men," we propose in this chapter to examine the ethical argument against slavery with some care.

§ 2. MISREPRESENTATIONS CLEARED.

But abolitionists, by their audacious assumptions, endeavour to throw the question out of the pale of discussion: they exclaim that it needs no wire-drawn inference, it is self-evident, that a system which dehumanizes a human being, and makes his very person like a brute's body, the property of another creature; which necessitates the entailing of ignorance and vice; which ignores the marital and parental rights; which subjects the chastity of the female to the brute will of her master, and which fills Southern homes with the constant outcry of oppression, is an iniquity: and that he who attempts to cite the testimony of reason and Scripture in defence of such wrongs, offers an insult to their minds and consciences which self-respect requires them to repel at once. The malignant industry of our enemies in propagating these monstrous slanders, compels us, therefore, to pause at the outset of the discussion, to rebut them, and disabuse the minds of readers. And it is here asserted, once for all, that the popular apprehension of the slave's condition and treatment, spread throughout Europe and the North, *is utterly false*: that it is the result of nothing less than persistent, wilful, and almost incredible lying on the part of interested accusers; and that this is recognized by every intelligent European and Northern man who has resided among us long enough truly to know the institution of slavery. The character disclosed by the Yankees in the war lately closed, has effectually taught the rest of the world to recognize the probability of our charge.

The reader is first, then, requested to recall the definition of American slavery admitted by us in the beginning of the fifth chapter. It is not an ownership of the servant's moral personality, soul, religious destinies, or conscience; but a property in his involuntary labour. And this right to his labour implies just so much controul over his person as enables his master to possess his labour. Our doctrine "hath this extent, no more." This we established beyond cavil by a reference to our laws and usages. Now, the abolitionist argues that the master's claim over the servant, if just, must imply a right to employ any means necessary to perpetuate it, such as to keep the mind of his slaves stupid and dark, because this is necessary to prevent his aspiring to his liberty. We reply that such means are not necessary in the nature of the case. To assert their necessity audaciously begs the question. If the master's claim were so essentially unrighteous, that any intelligent reflection in the slave would justify his indignation and resistance, then it might be more convenient for the master to make him an unreflecting animal. But the very subject in debate is, whether the claim is unrighteous. Suppose that the relation can be demonstrated to be right, reasonable, and beneficent for the servant, (which is what we assert,) then the only effect of intelligent reflection and of knowledge and virtue combined in the slave's character, will be to render him better satisfied with his condition. So that to degrade his soul is not a necessary means for perpetuating the master's authority, and not a part of the rights of masters. And now, it is emphatically asserted that Southern masters, as a class, did not seek or desire to repress either the mental or religious culture of their servants' souls; but the contrary. It is our solemn and truthful testimony, that the nearly universal temper of masters was to promote and not to hinder it; and the intellectual and religious culture of our slaves met no other general obstacle, save that which operates among the labouring poor of all countries, their own indifference to it, and the necessities of nearly constant manual labour. If there was any exception, it was caused by the mischievous meddling of abolitionists themselves, obtruding on the servants that false doctrine so sternly condemned by St. Paul. Southern masters desired the intelligence and morality of their servants. As a class, masters and their families performed a large amount of gratuitous labour for that end; and universally met all judicious efforts for it from others with cordial approval. An intelligent Christian servant was universally recognized as being, in a pecuniary view, a better servant. Is it asserted that there is still much degrading ignorance among Southern negroes? True: but it exists not because of our system, but in spite of it. There is more besotted ignorance in the peasantry of all other countries. It is the dispassionate conviction of intelligent Southerners, that our male slaves presented a better average of virtue and intelligence than the rank and file of the Federal armies by which we were overrun: and even the negro troops of our conquerors, although mostly recruited from the more idle and vicious slaves, were better than the white! The Africans of these States, three generations ago, were the most debased among pagan savages. A nation is not educated in a day. How long have the British people been in reaching their present civilization under God's providential tutelage? The South has advanced the Africans, as a whole, more rapidly than any other low savage race has ever been educated. Hence we boldly claim, that our system, instead of necessitating the ignorance and vice of its subjects, deserves the credit of a most beneficent culture.

We may here refer to the charge, that Virginian slavery condemned the Africans to mental and religious darkness, by forbidding them all access to letters; because the laws of the commonwealth forbade the teaching of them to read. Will not even the intelligent reader, after the currency of this charge, be surprised to learn that *there has never been such a law upon the statute books of Virginia*? To assert that there has been such a law, is an unmitigated falsehood. The only enactment which touches the subject is the following sentence, in the statute defining what were "unlawful assemblages" of negroes. "And every assemblage of negroes for the purpose of instruction in reading and writing, or in the night time for any purpose, shall be an unlawful assembly." Stat. 1830-31, p. 107. The previous section, commencing the definition of these unlawful assemblies, expressly states that they are unlawful if held *without the master's consent*. Our courts and lawyers uniformly held that, without this feature, no assemblage of negroes, to do any thing not criminal *per se*, can be unlawful; because the whole spirit of Virginian laws recognized the master's authority. His slaves were subject to his government. His authorization legalized everything not intrinsically criminal. Accordingly, the uniform interpretation given to the above words was, that it was the assembling of slaves for instruction in letters by others than their master or his authorized agents, which constituted the unlawful assembly. The whole extent of the law was, to arm masters with the power to prevent the impertinent interference of others with his servants, under the pretext of literary instruction; a power which the meddlesomeness of abolitionists pointed out as most wholesome and necessary. There was no more law to prevent the master from teaching his slaves than his children; either by himself, or his authorized agent; and thousands of slaves in Virginia were taught to read by their masters, or their children and teachers. As many Virginian slaves were able to read their Bibles, and had Bibles to read, as could probably be found among the labouring poor of boasted Britain. Here let another unmitigated falsehood be exposed. Since the ill-starred overthrow of our system, the most noted religious newspaper of the North, mentioning an appropriation of Bibles by the American Bible Society for gifts to negroes of the South, applauded the measure, because, as it asserted, "the Southern States had hitherto forbidden the circulation of the Scriptures among their slaves." It would be mere puling in us, to affect the belief that this amazing statement was made in ignorance; when the officials of the Society whose organ this slanderer professed to be, well know that, ever since the institution of the Bible Society, they were scarcely more familiar with any species of applications, than those of Christian masters and mistresses, and of Southern ministers, for Scriptures suitable for their servants. There has never been a law in Virginia preventing the gratuitous circulation of the Bible among slaves, or the possession or reading of it by slaves: and it is confidently believed that there has never been a single man in Virginia who desired such a law, or who would have executed it, had it defiled our statute book; unless, perchance, it was some infidel of that French school which invented abolitionism.

It is charged again, that slavery impiously and inhumanly sacrificed the immortal soul of the slave, to secure the master's pecuniary interest in him. This slander is already in part answered. We farther declare that neither our laws, nor the current temper and usage of masters, interfered with the slave's religious rights. On the contrary, they all protected and established them. The law protected the legal right of the slave to his Sabbath, forbidding the master to employ him on that day in secular labours, other than those of necessity and mercy. Instances in which slaves were prevented by their masters from attending the publick worship of God, were fully as rare among us, and as much reprobated, as similar abuses are in any other Christian country. On the contrary, the masters were almost universally more anxious that their servants should attend publick worship, than the servants were to avail themselves of the privilege. There was scarcely a Christian church in the South, which had not its black communicants sitting amicably at the table beside their masters; and the whole number of these adult communicants was reported by the statistics of the churches, as not less than a half million. We can emphatically declare, that we never saw or heard of a house of worship in the South, where sittings were not provided for the blacks at the expense of the whites: and it is believed that if there was such a case, it was in a neighbourhood containing no negro population. And in nearly every case, these sittings were more ample than the blacks could be induced to fill. Nor was there any expenditure of money on ecclesiastical objects, which was more cheerfully and liberally made, than that for the religious culture of the slaves. Further, with a few exceptions they enjoyed the fullest religious liberty in the selection of their religious communions and places of worship. Masters refused them liberty to join the churches of their choice more rarely than parents in New England and Old England perpetrated that act of spiritual tyranny upon their wives and daughters. So punctilious was this respect for the spiritual liberty of the servants, that masters universally yielded to it their own denominational preferences and animosities, allowing their servants to join the sects most repugnant to their own, even in cases as extreme as that of the Protestant and Romanist. The white people of the South may consider themselves truly fortunate, if they preserve, under the despotism which now rules them, as much religious liberty as our negroes received at our hands.

Our system is represented as oppressive and cruel, appointing different penalties for crimes to the black man and the white man; depriving the slave of the privilege of testifying against a white in a court of justice; subjecting him to frequent and inhuman corporal punishments, and making it a crime for him to exercise the natural right of self-defence, when violently assailed by a white man. The reply is, that the penal code of Virginia was properly made different in the case of the whites and the blacks, because of the lower moral tone of the latter. Many things, which are severe penalties to the white man, would be no punishment to the negro. And the penal code for the latter was greatly milder, both in its provisions, and in the temper of its administration, than that which obtained in England over her white citizens, far into this century. The slave was not permitted to testify against a white man, and this was a restriction made proper by his low grade of truthfulness, his difference of race, and the fact that he was to so great a degree subject to the will of another. But the seeming severity of this restriction was almost wholly removed, among us, by the fact that he always had, in his master, an interested and zealous patron and guardian, in all collisions with other white men. From oppression by his own master he found his sufficient protection, usually, in affection and self-interest. But in most of the abolition States, the wretched free black was equally disqualified to testify against his white oppressor; and the vast difference against him was, that he had no white master, the legal equal of his assailant, eagerly engaged by self-interest, affection, and honourable pride, to protect him. The black "citizen" was the helpless victim of the white swindler or bully. And such was usually the hypocrisy of abolitionism.

It is true again, that our law gave the master the power of corporal punishment, and required the slave to submit. So does the law of England give it to parents over children, to masters over apprentices, and to husbands over wives. Now, while we freely admit that there were in the South, instances of criminal barbarity in corporal punishments, they were very infrequent, and were sternly reprobated by publick opinion. So far were Southern plantations from being "lash-resounding dens," the whipping of adult men and women had become the rare exception. It was far less frequent and severe than the whipping of white men was, a few years ago, in the British army and navy, not probably more frequent than the whipping of wives is in the Northern States of America, and not nearly so frequent as the whipping of white young ladies now is in their State schools. The girls and boys of the plantations received the lash from masters and agents more frequently than the adults, as was necessary and right for the heedless children of mothers semi-civilized and neglectful; but universally, this punishment by their owners was far less frequent and severe than the black parents themselves inflicted. We may be permitted to state our own experience as a fair specimen of the average. The writer was for eighteen years a householder and master of slaves, having the government of a number of different slaves; and in that time he found it necessary to administer the lash to adults in four cases; and two of these were for a flagrant adultery—(resulting in the permanent reform of at least one of the delinquents.) His government was regarded by his slaveholding neighbours as by no means relaxed. Indeed, Europeans and Yankees are always surprised at the leniency and tolerance of Southern masters. But to the vain modern notion, that corporal punishments are in any case barbarous and degrading, we give place not for an instant. God enjoined them, in appropriate cases, on Hebrew citizens. Solomon inculcates the rod as the most wholesome correction for children. The degradation is in the offence, and not in the punishment. This pretended exclusion of whipping is a part of that Godless humanitarianism, born of conceit and pride, which always shows itself as full of real ferocity as of affected mildness.

It is also an outrageous misrepresentation to say that our laws imposed no check upon the master's brutality in punishing, and took away the slave's natural right of self-defence. The slave whose life was assailed might exercise the natural right of self-defence, even against his own master. He did it, of course, under the same responsibility to the law, and the same risque of guilt, if it should appear that he had shed blood gratuitously in a moment of ill-justified passion, under which the white man acts. Cases actually adjudicated have clearly ascertained this principle. In the county of——, a slave, in the year 1861, turned upon his master during harvest, and with his scythe inflicted a mortal wound. He was arrested by his own fellow-slaves, and when questioned, replied to one, "I intended to kill him;" and to another, "I tried to cut him in two." It was proved by the defence, at his trial, (through the exclusive testimony of blacks,) that his master had, on previous days, and also on the morning of the same day, two hours previously, harassed him with barbarous and unusual punishments, by which, although none of them even in appearance assailed life, a just sense of outrage and high indignation must have been produced. The grave defect of this defence was, that the assaults of the master, although barbarous, never had implicated life, and that two or more hours had intervened, for the cooling of passion. The only immediate provocation at the time of killing was the repetition of some words of rebuke, with a comparatively slight chastisement. Such was the case. The court decided that, on the one hand, a verdict of justifiable homicide could not be given in the slave's favour, because the lawful present provocation was absent; but on the other, that it was not murder, because the barbarities which had preceded the act justified resentment. The crime was therefore ascertained as a mitigated homicide, with a milder punishment.

The laws of Virginia protected not only the life, but the limb of the slave against white persons, and even his own master. The statute against wounding, stabbing and maiming is in the following words: "If any free person maliciously shoot, stab, cut or wound *any person*, or by any means cause him bodily injury with intent to maim, disfigure, disable or kill, he shall, except where it is otherwise provided, be punished by confinement in the penitentiary not less than one, nor more than ten years. If such act be done unlawfully, but not maliciously, with the intent aforesaid, the offender shall, at the discretion of the jury if the accused be white, or of the court if he be a negro, either be confined in the penitentiary not less than one nor more than five years, or be confined in jail not exceeding twelve months, and fined not exceeding five hundred dollars." And in the chapter on trials it is added: "And on any indictment for maliciously shooting, stabbing, cutting or wounding a person, or by any means causing him bodily injury with intent to kill him, the jury may find the accused not guilty of the offence charged, but guilty of maliciously doing such act with intent to maim, disfigure or disable, or of unlawfully doing it, with intent to maim, disfigure, disable or kill, such person." These are but digests of repeated older statutes of Virginia, of date 1803, 1815, and 1819. Now the General Court, the highest tribunal of appeal in criminal cases, decided that the "*any person*," protected by these laws, included the slave; and that an indictment for the malicious stabbing of a slave could be supported under these acts. Thus, while the slave was required to accept the chastisement of his master, his life and limb were as fully protected as those of the white man.

The General Court, in 1851, decided the appeal of Simeon Souther, convicted in the County of Hanover of murder in the second degree, because his slave Sam had, according to evidence, died under an excessive and barbarous whipping, with other punishments, the whole evidently not intended to kill. Souther's counsel appealed from this sentence to the General Court, asking that the grade of the offence be reduced to manslaughter only, because it appeared in evidence that the punishments were not inflicted with intent to kill. The court, after reprobating Souther's conduct as a "case of atrocious and wicked cruelty," instead of reducing the grade of the sentence already ascertained, decided that it was already too low; and that it should have been declared murder in the first degree. This tribunal granted that it is lawful for the master to chastise his slave; and that the law, as expounded by the same authority, (5th Randolph, 678,) did not sustain an indictment of the master on the mere allegation of excess in chastisement, where it was not charged that any unlawful maiming or other injury ensued. Because "it is the policy of the law in respect to the relation of master and slave, and for the sake of securing proper subordination and obedience on the part of the slave, to protect the master from prosecution in all such cases." ... "But in so inflicting punishment for the sake of punishment, the owner of the slave acts at his peril; and if death ensues in consequence of such punishment, the relation of master and slave affords no ground of excuse or palliation. The principles of the common law in relation to homicide apply to his case, without qualification or exception; and according to those principles, the act of the prisoner, in the case under consideration, amounted to murder. Upon this point we are unanimous." And Souther, although a man of property, and supported by the most active and able counsel, was committed to the penitentiary, (in pursuance of the original sentence, of murder in the second degree,) where he died. Such was the law and its administration in Virginia.

It may further be asserted that the laws were at least as well administered among us, against the murderers and oppressors of slaves, as against those who killed their equals. Our people had unfortunately imbibed, to some degree, the infidel and fanatical notions prevalent at the North against capital punishments; so that crimes of bloodshed met with more tolerance from publick sentiment than was proper. But when a master took the life of his servant, especially if it were done by cruel punishments, the publick scorn for his meanness and tyranny, and the general feeling of kindliness for our dependent fellow-creatures, were apt to secure a far more faithful execution of the law against him, than if he had slain his white peer for any insult or wrong.

The laws of Virginia were equally just and careful in protecting the liberty of every person not justly held to bondage. The stealing or kidnapping of any human being with the purpose of selling him into slavery, is a felony, punishable by imprisonment in the penitentiary not less than three, nor more than ten years.

Any coloured person whatsoever, conceiving himself to be unlawfully detained in bondage, may apply to any justice of the peace, or county or circuit superior court, to enter a suit for his freedom. There is not, within the lids of the Virginian code, another statute, so generous, so careful, so tender, so watchful, in protecting every possible right of a plaintiff, as this law enabling the slave, unjustly detained, to sue out his freedom. First, it compels every magistrate, of every grade, and every court, of every grade, to hearken to the cry of the supposed oppressed man, and to take effectual steps to secure him release, if just. Next, it instantly takes the claimant out of the hand of his nominal master, and assigns him protection and maintenance, during the pendency of his claim. Next, it provides counsel, and all costs of suit for the oppressed man, at publick expense. Next, it orders that his case shall have precedence of all other cases, before whatever court he may select, at its first sessions, irrespective of its place on the docket. And last, if the claim to freedom be found just, the court is empowered to give him damages for his detention pending the suit.

Another charge against us is, that our laws abrogated the rights of marriage among slaves, authorized their capricious separation by masters, and thus consigned them to promiscuous concubinage, like that of beasts. Now, first, admitting defect in our legislation here, let us ask, how much of the blame of the continuance of this defect is chargeable upon the frantic attacks of abolitionists upon us? Every sensible man can understand, that a people so fiercely assailed in their vital rights should be occupied solely by righteous defence, and should feel the time unsuited for the discussion of innovations, however needful. And next, let it be understood what the South has really done, and has not done, herein, and it will appear that an amazing misrepresentation is made of the whole case. The form of the charge usually is, that our laws deprived the slaves of all marital rights. This is, first, a monstrous perversion of the facts, in that the Africans never had any marital rights or domestic institutions to be deprived of. Have men forgotten, that in their native country there was no marriage, and no marriage law, but the negroes either lived in vagrant concubinage, or held their plurality of wives as slaves, to be either sold or slain at will? They have, at least, lost nothing, then; and the utmost that could be charged upon our legislation is, that it did not undertake to innovate upon their own native usages; that it did not force upon them marital restraints, and penalties for their breach, which the Africans were disqualified either to understand or value, which they would have regarded as a more cruel burden than their bondage. Next, our laws did not, as many seem to represent, prohibit, or delegalize the marriage of slaves; but were simply silent about them. The meaning of this silence was, to leave the whole matter to the controul of the master. It appears almost impossible for anti-slavery men to be made to apprehend the nature of the institution, as described in the words, '*domestic* slavery.' Their minds, perverted with vain dreams of the powers and perfectibility of the State, cannot be made to apprehend that God has made other parties than the commonwealth and the civil magistrate, depositories of ruling power; and that this arrangement is right and benevolent. Now, it is the genius of slavery, to make the family the slave's commonwealth. The family is his State. The master is his magistrate and legislator, in all save certain of the graver criminal relations, in which the commonwealth deals directly and personally with him. He is a member of municipal society only through his master, who represents him. The commonwealth knows him as only a life-long minor under the master's tutelage. The integers of which the commonwealth aggregate is made up, are not single human beings, but single families, authoritatively represented in the father and master. And this is the fundamental difference between the theory of the Bible, and that of radical democracy. The silence of our laws, then, concerning the marriage of slaves, means precisely this: that the whole subject is remitted to the master, the chief magistrate of the little integral commonwealth, the family. Obviously, therefore, the question whether our laws were defective therein, is in no sense a question between the living of the slaves in marriage or in beastly license; it is only a question whether, in the distribution of ruling functions, those of the master were not made too large and responsible, herein. And if error be admitted in this respect, it cannot be one which makes the relation of servitude sinful; for then the same crime must be fixed on all the patriarchs, notwithstanding their care in rightly ordering and preserving, as family heads, the marital relations of their children and slaves, because, forsooth, there happened to be no commonwealth law above them, as patriarchs, regulative of these marriages. This is nonsense. Where the modern patriarch, the Southern master, rightly ordered and protected the marriage relations of his slaves, the silence of the commonwealth no more made their connexions concubinage, than were those of Isaac, and of Abraham's steward, Eliezer of Damascus. What magistrate or legislature, other than Abraham, issued their marriage license? Who else enforced their marriage law or defined its rights? What civic agent solemnized the ceremonial for them? And this leads to another remark: that that ceremonial is wholly unessential to the validity of marriage. Of course, where the laws enjoin it for any class, every good citizen will observe it. But the absence of such ordained ceremonial does not make lawful marriage impossible. In this sense, *consensus facit nuptias*. It was thus that the holiest wedlock ever seen on earth was instituted, that of Adam and Eve; thus Abraham and Sarah, Isaac and Rebekah, were united. The fact that our laws pronounce the unions of Quakers and of Jews, legitimate marriage, although announced with different forms, and indeed almost without form, evinces this truth.

Now, then, for the facts. These facts are, that marriage in its substance was as much recognized among our servants as among any other peasantry; that the union was uniformly instituted upon a formal written license of the two masters; that it was almost always sanctioned by a religious ceremonial conducted by a minister; that the regularity of the connexion was uniformly recognized by the master's assigning the husband and wife their own dwelling; that the moral opinion of both whites and blacks made precisely the same distinction between this connexion and the illicit ones, and between the fruits of it as legitimate, and the fruits of concubinage as illegitimate, which publick opinion establishes for white persons: and that even the criminal law recognized it as a regular connexion, by extending to the black man who slew the violator of his bed in heat of blood, the same forbearance which it extends to the outraged husband. How can it be said, in the face of these facts, that marriage did not exist among them?

But, it is asked, did not the master possess power to separate this union at his will; and was not this power often exercised? They did. The power, relatively, was not often exercised; and when the separation was not justified by the crimes of the parties, it met the steady and increasing reprobation of publick opinion. The instances of tyrannical separation were, at most, far fewer than the harsh tyranny of destitution imposes on poor whites in all other countries; and the pretended philanthropy of the Yankees has, in five years, torn asunder more families than all the slave dealers of the South did in a hundred. But the power of separating was sometimes abused by masters; and the room for this abuse was just the defect in our laws, which nearly all Southern Christians deplored, and which they desired to repair. Justice requires the testimony, on the other hand, that the relaxed morals which prevailed among the Africans was not the result of their marital relations, as arranged among us, but the heritage of their paganism; that under our system the evil was decreasing; and that since their emancipation and nominal subjection to the marriage law of the whites, a flood of licentiousness, vagrant concubinage, and infanticide, has broken out again among them. Clear proof this, that our abused system was better adapted to their character than the present.

Anti-slavery men often talk as though the right of slave parents to the controul and education of their children, were so indefeasible and native, that it is a natural wrong to permit the authority of the master over them to override that of the parents. This we utterly deny. We have the authority of Locke himself for saying that the parental authority is correlative to the parental obligation to preserve and train the child; that it is, therefore, not indefeasible; that if the father is clearly incompetent to or unwilling for his duty, his authority often is, and of right ought to be, transferred by society to another. When, therefore, the civilized master uses his authority against and over that of the semi-civilized, or savage parent, to train the slave child to habits of decency, industry, intelligence, and virtue, which his degraded natural guardians are unable or unwilling to inculcate, he does no crime against nature, but an act just and beneficent.

The most odious part of this charge is, that slavery made the chastity of the female slave the property of her master. We meet this with an emphatic denial. It is false. The laws of Virginia protect the virtue of the female slave by the very same statute which shields that of the white lady, even against her own master. The law of rape, until 1849, used these words: "If any man do ravish *a woman*," &c. The act of 1849 used the words: "If any white person do carnally know *a female* of the age of twelve years or more, against her will, by force, or carnally know *a female child*, under that age," &c. (If the ravisher were a negro the penalty was different.) The question is, whether the words "*a woman*," and "*a female*," were intended to include coloured persons and slaves. The answer uniformly given by Virginian lawyers to this question is affirmative. They say that the terms are the most general in our statutory vocabulary. The law of 1849, just quoted, clearly implies that the terms "a female," in § 15, are inclusive of coloured females, by expressly introducing the word "white," "a white female," in § 16, when its purpose was to enact a special penalty for the forcible abduction of that class. The General Court has held that *female* is synonymous with *woman*, and may be substituted for it even in an indictment. Is it asked, why the appeal is not made to judicial decisions, as conclusive authority of the true intent of the statute? We have caused a thorough search to be made by the most competent authority in Richmond; and while many indictments are found against black men for rape of white women, none exist, in the history of our jurisprudence, against white men for rape of black women. And this, not because there would have been any difficulty in making the indictment lie: *but because*, as the most experienced lawyers testify, *the crime is unheard of on the part of white men amongst us.*

It is undoubtedly true, that the moral sense of the Africans on this subject is low: that many voluntary breaches of chastity occur among themselves, and some between them and whites. But the latter are far less frequent than similar sins in Philadelphia, in Boston, in London. Notwithstanding the sad inheritance of vice drawn by the Africans from their pagan ancestors, Southern slavery had elevated them so far, that illegitimate births among them had become far fewer than among the boasted white peasantry of Protestant Scotland, with all its Bibles and churches, and parochial schools. This fact can be proved by Scotch statistics. The odious and filthy charge which the abolitionists make against the Southern people and against slavery, as a system of lust, also receives a terrible reply from the returns of the American census. When illicit cohabitation takes place between the whites and the blacks, nature tells the secret with infallible accuracy, in the yellow skin of the offspring. The census of 1850 distinguished the full blacks from the mulattoes, both among the slave and free. Of the slaves, one in twelve was mulatto, taking the whole United States together. Of the slaves in Virginia the ratio of mulattoes to blacks was about the same. In South Carolina there was only one mulatto to thirty-one black slaves! The explanation is, that the latter State, being less commercial and manufacturing than Virginia, and having a system of more perfect agricultural slavery, exposed her slaves less to intercourse with immigrant and transient whites. But taking the United States as a whole, the free mulattoes were more than half as numerous as the free blacks! In several of the slave States they are more numerous; and in Ohio, the stronghold of Black Republicanism, there were fourteen thousand mulattoes to eleven thousand blacks. Since the regular marriage of free blacks to the whites was as unknown at the North as at the South, these figures tell a tale as to the comparative prevalence of this infamous and unnatural form of uncleanness among the Yankees, which should forever seal their lips from reproaches of us. They also show that at the South the state of slavery has been far more favourable to chastity among the coloured people than that of freedom.

The reader probably feels by this time, that if we speak truth, then was slavery a very different thing practically from its usual picture abroad. He will perhaps feel with a shade of skepticism, that it is strange the world should have been so much mistaken. The chief explanation we offer of so strange a fact, is that trait of abolitionists, our interested and unscrupulous accusers, predicted by St. Paul: ("men of corrupt minds and destitute of the truth.") The world will find them out in due time: the statements made of the events of the late war have done much to unmask them. Still another cause is that Europeans, and even Yankees, are so ignorant of Southern society. Still another explanation is, that slavery in the British colonies, from which the people of that Empire have chiefly derived their conceptions, actually was far more harsh and barbarous than in this country. The reader is emphatically cautioned that he must not judge slavery in Virginia by slavery in Jamaica or Guiana. Whether the charge of the great Paley is correct, who accounts for this difference by the greater harshness of British character, politeness may forbid us to decide. But the comparative fates of the Africans in the British colonies, and those in our States, tell the contrast between the humanity of our system, and the barbarity of theirs, in terms of indisputable clearness. If political science has ascertained any law, it is that the well or ill-being of a people powerfully affects their increase or decrease of numbers. The climate of the British Indies is salubrious for blacks. Yet, of the one million seven hundred thousand Africans imported into the British colonies, and their increase, only six hundred and sixty thousand remained to be emancipated in 1832. The three hundred and seventy-five thousand (the total) imported into the Southern States, had multiplied to four millions. Such is the contrast! How grinding and ruthless must have been that oppression which in the one case reduced this prolific race, in the most fertile and genial spots of earth, in the ratio of five to two! And how generous and beneficent that government which, in the Southern States, nursed them to a more than ten-fold increase, in a less hospitable and fruitful clime! Well may we demur to have the world take its conceptions of our slavery from the British.

We trust that we shall proceed, then, to the remaining discussion of the moral character of slavery, with a just understanding of what is to be defended. It is simply that system which makes the involuntary labour of the servant the property of the master, and gives the latter such controul over the former's person, as will secure his possession of the labour. We conclude this section with a few words touching the admitted abuses of the system. That such existed among us, both legislative and individual, is fully admitted. There were cruel masters. Slaves were sometimes refused that which the apostle enjoined masters to give them, as "just and equal." Some cruel punishments were inflicted. A few slaves have been tortured to death. Some wives and children were wickedly torn from their husbands and parents. And our laws in some points failed to secure to the slaves that to which their humanity entitled them. But we repeat, these things prove only the sinfulness of the individual agent, and not of the system of which they are incidents. Fathers have been known to maltreat, scourge, maim and murder their children; and husbands their wives; but no one dreams that these things evince the unrighteousness of the family relations. Wife-murder is doubtless more frequent in the State of New York, than slave-murder was in Virginia. The laws of the State of Indiana concerning divorce are, in some particulars, glaring violations of God's laws. Yet no one dreams of arguing thence, that to have a wife in those States is a sin. Unless the abuse can be shown to be an essential part of the system, it proves nothing against the lawfulness of the system itself. But that none of these crimes against slaves are essential parts of slavery, is proved by the fact, which we fearlessly declare, that the vast majority of slaves in our country never experienced any of them. The unfairness of this mode of arguing cannot be better stated than in the words of Dr. Van Dyke, of New York:

"Their mode of arguing the question of slaveholding, by a pretended appeal to facts, is a tissue of misrepresentation from beginning to end. Let me illustrate my meaning by a parallel case. Suppose I undertake to prove the wickedness of marriage, as it exists in the city of New York. In this discussion suppose the Bible is excluded, or, at least, that it is not recognized as having exclusive jurisdiction in the decision of the question. My first appeal is to the statute law of the State.

"I show there enactments which nullify the law of God, and make divorce a marketable and cheap commodity. I collect the advertisements of your daily papers, in which lawyers offer to procure the legal separation of man and wife for a stipulated price, to say nothing, in this sacred place, of other advertisements which decency forbids me to quote. Then I turn to the records of our criminal courts, and find that every day some cruel husband beats his wife, or some unnatural parent murders his child, or some discontented wife or husband seeks the dissolution of the marriage bond. In the next place, I turn to the orphan asylums and hospitals, and show there the miserable wrecks of domestic tyranny in wives deserted and children maimed by drunken parents. In the last place, I go through our streets, and into our tenement houses, and count the thousands of ragged children, who, amid ignorance and filth, are training for the prison and gallows.

"Summing all these facts together, I put them forth as the fruits of marriage in the city of New York, and a proof that the relation itself is sinful. If I were a novelist, and had written a book to illustrate this same doctrine, I would call this array of facts a 'Key.' In this key I say nothing about the sweet charities and affections that flourish in ten thousand homes, not a word about the multitude of loving-kindnesses that characterize the daily life of honest people, about the instruction and discipline that are training children at ten thousand firesides for usefulness here and glory hereafter;—all this I ignore, and quote only the statute book, the newspapers, the records of criminal courts, and the miseries of the abodes of poverty. Now, what have I done? I have not misstated or exaggerated a single fact. And yet am I not a falsifier and a slanderer of the deepest dye? Is there a virtuous woman or an honest man in this city whose cheeks would not burn with indignation at my one-sided and injurious statements? But this is just what abolitionism has done in regard to slaveholding. It has undertaken to illustrate its cardinal doctrine in works of fiction; and then, to sustain the creation of its fancy, has attempted to underpin it with an accumulation of facts. These facts are collected in precisely the way I have described. The statute books of slaveholding States are searched, and every wrong enactment collated, newspaper reports of cruelty and crime on the part of wicked masters are treasured up and classified, all the outrages that have been perpetrated 'by lewd fellows of the baser sort'—of whom there are plenty, both North and South—are eagerly seized and recorded; and this mass of vileness and filth, collected from the kennels and sewers of society, is put forth as a faithful exhibition of slaveholding. Senators in the forum, and ministers in the pulpit, distil this raw material into the more reined slander 'that Southern society is essentially barbarous, and that slaveholding had its origin in hell.'"

Such are the words of one who is himself no advocate of slavery, but who is moved to utter them solely by his regard for truth. His reprobation is just. To take the exceptional abuses of any institution, and exhibit them as giving the ordinary state of society under it, is the very essence of slander.

But the enemies of the South say, that still the system of slavery is unrighteous, even though the generosity of a majority of masters prevents its oppressions from being felt, because it confers a power which is irresponsible. We reply, that this is true, although to a vastly less degree than has been charged; but it is also true of every form of authority under heaven; and it is simply impossible to place authority in any human hands at all, without some degree of this risque of irresponsible abuse. The authority of the master is no more irresponsible than that of the husband, father, or mechanic, over his wife, child, or apprentice. The father, in order to have authority, must have discretion: and he may abuse it: for he is imperfect; and against this abuse the child has no legal remedy. For this imperfection in the family law there is no help, save by abolishing all family government; a remedy fraught with ten thousand times the mischief and misery which all the occasional severities of unnatural parents have caused. All human government must have this defect, for man, who administers it, is a sinner. So that the objection of the abolitionist amounts to this: that the institution of slavery is unlawful, because it is not perfect; which nothing human can be. It is so true that any grant of power whatsoever confers some irresponsibility; that the fact remains even where the rights of free citizens are most carefully guarded under republican governments. See, for example, the courts of law, which judge concerning our lives and property. We attempt to limit the abuse of power of the lower courts, by passing their decisions in review before a higher; but there must be some highest, beyond which no appeal can go. Yet the judges of that highest court are also capable of wrong and error; and if they commit them, the victim has no human help; he must submit. All that just and humane legislation can do, then, is so to adjust and limit powers, that the chances of uncompensated wrong may be as small as possible. Now we shall see that in this case of employer and labourer, such as they are in Virginia, the chances of unredressed wrong were reduced to their *minimum* by our system of domestic slavery. For we thereby raised the most efficient motives, those of self-interest and affection, in the stronger party, to treat the weaker equitably. If the irresponsibility of a part of the master's power proved the relation sinful, all government would be wrong.

§ 3. THE RIGHTS OF MAN AND SLAVERY.

The radical objection to the righteousness of slavery in most minds is, that it violates the natural liberty and equality of man. To clear this matter, it is our purpose to test the common theory held as to the rights of nature, and to show that this ground of opposition to slavery rests upon a radical and disorganizing scheme of human rights, is but Jacobinism in disguise, and involves a denial of all authority whatsoever. The popular theory of man's natural rights, of the origin of governments, and of the moral obligation of allegiance, is that which traces them to a *social contract*. The true origin of this theory may be found with Hobbes of Malmesbury. It owes its respectability among Englishmen, chiefly to the pious John Locke, a sort of baptized image of that atheistic philosopher; and it was ardently held by the infidel democràts of the first French revolution. According to this scheme, each person is by nature an independent *integer*, wholly *sui juris*, absolutely equal to every other man, and naturally entitled, as a "Lord of Creation," to exercise his whole will. Man's natural liberty was accordingly defined as *privilege to do whatever he wished*. True, Locke attempts to limit this monstrous postulate by defining man's native liberty as privilege to do whatever he wished within the limits of the law of nature. But this virtually returns to the same; because he teaches that man is by nature absolutely independent, so that he must be himself the supreme, original judge, what this law of nature is. According to the doctrine of the social contract, man's natural rights are confounded with this so-called natural liberty. Each man's natural right is to protect his own existence, and to possess himself of whatever will render it more happy, (Locke again adds, within the limits of natural law.) And this scheme most essentially ignored the originality of moral distinctions. Hobbes explains them as the conventional results of the rules which man's experience and convenience have dictated to him. For, the experience of the mutual violences and collisions of so many independent wills, in this supposed "state of nature," induced men, in time, to consent to the surrender of a part of this native independence, in order to secure the remainder of their rights. To do this, they are supposed to have conferred together, and to have formed a compact with each other, binding themselves to each other to submit to certain stipulated rules, which restrained a part of their natural liberty, and to obey certain men selected to govern. The power thus delegated to these hands was to be used to protect the remaining rights of all. The terms of this compact form the organic law, or constitution. Subsequent citizens entering the commonwealth by birth or immigration, are assumed to have given an assent, express or implied, to this compact. And if the question be asked, why men are morally bound to obey magistrates, who naturally are their equals and fellows, the answer of this school is: because they have voluntarily bargained to do so in entering the social compact; and they receive a *quid pro quo* for their accession to it. Such is the theory of the origin of government, from which the natural injustice of slavery is deduced. For, obviously, if man's obligation to civil society originates in the voluntary social contract of independent integers, none can be rightfully held to a compulsory obedience, which enters into all servitude, both domestic and political.

Some liberal writers, as Blackstone, and the great Swiss publicist, *Burlemaqui*, are too sensible not to see that this scheme is false to the facts of the case. But they still hold, that although individual men never, in fact, existed in the independent insulation supposed, and did not actually pass into a state of society by a formal social contract, yet such a transaction must be assumed as the implied and virtual source of political power and civic obligation. To us it appears, that if the contracting never occurred in fact, but is only a theoretical fiction, it is no basis for any thing, and no source of practical rights and duties. Civil society is a universal fact; and its existence must be grounded in something actual. We object, then, to this dream of a social contract preceded by a native state of individual independence, that it is false to the facts of the case. Human beings never rightfully existed, for one moment, in this state, out of which they are supposed to have passed by their own option. God never gave them such independency. Their responsibility to him, and to the civil society under which He has placed them, is as *native* as they are, being ordained by God to exist from the first. Men do not choose civic obligation, but are born to it, just as the child to his filial obligation. And the simple, conclusive proof is, that if any man were to claim this native option to assume or to decline civic obligations, (in the latter case relinquishing also their advantages,) there is not a government on earth, not the most liberal, that would not laugh his claim to scorn, and at once compel his allegiance. The very assumption of what this theory calls man's normal state, and the very attempt to exercise the option which, as it babbles, originated civil society, would constitute a man an outlaw, the radical enemy of civic society, and would give it a natural right, that of self-preservation, to destroy him. The scheme is not only fictitious, but absurd.

Second: We object that it is atheistic, utterly ignoring the existence of a Creator, and his relations to, and proprietorship in, man. It affects to treat men as though their existence were underived, and independent of any Supreme Being. It boldly discards God's right to determine under what obligations man shall live, and quietly contemns the great Scriptural fact that He has determined man shall live under social law.

Third: This scheme is thoroughly unphilosophical, in that whereas the science of government should be an inductive one, this theory is, and in its nature must be, purely hypothetical. No body, no history pretends to relate in a single instance, any such facts as it professes to rest upon. This Locke admits, and even claims, absurdly seeking in this mode to evade this vital objection. Hence we assert that it has no claims to be entertained *in foro scientiæ*, even for discussion.

Fourth: If man at first possessed that natural liberty, and passed from it under the obligation of constitutions and laws by a social contract, then sundry most inconvenient and preposterous consequences must logically follow. One of these is, that when once men had established their constitution, (in other words, their compact,) so long as its terms were observed by the magistrates and the minority, the majority could never righteously change it, no matter how inconvenient, or even ruinous, new circumstances might have made it, against the will of the minority or of the rulers. For when one has made a voluntary bargain, subsequent inconveniences of it do not justify its breach. The just man is one who changeth not, though he "sweareth to his own hurt." Another consequence would be, that it could never be settled what were the terms agreed upon in the original compact, and what part of existing laws were the accretions of unwarranted power, except in the case of written constitutions. Few nations have such. But a far worse consequence would be, that if the duty of allegiance originated in such compact, then any one unconstitutional act of the rulers or majority would dissolve it. For it is a covenant; but a covenant broken by one party is broken for both. Now, who believes that a single unconstitutional act of the ruler voids the whole allegiance of the aggrieved citizen? Where would be the government which would not be plunged into anarchy?

Last, all commonwealths have found it necessary to arm the magistrate with some powers, which individuals could not have conferred by a social compact, because they never possessed them. One of these is the power of life and death. No man's life is his own: it belongs to God alone. One cannot bargain away what is not his own. Besides, it is absurd to represent men as bargaining away this tremendous power for some smaller advantages and securities; because life is the most precious of all. "What shall a man accept in exchange for his life?" It is of no avail to say that the community is entitled, by the law of self-preservation, to assume this power; because, on this theory, there is no community as yet. There is only a number of independent integers, sovereignly treating with each other. The community cannot assume powers before it exists! It is, if possible, still more difficult to explain, on this theory, how political societies came by the power of capital punishment, against aliens who assail their members. But all governments hold aliens living among them, and invading enemies, subject to their capital penalties. How is this? The foreigner certainly has not assented to the social compact of this society; for he claims to be alien, and to owe no allegiance. His consent, the supposed fountain of all right over him, is utterly lacking. Once more, this theory draws a broad distinction between man's civil liberty as a subject of government, and his natural liberty. The latter it defines as *privilege to do whatever the man pleases*, within the limits of natural law as interpreted by himself. And his natural rights are just the same. Some of these he voluntarily surrenders to society, to secure the rest. All government, therefore, is not only of the nature of restraint; it is essentially *restraint upon one's rights*. The advocates of the theory distinctly represent government as of the nature of a natural evil and wrong, but adopted as an expedient against the worse evil, anarchy; and therefore the obligation to obey it has no higher source than expediency. But worse yet; if there is any such thing as intrinsic morality, government is an immoral restraint, for it is a *restraint upon rights*. Whatever good government may bring us, it is of that species which St. Paul reprobates, as "doing evil that good may come." The great Hobbes was therefore perfectly consistent, in teaching that there is no original morality in acts, and that there was at first no such thing as right, distinct from might. Morals are factitious distinctions invented under civil society for expediency. Let the thoughtful reader consider how this monstrous conclusion uproots all obligation, and order, and allegiance. No man can hold the theory of the origin of government in the social contract, unless he either holds, with Hobbes, this damnable error, or with some abolitionists, (who are thoroughly consistent here,) that *all government is immoral.*

But its advocates urge that it does give the correct origin of government, because they can point to specific rights, which must have been natural in the individual, but which we now find vested in the government. The instance they most cite, is that of self-defence. We accept it, and assert that it confirms our view. For, if the right of self-defence means privilege of forcible resistance to violence at the time it is offered, we utterly deny that it has been surrendered by the individual, or can be justly limited one iota by government. If it means the savage privilege of retaliation after the collision has passed away, which claims to make the angry defendant accuser, judge, jury, and executioner in his own case, we utterly deny that nature ever gave such right to any man. "Vengeance is mine: I will repay, saith the Lord." Another instance alleged, is when the citizen is restrained by society from certain acts, moral *per se*: as selling his corn out of the country when there is dearth. Yet the good citizen obeys. The answer is, that if the restriction is not unjust, it is because there exists among the citizens such danger of suffering for corn, that the sending it out of the country would be a breach of the natural law of love and equity. Natural rights may change with circumstances, a simple truth often strangely forgotten on this subject.

Now, it is from this vicious theory of human rights, that abolitionism sucks its whole life. The whole argument is but this: no restraint of government on man's will can be righteous, which is forcible and involuntary, because the obligation of all just government originates in the option of the individuals governed, who are by nature sovereign. Before we indicate the relationship of this conclusion with its disorganizing brood of kindred, we must pause to meet a question which arises. It is this: if this pet hypothesis is relinquished, on what basis shall we defend free government? Let us see if a better foundation for its blessings cannot be found.

Political and ethical philosophers have been perpetually victims to the notion, that because theirs are natural sciences, as distinguished from revealed or theological, therefore they must banish from them all reference to God, his nature, his acts, and his will, and our relations to it. The true inference should be, only, that they must abstain from the introduction of those peculiar revealed facts, which belong to man as an object of redemption and subject of the Church of Christ. If we are not atheists, the facts that God is, that our being proceeds from his act, that we are his property, are as truly *natural* as man and his attributes are. They should therefore be embraced as a part of the facts of the case, to be treated just as all other natural facts, save that these are the most rudimental of all. For, how can that treatment be truly scientific, which proceeds upon a partial induction of the facts of the case, leaving out the most primary? It is this illusion which has led so many moralists to attempt the discussion of the nature and origin of moral distinctions, without introducing a Creator, or a divine will. Whereas, a true science accepts God as the first fact in ethics; his attributes as the primary standard of the moral distinction; his will as the fountain of moral obligation. What wretched impotency and confusion has not this omission caused in ethical discussions!

In like manner, this impotent and infidel theory of government sets out, (as was consistent with its atheistic inventors,) without reference to the fact that man's existence, nature, and rights originated in the personal will of a Creator, without reference to original moral distinctions, or to original responsibilities to God, or to the moral quality of God's will towards man. It quietly ignores the fact that man's will, if he is the creature of an intelligent and moral personal Creator, never could, by any possibility, be his proper rule of acting. It passes over, in the insane pride of human perfectionism, the great fact that man is also a naturally depraved creature. It falsely supposes a state of nature, in which man's will made his right: whereas no being, save an eternal and self-existent God, has a right to exist in that state for one instant. But all these are *facts of nature*, belonging to the case, ascertainable by experience and reason. If, then, we would have a correct theory of natural rights, all of them must be embraced in our view. And the proper account of the matter is simply this: Inasmuch as man did not make himself, *he enters existence the subject of God*. This subjection is not only of force, but also of moral right. Moral distinctions are original, being eternally expressed in God's perfections, and sovereignly revealed to the creature in his preceptive will; which is, to man, the practical source and rule of obligation. This moral obligation is therefore as *native* as man is. The rudimental relations to his God and his fellows imposed on man are binding on him *ab initio*; not at all by force of any assent of his will, but merely by the rightful force of God's will: man's virtue is to conform his will freely to God's.

This will also defines his rights; by which we mean those things which other creatures are morally obliged to allow him to have and to do. Man, we repeat, enters existence with these moral relations resting upon him. And among them, are his social relations to his fellows; as is shown by the fact that he has a social nature. Now civil government is nothing more than the organization of a part of these social relations. God's will and providence, then, as truly as his word, has placed man naturally under civil government. It is as natural as man is. Again: the rule of action imposed by just government is *the moral rule*. That is to say, an equitable government enjoins on its members or subjects the doing of those things which are morally right, and the refraining from those things which are morally wrong.

We trace civil government, then, not to any social contract, or other human expediency, but to the will and providence of God, and to original moral obligation. If asked, whence the obligation to obey the civil magistrate who, personally, is but our fellow, we answer, from God's will, which is the source and measure of duty. Man's will is wayward and depraved. Hence practical authority to enforce this rule of right upon him must be lodged in some hands; and since God does not rule statedly by miracle, it must be in human hands. Civil government is God's ordinance, and its obligations are those of original moral right. The advantage and convenience resulting illustrate and confirm, but do not originate, the obligation. This is the theory of government plainly taught by St. Paul (Rom. xiii. 1 to 7) and St. Peter (1 Ep. ii. 13 to 18.) For we are here told that the civil magistrate is God's minister, to uphold right and repress wrong; that obedience to him in this is not only of moral, but religious obligation; and that he who resists this function disobeys God.

What, then, is man's natural liberty? We answer, that it is only *privilege to do whatever he has a moral right to do*. Freedom to do whatever a man wills, is not a liberty, either natural or civil, but an unnatural license, a natural iniquity; man's will being naturally depraved. What then is man's civil liberty? We reply, that under an equitable government, it is the same—the privilege to do whatever he has a moral right to do. No government is perfectly equitable: none are wholly unjust. Some withhold more, some fewer, of the citizen's moral rights. None withhold them all. Hence, under the most despotic government there are some rights left, and so, some liberty. A perfectly just government would be one which would allot to each citizen freedom to do all the things which he had a moral right to do, and nothing else. Such a government would not restrain the natural liberty of any citizen in any respect; each man's civil liberty would be identical with his natural. Government does not originate rights, neither can it justly take them away. But practically, it confirms, instead of impairing, our natural liberty; because it secures us in the exercise of it.

But the friends of liberal government may feel a lurking suspicion of this plain statement; because it is on a theory of pretended 'divine right' that the arguments for legitimacy, passive obedience, and despotism repose. Let us, then, pause to inquire whether the true scheme looks in that direction. And we ask first: Whether it is not much more likely that tyrannical conclusions will be drawn from those principles which ignore God, the great standard of right, and original moral distinctions, which are the basis of all rights, and so of all liberty—from principles which make man's might his natural right; rather than from our principles, which solidly found man's rights in eternal moral distinctions, and in the will of a just and benevolent God, the common Father, before whom rulers and ruled are equal? And when we turn to the history of opinion, we see that while Locke illogically deduced from this theory of the social contract a scheme of liberal government, his greater master, Hobbes, inferred that the most complete despotism was the most consistent. And both the French and the Yankee Jacobins, deriving from it an impious deification of the will of the mob which happens to be the larger, as the supreme law, have reduced their theory to practice in the most violent, ruthless, and mischievous oppressions ever perpetrated on civilized communities. Let the tree be judged by its fruits.

We repeat, that the glory and strength of the Christian theory of human government and liberty is this: that *it founds man's rights on eternal moral distinctions*. The liberty it grants each man is privilege of doing all those things which he, with his particular character and relations, is morally entitled to do. Privilege of doing all other things it retrenches; for what would this be but sin? Now the epitome of moral distinctions is, 'Love thy neighbour as thyself.' It is the same law expressed in the "Golden Rule." The meaning of this, as we saw, is, not that we must do to our fellow all that our caprice might desire, if our positions were inverted; but what we should believe ourselves morally entitled to require of him, in that case. Here, then, is the true basis of human equality. Men are all children of a common Father, brethren of the same race, each one entitled by the same right to his own appropriate share of well-being.

Hence, by a single and conclusive step, as the foundation of civil government is moral, its proper object is the good of all, governors and governed. Government is not for the behoof of rulers, but of the ruled also. Subjects were not made for kings, but kings for subjects. Indeed, rulers are themselves subjects, owing allegiance to the universal law of right, and members of the brotherhood for whose common good this law reigns. In the sublime Words of Samuel Rutherford, *Rex, Lex*. Neither Scriptures nor providence give to rulers any of that paternal right over the people, of which the legitimatists prate. They neither have for their subjects the father's instinctive love, nor the father's natural superiority in virtue, experience, or powers. The Scriptural governments over Israel were none of them legitimatist; and that to which Paul, Peter, and Christ owned conscientious allegiance, the Empire of the Cæsars, was not hereditary, and was a recent novelty. Again: while it is God's ordinance that men shall live under governments, no one form of government is ordained. "The powers that be are ordained of God." The one which, in His providence, actually subsists, is the legitimate one to the individual conscience. Still less has God indicated the individuals who shall govern as His agents. There is no divine nomination of the particular person. Hence, as government is for the common good of all, the selection of these agents belongs to the common wisdom and rectitude of the whole. And it is in this sense, (and only this,) that the Christian holds that the power of rulers is delegated from the ruled. In the higher sense, it is delegated from God, who is our true, rightful, and literal despot. The despotism of perfect, infinite rectitude is the most perfect freedom.

Now it is clear, that the several rights of different individuals in the same society must differ exceedingly, because the persons differ indefinitely in powers, knowledge, virtue, and natural relations to each other. From that very law of love and equity, whence the moral equality of men was inferred, it must also follow, that one man is not morally entitled to pursue his natural well-being at the expense of that of other men, or of the society. Each one's right must be so pursued, as not to infringe others' rights. The well-being of all is inter-connected. Hence equity, yea, a true equality itself, demands a varied distribution of social privilege among the members, according to their different characters and relations. In other words, an equal government must confer very different degrees of power, and impose very different degrees of restraint, upon different classes of members. To attempt an identical and mechanical equality; to confer on those who are incompetent to use them, the same privileges granted to others who can and will use them rightfully, would be essential inequality; for it would clothe the incompetent and undeserving with power to injure the deserving and capable, without real benefit to themselves. Hence, the civic liberties of all classes in the same society ought not to be the same. Thus, of the adult members, half are females, inexorably separated by sex, strength, social relations, and natural duties. Hence different civic rights are properly given to the male, in some respects; not because it is right to empower him to consume upon the promotion of his natural well-being that of his sister, but because, on the whole, the well-being of both sexes is thus most promoted. Whether this result does follow, must be a question of fact, to be decided by experience, if not settled in advance by God's Word. There is in the society another class of members, the children, who are not only different from, but inferior to, the adults, in knowledge, strength, experience, and self-controul. Hence, it is equitable to withhold from them still other privileges of the full citizenship. Again: the amount of privileges properly conceded to the body of citizens of the first class, should vary in different commonwealths with their average character. If intelligence and virtue are, in the average, more developed, the restraints of government should be fewer; if less cultivated, more numerous. Different frames of government may be best for different communities.

Once more: If the society contains a class of adult members, so deficient in virtue and intelligence that they would only abuse the fuller privileges of other citizens to their own and others' detriment, it is just to withhold so many of these privileges, and to impose so much restraint, as may be necessary for the highest equity to the whole body, inclusive of this subject class. And how much restraint is just, must be determined by facts and experience. Any degree of it is righteous, which is necessary to the righteous end. This is so obvious, that even abolitionists admit it, when they lose sight for the moment of their hobby. Of this Dr. Francis Wayland, a prominent abolitionist, gives us a striking instance in his "Moral Science." (Boston, 1838, p. 351.) He says: "Whatever concessions on the part of the individual, and whatever powers on the part of society, are *necessary* to the existence of society, must, by the very fact of the existence of society, be taken for granted." On p. 356, he adds: "If it be asked which of these" (hereditary, mixed, or republican) "is the preferable form of government, the answer, I think, must be conditional. The best form of government for any people, *is the best that its present social and moral condition renders practicable.* A people may be *so entirely surrendered to the influence of passion,* and so feebly *influenced by moral restraints,* that a government which relied upon moral restraints could not exist for a day. In this case a subordinate and inferior principle yet remains,—*the principle of fear:* and the only resort is to a government of force, or a military despotism."

If then the necessities of order justify the subjection of a whole nation, with their labour, property, and lives, to one man, will not the same reasons justify the far milder and more benevolent authority of masters over their servants? If it appear that the Africans in these States were by recent descent pagans and barbarians, men in bodily strength and appetite, with the reason and morals of children, constitutionally prone to improvidence, so that their possession of all the franchises of a free white citizen would make them a nuisance to society and early victims to their own degradation; and if sound experience teaches that this ruin cannot be prevented without a degree of restraint approaching that proper for children; that is, by giving to a guardian the controul of their involuntary labour, and the expenditure of the fruits for the joint benefit of the parties; how can we be condemned for it? And that social welfare and order, and the happiness of the African himself, do call imperiously for this degree of controul, is confessed by all who have a practical knowledge of his character, as it is proved by the disasters resulting from his emancipation.

Every government in the world acknowledges this necessity, and applies, in some form, this remedy. The abolition government of the United States, for instance, imposed compulsory restraints and labour upon multitudes of fugitive slaves, during the war. The only difference was, that whereas our system of domestic slavery placed this power in hands most powerfully interested to employ it humanely and wisely, the anti-slavery authorities placed it in hands which had every selfish inducement to abuse it to the misery of the slave, and the detriment of the publick interest. And the same government is to-day avouching every word of the above argument, by justifying itself, from a pretended political necessity, for placing the white race of the South under a much stricter bondage than that formerly borne by the negroes; a bondage which places not only labour and property, but life, at the irresponsible will of the masters. If slavery is wrong, then the abolitionists are the greatest sinners; for they have turned their own brethren into a nation of slaves.

Domestic servitude, as we define and defend it, is but civil government in one of its forms. All government is restraint; and this is but one form of restraint. As long as man is a sinner, and his will perverted, restraint is righteous. We are sick of that arrogant and profane cant, which asserts man's 'capacity for self-government' as a universal proposition; which represents human nature as so good, and democratic government as so potent, that it is a sort of miraculous *panacea*, sufficient to repair all the disorders of man's condition. All this ignores the great truths, that man is fallen; that his will is disordered, and therefore ought not to be his rule; that God, his owner and master, has ordained that he shall live under authority. What fruit has radical democracy ever borne, except factious oppression, anarchy, and the stern necessity for despotism?

It has been stated that each man's civil liberty, which, under a just government, is the same with his natural liberty, consists in the privilege of doing and having those things to which he is morally entitled. It has been shown, that as different persons in the same society differ widely in character, powers, and relations, their specific natural rights differ also. But under all forms of government, all still have some liberty. And under a perfectly equitable form, the different classes of persons would properly have different grades of liberty. So that, even in the relation of involuntary servitude for life, if it be not abused, there is an appropriate liberty. Such a servant has privilege to do those things which he is morally entitled to do. If there are certain things which he is restrained by authority from doing, which the superior grades may do, these things are not rights to him. His inferior character, ignorance, and moral irresponsibility, have extinguished his right to do them. And this properly, because his privilege of doing them would injure others and himself, and thus violate the law of equity. If his slavery restrains him from doing more things than these, then the laws do him injustice, and mar his rightful liberty.

This degree of domestic servitude supposes that the end of the restraints it imposes is, to secure, on the whole, the best well-being of both parties to the relation, servant as well as master. Here we may notice a forensic trick practised by Dr. Wayland and the abolitionists. It is that of giving to the proposition which they wish to overthrow, such an exposition as makes it absurd in itself. Says this professed moralist, in his chapter on slavery: "Domestic slavery proceeds upon the principle that the master has a right to controul the actions, physical and intellectual, of the slave, for his own, that is, the master's individual benefit; and of course, that the happiness of the master, when it comes in competition with the happiness of the slave, extinguishes in the latter the right to pursue it." If this were true, it would need no argument to show that slavery is a natural injustice. But slavery proceeds on no such principles. All men ought to know that our slave laws proved the contrary, in that they protected the slave, in many particulars, against the master's will, when it became unrighteous. All know that the publick sentiment of our people proved the contrary; in that the vast majority laboured and gave heartily for the welfare of their servants. And all men who have informed themselves know, that the grand result stamps the definition as a misrepresentation; in that domestic slavery here has conferred on the unfortunate black race more true well-being than any other form of society has ever given them. But it may be asked: Do not many masters selfishly use their slaves according to that definition? We reply: Do not many parents selfishly use their children according to that definition, neglecting their culture and true well-being, temporal and eternal, for the sake of gain? And is it not in the "thrifty" North that most of these instances of greedy, grinding parents are found? Yet who dreams of accusing the parental relation as therefore unrighteous and mischievous? This selfish tyranny is not the parental relation, but the abuse of it. So, every intelligent master defends his slaveholding, because it was, in the main, as preferable for the slave's interest as for his own.

§ 4. ABOLITIONISM IS JACOBINISM.

The promise was made above, to unmask some of the hideous affinities of the anti-slavery theory. This is now easy. If men are by nature sovereign and independent, and mechanically equal in rights, and if allegiance is founded solely on expressed or implied consent, then not only slavery, but every involuntary restraint imposed on a person or a class not convicted of crime, and every difference of franchise among the members of civil society, is a glaring wrong. Such are the premises of abolition. Obviously, then, the only just or free government is one where all franchises are absolutely equal to all sexes and conditions, where every office is directly elective, and where no magistrate has any power not expressly assented to by the popular will. For if inequalities of franchise may be justified by differences of character and condition, of course a still wider difference of these might justify so wide an inequality of rights as that between the master and servant. Your true abolitionist is then, of course, a Red-Republican, a Jacobin. Is not this strikingly illustrated by the fact, that the first wholesale abolition in the World was that enacted for the French colonies by the frantic democrats of the 'Reign of Terror?' And this hint may serve to explain to the aristocracy of Great Britain the popularity of the authoress of 'Uncle Tom's Cabin,' and of her slanderous book, among the masses there. It was not because Britain was so exempt from cases of social hardship and oppression at home, that its people had all its virtuous sympathies at leisure and unoccupied, to pour forth upon the imaginary wrongs of Uncle Tom: but it was because the Jacobinism of the abolitionist theory awakened an echo in the hearts of the lower classes, still seething with the recent upheaval of 1848. The community of agrarian sympathies made itself felt. The noble Lords and Ladies, who patronized the authoress and her book, were industriously fanning the very fires which are destined to consume their vested privileges.

Again, it follows of course from the premises of abolitionism, that hereditary monarchy, no matter how limited, is a standing injustice. A hereditary branch of the legislature is, if possible, still worse. Any such thing as a privileged class in the State is a fraud upon the others; for "all men are equal." The limitation of the right of suffrage, by property or sex, is a crime against human right; for the non-voting classes are ruled without their own consent; but consent is, according to them, the source of rightful authority. Thus are condemned at once the three branches of the hoary and honoured British constitution, kings, lords, and commons; under which men have enjoyed regulated liberty longer, and to a greater degree, than under any government on earth. And here it may be remarked that abolitionist ideas, so current in Great Britain, should have been as alien to the prevalent turns of thought of that people, as they certainly are to their welfare and the genius of their institutions. That a fantastic sciolist, intoxicated with vanity and dazzled by some glittering sophisms, should be an abolitionist, is natural. But Englishmen have ever been esteemed a solid and practical race. Their political conclusions have usually been, to the credit of their good sense, historical rather than theoretical. Their temper has been rather to guard the franchises inherited from their fathers, and approved by the national experience, than to gape after visionary and abstract rights of man. But despite all this, Great Britain has also been leavened with this fell spirit. Her political managers imagined that they found in abolitionism the convenient 'apple of discord' to destroy the peace of a great rival, and they therefore fostered it. To this great injustice they have added the condemnation of the South unheard, upon the testimony of our interested accusers. And the majority of Englishmen, with a dogmatism as unjust as senseless, have refused to permit either explanation or defence, proudly wrapped in impenetrable prejudice, while an innocent and noble people were condemned and overwhelmed by baseless obloquy. But it requires no spirit of prophecy to see that Divine Providence is speedily preparing a retribution by means of their own sin, which will be tremendous enough to satisfy the resentment of any injured Southerner. Abolitionized America is manifestly to be the Nemesis of Britain, through her Jacobin ideas, or arms, or both. The principles of abolition are, as we have proved, destructive of the foundations of the British constitution. Her own statesmen have insanely taught them to her people. The masses do not, indeed, reason very continuously or consistently; yet principles once fixed in their minds always work themselves out, in time, to their logical results. The so-called "Liberal Party" of Great Britain, which draws its inspirations from the abolition democracy of America, is unveiling itself more and more, as a party of true Jacobinism; and other parties have now paltered and dallied so long, that it will speedily show itself irresistible. And when the policy of England is swayed by moneyless votes, instead of capital and land, the caution and forbearance, bred by financial interests, which has thus far scarcely kept the peace between her and the United States, will speedily be changed. The two Jacobinisms, now so sweetly fraternizing over the ruin of the South, will disclose their innate and uniform aggressiveness, and will rush at each other's throats. This the immemorial rivalries and opposition of dearest interests will insure. Then will England feel, in the disintegration of her whole social fabrick by radical American ideas, and the Yankee invasions of Canada and Ireland, the folly of her own policy.

But other consequences follow from the abolitionist dogmas. "All involuntary restraint is a sin against natural rights," therefore laws which give to husbands more power over the persons and property of wives than to wives over husbands, are iniquitous, and should be abolished. The same decision must be made upon the exclusion of women, whether married or single, from suffrage, office, and the full franchises of men. There must be an end of the wife's obedience to her husband. Is it said that these subordinations are consistent, because women assent to them voluntarily, in consenting to become wives?

This plea is insufficient, because the female sex is impelled to marriage by irresistible laws of their nature and condition. How tyrannous is this legislation which shuts woman up to the alternative of foregoing the satisfaction of the prime instincts of her existence; or else of submitting to a code of natural injustice! As to the disabilities of single women, this plea has no pretended application. Thus the abolitionists will reason, yea, are reasoning. What was the strange prediction of prophetic wisdom, a few years ago, is now already familiar fact. Female suffrage is already introduced in one State, and will doubtless prevail as widely as abolitionism. But when God's ordinance of the family is thus uprooted, and all the appointed influences of education thus inverted; when America has had a generation of women who were *politicians*, instead of *mothers*, how fundamental must be the destruction of society, and how distant and difficult must be the remedy!

Once more: The same principles have consistently led some abolitionists to assail the parental relation itself. For although none can deny that, in helpless infancy, subjection should be the correlative of protection and maintenance, when once the young citizen has passed from the age of childhood, by what reason can the abolitionist justify his compulsory government by the father? Are not all men by nature equal?

It has been currently asserted that the premises of the abolitionists were embraced in the Declaration of Independence; so that the United States have been committed to them from the beginning. The words usually referred to are the following: "That all men are created equal: that they are endowed by their Creator with certain inalienable rights: that among these are life, liberty, and the pursuit of happiness. That to secure these rights governments are instituted among men, deriving their just powers from the consent of the governed," etc. If by these celebrated propositions it was meant that there ever was, or could be, a government where all men enjoyed the same measure of privilege, then it is false. If it was meant that there ever was, or could be, a state of society in which all men could indulge their volitions to the same extent, and that, in every case, the full extent, it is false; for natural and unavoidable differences of persons must ever prevent this. If it were meant that all men are naturally equal, then it would be false; for men are born with different bodily and mental powers, different moral qualities, and different inheritances of rights. If it was meant that every person enters life free from just controul, it is false; for we all begin our existence rightfully subject, irrespective of our consent, to authority in family and State. Neither God nor nature makes it optional with us whether we will be subject to government. But if it be meant that all men are created equal in this sense, that all are children of a common heavenly Father, all common subjects of the law of equity expressed in the "Golden Rule," each one as truly entitled to possess the set of rights justly appropriate to him, (and by the same reason,) as any other is entitled to his set of rights; this is true, and a glorious truth. This is man's moral equality. It means that, under God, the servant is as much entitled to the rights and privileges of a justly-treated servant, as the master is to the rights of a master; that the commoner is as much entitled to the just privileges of a commoner, as a peer to those of a peer. It is the truthful boast of Englishmen, that in their land every man is equal before the law. What does this mean? Does it mean that Lord Derby has no other franchises and privileges than the day-labourer? By no means. But the privileges allotted to the day-labourer by the laws are defended by the same institutions, and adjudicated by the same free principles, and made legally as inviolable, as the very different and larger privileges of Earl Derby. It is in this sense that a just and liberal government holds all men by nature equal. And if, when the Declaration of Independence says that the right of all men to their liberty is "inalienable," the proper definition of civil liberty is accepted, (that it only means privilege to do what each man, in his peculiar circumstances, has a moral right to do,) this also is universally true. But all this is perfectly consistent with differences of social condition, and station, and privilege; where characters and relations are different. As we have seen, the servant for life, who as a slave receives "those things which are just and equal," has his true liberty, though it is different from that of the free citizen; and the servant can no more be justly stripped of this his *modicum* of liberty, than the master of his. Last, when it is declared that "governments derive their just powers from the consent of the governed," there is a sense in which it is true, and one in which it is false. In one sense, they derive their just powers from God, his law, and providence. In the other sense, that the people are not for their rulers, but the rulers for their people, the selection of particular forms of constitution and of the individuals to execute the functions, belongs to the aggregate rectitude and intelligence of the commonwealth, expressed in some way practically fair. But by "the consent of the governed," our wise fathers never intended the consent of each particular human being, competent and incompetent. They intended the representative commonwealth as a body, the "*populus*," or aggregate corporation of that part of the human beings properly wielding the franchises of full citizens. Their proposition is general, and not particular. The men of 1776 were not vain *Ideologues*; they were sagacious, practical Englishmen. Thus understood, as every correct thinker does, they teach nothing against difference of privilege among the subjects of government; and consequently, nothing inconsistent with the servitude of those who are found incapable of beneficially possessing a fuller liberty.

Now, the evidence that this only was their meaning is absolutely complete. Had their proposition been that of the Jacobin abolitionist, (that just claim on men's obedience to authority is founded on the individual's consent,) they must have ordered every thing differently from their actual legislation. They could not have countenanced limited suffrage, of which nearly all of them were advocates. They must have taught female suffrage, which the most democratic of them would have pronounced madness. Not only did they retain the African race in slavery, in the face of this declaration, but they refused to adopt full democratic equality, in reconstructing their constitutions. Were these men fools? Were they ignorant of the plain meaning of their own propositions? Did they, like modern Radicals, disdain the plainest obligations of consistency? Some attempt to evade their retention of slavery, by saying that they did not defend its consistency, nor contemplate it as a permanent relation; but the other facts are unanswerable. It may be true that Jefferson, the draughtsman of the Declaration, did heartily adopt his propositions in the sense of the advocates of the social contract; for it is well known that he was properly a Democrat, and not, like the other great Whigs of Virginia, only a Republican; that he had drank deeply into the spirit of Locke's political writings; and that he had already contracted a fondness for the atheistical philosophy of the French political reformers. But who can believe that George Mason, of Gunston, could fail to see the glaring inconsistency between these propositions, taken in the extravagant and radical sense now forced upon them by the abolitionists, and the constitution which he gave to the State of Virginia? According to that immortal instrument, our commonwealth was as distinctly contrasted with a levelling democracy, as any monarchy regulated by laws could possibly be. It was, indeed, a liberal, aristocratic republic. None could vote save the owners of land in fee-simple; and these were permitted to exercise their elective powers directly, only in one sole instance, the election of the General Assembly. This Assembly then exercised, without farther reference to the freeholders, all the powers of the commonwealth. The Assembly elected the Governor of the State. The Assembly appointed all judges of law, and executive officers of State. The county courts, to whom belonged the whole power of police, of local taxation, and of administration of local justice in cases beneath the grade of a felony, formed a proper aristocracy, serving for life, appointing their own clerks and sheriffs, and filling vacancies in their own numbers by a nomination to the Governor, which was always virtually imperative. Such was the government which the statesmen of Virginia deliberately adopted, after signing the Declaration of Independence; than which none could have been devised by human wit, so well adapted to the character and wants of their people, and under which they exhibited the highest political stability and purity which our commonwealth has ever known. Any one who knows the British Constitution will see at a glance, that our Virginian frame of government was not the work of men led by the Utopian dream of "liberty, fraternity, and equality," but of practical statesmen, establishing for their posterity the historical rights of British freemen.

But were the language of the Declaration of Independence as decisive as anti-slavery men suppose, it would concern us exceedingly little. We regard it as no political revelation. When we formed a part of the United States, it was no article of our constitution; and still less are we responsible for it now. If it should be even convicted of embodying some error, this would be neither very surprising, nor very disgraceful to its authors. For what more probable than that men inflamed by the spirit of resistance to tyranny, and surrounded by the excitements of a revolution, in the indiscreet effort to propound a set of abstract generalities as the basis of their action, should mix the plausible errors of the advocates of freedom with the precious truth?

§ 5. LABOUR OF ANOTHER MAY BE PROPERTY.

By confounding the master's right to the slave's labour with a pretended property in his conscience, soul, and whole personality, abolitionists have attempted to represent "property in man" as a self-evident wrong. But we shall show that, in the only sense in which we hold it, property in man is recognized by the laws of every commonwealth. The father has property in his child, the master in his apprentice, the husband in his wife, the wife in her husband, and the employer in his hireling. In every one of these cases, this property is recoverable by suits at law, and admits of being transmuted for money, just as any other possession. When the husband is killed by the culpable negligence of a railroad company which had engaged to transport him for hire, the wife sues and recovers money damages. When the daughter is seduced from her father's house, he may sue for compensation, and the court will assess the value of her remaining services until her majority, at such a sum as they judge proper. How is this to be explained, save by regarding the wife as having lawful property in the industry of her husband, and the father as having property in the labour of his daughter? The labour of a minor son is often sold by the father, and thus becomes the property of the purchaser. It is of no avail to say that this labour is voluntary, and that the property originates in the virtual compact between the parties; for this is not true of the parental relation. Still another striking instance of lawful property in the involuntary labour of a fellow-man, appears in the apprenticeship of the children of paupers. Pauperism is not a crime; yet these children are, with undisputed moral propriety, indentured to householders, during their minority; and the labour thus conveyed is hired, sold, bequeathed, just as any other property. Dr. Wayland argues that there cannot be ownership in man, because ownership as he defines it, consists in our "*right to use the property as we please!*" This definition was made to suit abolitionism, and is not the truth. May we, because we have property in our horses, use them living as we would our logs of wood, for fuel? The ethics of common sense, as that of all true science, (what Dr. W. should have known, if he had been fit to do what he assumed, teach science,) define ownership to be *a right to use our property according to its nature*. Thus defined, property in man presents no solecism whatever, inconsistent with righteousness.

§ 6. THE SLAVE RECEIVED DUE WAGES.

But it is charged that the injustice of our system is apparent in this, that it takes the slave's labour without compensation. It is simply untrue. Southern slaves received, on the average, better and more certain compensation than any labouring people of their capacity in the world. It came to them in the form of that maintenance, which the master was bound by the laws, as well as his own interests, to bestow upon them. During childhood, they were reared at his expense; in sickness they received maintenance, nursing, and the same medical advice which he provided for his own children; all at his expense. When they married and had children, (which all did, single-blessedness was unknown among them,) their families were provided for by the masters without one additional toil or anxiety on their part. When they died, their orphans had, in the master's estate, an unfailing provision against destitution; and if old age overtook them, they received, without labour, the same supplies and comforts which were allotted to them in their prime. How many of the sons of toil in nominally free countries would seize with rapture the offer of such wages for their labour, if the name of slavery were detached from them? To be able to secure, by the moderate labours of their active years, a certain and liberal provision for their daily wants, for their families, however large, and for sickness and old age, would be a contract so advantageous, in comparison with the hardships and uncertainties of the peasant's usual life, that few thoughtful persons of that class would hesitate, from love of novelty or dim hope of a more lucky career, to embrace it. But this is just what our laws and customs gave to our slaves, as wages of their easy labour. But the anti-slavery man objects, that the adjustment of this compensation is made at the will of the master alone, while the slave has no power to influence it. This is precisely the same objection, in effect, with the one that the labour is involuntary. We have already shown that this circumstance alone does not make the claim on the labour unjust. And if the system makes for the slave, on the average, a better bargain than he could make for himself, where is his hardship? Is he injured by being restrained of the liberty of injuring himself? Surely, the fairness of any system should be judged by the fairness of its average results. If some masters withhold a part of the due wages, by failing to "render to their servants that which is just and equal," this is their individual fault, not that of the system. St. Paul, in the passage quoted, manifestly thought that we might hold the involuntary labour of our slaves, and yet be no robbers.

But our enemies return to the charge, urging that we robbed our slaves, because we engrossed to ourselves the lion's share of the bondsman's labour. The master and his family, say they, who did no work, rolled in luxury, while the poor slaves, who did all, got only such a pittance as was needed to preserve their capacity for toil. This is false in every part. Masters and their families were not idlers. Their life was not relatively luxurious. The slave's share was not a pittance, but much more like the lion's share. But, they exclaim: "Let the masters stand aside and allow the slaves to enjoy the whole fruits of the estates they cultivate: then only will the former cease to be robbers." This astonishing folly is exposed by simply asking, whether capital and superintending skill are not entitled to wages, as well as labour? The crops of the Southern plantation were the joint fruit of the master's capital, the master's labour and skill of oversight, and the slaves' labour. If capital be denied all remuneration, the wheels of productive industry would stop everywhere, to the especial ruin of the labouring classes. Does the anti-slavery manufacturer of Lowell or Manchester think it fair, after investing his thousands in fixtures and material, and bestowing his anxious superintendence, that his operatives should claim the whole profits of the factory, leaving him not a penny, because, forsooth, he never spun or wove a thread? Away with the nonsense! Southern slaves enjoyed a larger share of the proceeds of conjoined capital, superintending skill, and labour, than any operatives in the world. This is not only allowed, but virtually asserted, by anti-slavery men, when they reason that slavery is an economical evil, because the maintenance of slaves is more costly, in proportion to the value of their labour, than that of free labourers. Thus, in one place, they object that slaves receive too much compensation, and in another, that they receive too little. Nor is it true that Southern masters usually make no contribution of labour to the products of their farms. There is nowhere a population of equal wealth, more industrious than slaveholders. The master usually contributes far more to the common production than the strongest labourer on his estate; and the mistress more than the most industrious female servant, partly in the labours of superintendence, but also in actual toil.

§ 7. Effects of Slavery on Moral Character.

It is argued by abolitionists, that slavery regularly exerts many influences tending to degrade the moral character of both masters and servants. Their charge cannot be better stated than in the Words of Dr. Wayland. ["Moral Science," Personal Liberty, Ch. I., § 2.]
"Its effects must be disastrous upon the morals of both parties. By presenting objects on whom passion may be satiated without resistance, and without redress, it tends to cultivate in the master, pride, anger, cruelty, selfishness, and licentiousness. By accustoming the slave to subject his moral principles to the will of another, it tends to abolish in him all moral distinctions, and thus fosters in him, lying, deceit, hypocrisy, dishonesty, and a willingness to yield himself up to minister

to the appetites of his master. That in all slaveholding countries there are exceptions to this remark, and that there are principles in human nature which, in many cases, limit the effect of these tendencies, may be gladly admitted. Yet that such is the tendency of slavery as slavery, we think no reflecting person can for a moment hesitate to allow."

This is a flattering picture of us, truly! By good fortune, it is drawn by one who knows nothing of us. Just such are the current representations which Yankees have made of Southern morals, down to the notable instance of Senator Sumner's speech on the "Barbarism of Slavery." The question whether the system of slave labour deteriorates the morals of master and servant, as compared with that of free labour, may be treated as one of deduction and reasoning, or one of fact. The latter is the more trustworthy way to decide it. Dr. Wayland undertakes to settle it solely by the former. And it is manifest to the first glance, that his whole reasoning begs the question. If the very relation is wicked, if every act of authority on the master's part is a wrong, and of submission on the servant's part is a surrender of his right, then the reasoning is plausible. But let us suppose, for argument's sake, (what may be true, as it is the very point undecided,) that the relation may be right, the authority exercised lawful, and the things our servants are usually enjoined to do, innocent acts. Then, the fact that there is authority on one side and obedience on the other, cannot tend, of itself, to degrade ruler and ruled: for if this were so, the parental relation itself (ordained by God as His school of morals for young human beings) would be a school of vice. But the argument is a sophism, in a yet more audacious and insulting sense. Its author argues the degradation of the slave, chiefly because his wicked master compels him by fear to do so many wicked things. But suppose the master to be a gentleman, and not a brute, so that the things he customarily compels the slave to do, are right things; where, then, is the argument? Which of the two characters masters usually bear, is the question to be solved at the conclusion of the reasoning, and, yet more, to be decided by the surer testimony of fact. But Dr. Wayland chooses to begin by presuming, *à priori*, that masters are generally rascals.

Wisdom would infer, on the contrary, that the habitual exercise of authority, approved as righteous by the ruler's conscience, tends to elevate his character. He who would govern others must first govern himself. Hence, we should expect to find him who is compelled to exercise a hereditary and rightful authority, a man more self-governed, thoughtful, considerate, firm, and dignified, than other men. The habit of providing constantly for a number of persons, whom he is impelled by the strongest self-interest to care for efficiently, should render a man considerate of others, and benevolent. Experience will soon teach the head of such an estate, that his relation with his dependents must be any thing else than a carnival of self-indulgence, violence, and tyranny; for such a life will speedily leave him no servants to abuse. On the contrary, the very necessities of his position compel him to be, to a certain extent, provident, methodical, and equitable. Without these virtues, his estate slips rapidly away. And who, that knows human nature, can fail to see the powerful effects of the institution in developing, in the ruling caste, a higher sentiment of personal honour, chivalry, and love of liberty? This was asserted of the slaveholders of Virginia and the Carolinas by the sagacious Burke. It is very true, that if every man in the country were under the vital influence of Christian sanctification, he would not need these more human influences to elevate his character. But the wise statesman takes men as they are, not as they should be. Until the *millennium*, the elevating influences of social position will continue to be of great practical value. Yankeedom, at least, continues thus far to exhibit a great want of them.

But now, in considering the actual influences of slavery on the morals of the Africans, let the reader remember what they actually were before they were placed under this tutelage. He may be sure they were not what abolitionism loves to picture them, a sort of Ebony Arcadians, full of simple, pastoral purity, and of what infidels vainly prate as the dignity of native virtue. It is not slavery which has degraded them from that imaginary elevation. On the contrary, they were what God's word declares human depravity to be under the degrading effects of paganism. Let the reader see the actual and true picture, in the first chapter of Romans, and in authentic descriptions of the negro in his own jungles, such as the invaluable work of Dr. John Leighton Wilson, on the tribes of the Guinea coast. And here, moreover, he will find proof, that the type of savage life brought to America originally by the slave trade, was far below that witnessed in Africa among the more noticeable tribes; because the great bulk of the slaves were either the Pariahs of that barbarous society, or the kidnapped members of the feeble fragments of bush tribes, who had nearly perished before the comparative civilization of the Mandingoes and Greboes, living but one remove above the apes around them. Now cannot common sense see the moral advantage to such a people, of subjection to the will of a race elevated above them, in morals and intelligence, to an almost measureless degree? Is it no moral advantage to be compelled to wear decent clothing, and to observe at least the outward proprieties which should obtain between the sexes? None to be taught industry, in place of pagan laziness; and methodical habits, in place of childish waste and unthrift? The destructive effects of the savage's common vices, lying, theft, drunkenness, laziness, waste, upon business and pecuniary interests, will of course prompt masters to repress those vices, if no higher motive does. Is this no gain for the poor pagan? Especially does the matter of drunkenness illustrate, in a splendid manner, the benign effects of our system on African character and happiness. Place any savage race beside a civilized and commercial people, and leave them free; and the speedy result is, that the "fire-water" consumes and depopulates them. Witness the North American Indians. But here was just such a race, in the midst of the temptation and opportunity, and yet preserved from all appreciable evil from this source, and advancing in physical comfort, manners, and numbers, more rapidly than any white race in Christendom. While numbers of Africans exhibited just that weakness for ardent spirits, which is to be expected in people lately barbarians, yet so wholesome were the restraints of that regular and constant occupation enforced upon them, it was the rarest thing in the world that a farm-servant filled a drunkard's grave among us. But now the flood-gates are opened. Was not Dr. Wayland a temperance man? Southern slavery was the most efficient temperance society in the world.

Once more, was it nothing, that this race, morally inferior, should be brought into close relations to a nobler race, so that the propensity to imitation should be stimulated by constant and intimate observation, by domestic affection, by the powerful sentiment of allegiance and dependence? And above all, was it nothing that they should be brought, by the relation of servitude, under the consciences and Christian zeal of a Christian people, in circumstances which most powerfully enlisted their sense of responsibility, and gave free scope to their labour of love? Let the blessed results answer, of a nation of four millions lifted, in four generations, out of idolatrous debasement, "sitting clothed, and in their right mind;" of more than half a million adult communicants in Christian churches! And all this glorious work has been done exclusively by Southern masters; for never did foreign or Yankee abolitionist find leisure from the more congenial work of slandering the white, to teach or bless the black man in any practical way. This much-abused system has thus accomplished for the Africans, amidst universal opposition and obloquy, more than all the rest of the Christian world together has accomplished for the rest of the heathen. It is the delight of abolitionists to impute to slavery a result peculiarly corrupting as to sins of unchastity. Witness the repetitions charges by Dr. Wayland, of these sins, as contaminating both masters and slaves, in consequence of slavery. The evidence of facts has been already given as to the comparative justice of this charge. But reason itself would suggest to the least reflection, that Southern households are not the only ones where young men and female domestics are thrown together, amidst all the temptations and opportunities of privacy and domestic intimacy; that the power of corporal punishment, unlawful here for this end, is not the only power which a superior may apply to an inferior to overcome her chastity, nor the most effective. But, on the other hand, reason would suggest that the employment of free persons of the same colour and race would greatly enhance the force of those temptations; while among us, the differences of colour, race, and personal attractions, would greatly diminish them; while the very sentiment of superior caste would render the intercourse more repulsive and unnatural.

The testimony of facts, however, is the conclusive evidence on the question, whether our system is relatively more corrupting than that of free labour. In this department of the discussion, Providence has given us a refutation against the Yankees so terribly biting, as fully to satisfy any indignation which their arrogant railings may have excited in our bosoms. We were placed together at the beginning of our national existence, under the same Federal government, and under similar religious and State institutions. Our union presented a common field for constant meeting and comparison. And what were the results disclosed? It has been shown that while the South, as a great section of the Union, never, in one single instance, made any general or united movement to pervert Federal laws and powers for unfair local purposes; while the South ever manifested a chivalrous patriotism against any assaults upon the common rights; the North has never failed, from the first year of the government, to use it as a machine for legislative extortion and local advantage; and the North has usually played the traitor to the common cause when assailed from without, even when, as in the second war with England, the interests assailed by the foreign enemy, and generously defended by the South, were more peculiarly her own. It has appeared that when at last legislative peculation grew so foul that the publick demanded inquiry, every member of the Congress convicted of that disgraceful iniquity, was from the North, and not one from the South. If we pass to personal comparisons, the publick men of the South have shown themselves, on the federal *arena*, superior, in general, in the talent of command, in personal honour, in dignity, in the amenities of life, in forbearance and self-controul; while that very petulance, wilfulness, and love of arbitrary power, which, abolition philosophers infer, must be the peculiar fruits of slaveholding, were exhibited in marked contrast, by the few Northern Presidents who had the fortune to reach that high position. Compare, for instance, the benign Washington, a great slaveholder, with that petty tyrant, the elder Adams; or Jefferson, Madison and Monroe with his son, (worthy son of such a sire,) John Quincy Adams; or Jefferson Davis with Abraham Lincoln; or our Lee, Johnstons, Jackson and Beauregard, with a McNeill and a Butler! So well proved are the superior courtesy, liberality, and humanity of the Southern gentleman, that the very porters on the wharves, and waiters in the hotels, of Northern cities, recognize them by these traits. It has been the fashion of a certain type of poltroons among the Yankees, who wish to indulge the anger and malignity of the bully, along with the safety and impunity of the Quaker, to represent the resort of Southerners to the code of honour, as a peculiar proof of their uncivilized condition. They exclaim triumphantly that we fight duels, while Yankees do not. Now the code of honour is certainly irrational, unchristian, and wicked. But there is another thing that is greatly more wicked; and this is the disposition to inflict upon a fellow-man the injuries and insults which that code proposes to prevent; and then cloak one's self under the cowardly pretence of a conscience which forbids to fight. The duellist sins by anger and revenge: these sneaking hypocrites sin by anger and revenge, and cowardice and lying, at once. The truly good man is forbidden by his conscience from seeking retaliation; but the same conscience equally forbids him to inflict on others the injuries which provoke retaliation. The man who wilfully injures his fellow, has therefore no right to plead conscience, for refusing satisfaction. It is not conscience, but cowardice. While, then, we mourn the crimes of violent retaliation which sometimes occur at the South, the citizens of the North have occasion for a deeper blush, at the crimes of malignant slander and vituperation which their people are accustomed to launch at us from the vile hiding-place of their hypocritical puritanism.

It will be seen by every one, that the females of the ruling class must be very intimately concerned in the duties of the relation of master and servant. It is properly termed *domestic* slavery; and woman's functions are wholly domestic. If then, slavery is morally corrupting, Southern ladies should show the sad result very plainly. But what says fact? Its testimony is one which fills the heart of every Southern man with grateful pride; that the Southern lady is proverbially eminent for all that adorns female character, for grace, for purity and refinement, for benevolence, for generous charity, for dignified kindness and forbearance to inferiors, for chivalrous moral courage, and for devout piety.

We might safely submit the comparative soundness of Southern society to this test: that it has never generated any of those loathsome *isms*, which Northern soil breeds, as rankly as the slime of Egypt its spawn of frogs. While the North has her Mormons, her various sects of Communists, her Free Lovers, her Spiritualists, and a multitude of corrupt visionaries whose names and crimes are not even known among us, our soil has never proved congenial to the birth or introduction of a single one of these inventions.

But the crowning refutation of this slander against Southern morals, is presented by the great war lately concluded—a refutation whose glory repays us for long years of reproach. Dispassionate spectators abroad have passed their verdict of disgust upon the combination of feebleness in the field, boasting and falsehood at home, venality and peculation towards their own treasury and the property of private citizens, with ruthless violation of all the laws of humanity. Dispassionate spectators! No; there were none such: but from ignorant and prejudiced minds stuffed with misconceptions by our interested assailants, the splendid disclosure of civic and military genius, bravery, fortitude under incredible hardships, magnanimity under unspeakable provocations, and dignity under defeat, which appeared at the South, drew a general acclaim of admiration from the whole civilized world. This war, among its many evils, has done us this good, that it has settled for this century the charge of the "barbarism of Southern slavery."

But it may not be amiss to reveal those vices which are peculiarly opposed to the Yankees' own boasts, as the inhabitants of "the land of steady habits." Our soldiers who have been prisoners of war among them, all report that their camps were *Pandemoniums*, for their resounding blasphemies and profanities. Nothing was more common than the capture from them of prisoners of war, too drunk to walk steadily. The mass of the letters found upon their slain, and about their captured camps, disclosed a shocking prevalence of prurient and licentious thought, both in their armies and at home. And our unfortunate servants seduced away by their armies, usually found, to their bitter cost, that lust for the African women was a far more prevalent motive, than their pretended humanity, for their liberating zeal. Such was the monstrous abuse to which these poor creatures were subjected, that decent slave fathers often hid their daughters in the woods, from their pretended liberators, as from beasts of prey.

We freely avow that the line of argument which occupies this section is not to our taste; nor, as was intimated in the introduction, do we regard it as the safest means of ascertaining the moral influences of the two systems. But it has not been by our choice that it has been introduced. The slanders of our accusers have thrust it upon us. We now gladly dismiss it with this general concluding remark; that the comparative general virtue of Southern masters, and the purity of Southern Christianity, are a strong evidence that we were not living in a criminal relation, as to the African race. For sins are always gregarious. One sin, permanently established in the heart and life, always introduces its foul kindred. Sin is contagious. An unsound spot in the character ultimately taints the whole. The misguided gentleman who first yields to the passion of gaming, solely for its amusement and excitement, cannot continue a habitual gamester and a gentleman. The ingenuous youth who harbours the habit of intoxication, in due time ceases to be even ingenuous. These unhallowed passions, once established, introduce fraud, selfishness, meanness, falsehood. So, we argue, if slaveholding were a sin, its practice would surely tell upon the honour and integrity of those who continue in it. But Southern character exhibits no such general effect.

§ 8. SLAVERY AND THE AFRICAN SLAVE TRADE.

It is a plausible ground of opposition to slavery, to charge it with the guilt of the slave trade. It is argued that unless we are willing to justify the capture of free and innocent men, on their own soil, and their reduction from freedom to slavery, with all the enormous injustice and cruelty of the African slave trade, we must acknowledge that the title of the Southern master to his slave at this day is unrighteous; that a system which had its origin in wrong cannot become right by the lapse of time; that, if the title of the piratical slave catcher on the coast of Africa was unrighteous, he cannot sell to the purchaser any better title than he has; and that an unsound title cannot become sound by the passage of time. It need hardly be said that we abhor the injustice, cruelty, and guilt of the African slave trade. It is justly condemned by the public law of Christendom—a law which not Wilberforce, nor the British Parliament, nor British, nor Yankee Abolitionists, have the honour of originating, but the slaveholding Commonwealth of Virginia. It is condemned by the law of God. Moses placed this among the judicial statutes of the Jews: "And he that stealeth a man and selleth him, or if he be found in his hand, he shall surely be put to death." We fully admit, then, that the title of the original slave catcher to the captured African was most unrighteous. But few can be ignorant of the principle, that a title, originally bad, may be replaced by a good one, by transmission from hand to hand, and by lapse of time. When the property has been acquired, by the latest holder, fairly and honestly; when, in the later transfers, a fair equivalent was paid for it, and the last possessor is innocent of fraud in intention and in the actual mode of his acquisition of it, more wrong would be effected by destroying his title, than by leaving the original wrong unredressed. Common sense says, that whatever may have been the original title, a new and valid one has arisen out of the circumstances of the case. If this principle be denied, half the property of the civilized world will be divorced from its present owners. All now agree that the pretext which gave ground for the conquest of William of Normandy was wicked; and however just it might have been, by the laws of nations, the conquest of the government of a country ought not to disturb the rights of individuals in private property. The Norman Conquest resulted in a complete transfer of almost all the land in England to the hands of new proprietors; and nearly all the land titles of England, at the present day, are the legal progeny of that iniquitous robbery, which transferred the territory of the kingdom from the Saxon to the Norman barons. If lapse of time, and change of hands, cannot make a bad title good, then few of the present landlords of England have any right to their estates. Upon the same principles, the tenants leasing from them have no right to their leases, and consequently they have no right to the productions of the farms they hold. If they have no right to those productions, then they cannot communicate any right to those who purchase from them;

so that no man eating a loaf of English bread, or wearing a coat of English wool, could be certain that he was not consuming what was not his own. Thus extravagant and absurd are the results of such a principle. Let us apply to the abolitionists their own argument, and we shall unseat the most of them from the snug homes whence they hurl denunciations at us. It is well known that their forefathers obtained the most of that territory from the poor Indians, either by fraud or violence. If lapse of time and subsequent transfers cannot make a sound title in place of an unsound one, then few of the people of the North have any right to the lands they hold; and, as honest men, they are bound to vacate them. To this even as great a man as Dr. Wayland, the philosopher of abolitionism, has attempted an answer, by saying that this right, arising from possession, only holds so long as the true, original owner, or the inheritor of his right, does not appear; and that, when he appears, the right of possession perishes at once. But he argues, the original and true claimant to the ownership of the slave is always present, in the person of the slave himself; so that the right originating in possession cannot exist for a moment. Without staying to inquire whether the presence of the inheritor of the original right necessarily puts an end to this right of possession—a proposition worse than questionable—I would simply remark, that, to represent the slave himself as the possessor of the original right, is a complete begging of the question. It assumes the very point in dispute, whether the right of the master is sound or not. And we would add, what would the courts of New England, what would Dr. Wayland say, should the feeble remnants of the New England Indians, who are yet lingering in those States, claim all the fair domains of their tribe? And what would be said in England, if the people of Saxon descent should rise upon all those noble houses who boast a Norman origin, and claim their princely estates?

But we carry this just *argumentum ad hominem* nearer home. If the Virginian slaveholder derived from the New England or British slave-trader, no valid title to the African, then the trader had no valid title to the planter's money. What can be clearer than this? And if continued possession, with lapse of time, and transmission from hand to hand, cannot convert an unsound title into a sound one, all the wealth acquired by the African slave trade, together with all its increase, is wrongfully held by the heirs of those slave dealers: it belongs to the heirs of the planters from whom it was unjustly taken. Now it is well known that the New England States, and especially the little State of

Dr. Wayland, Rhode Island, drew immense sums from the slave trade; and it was said of the merchants of Liverpool and Bristol, that the very bricks of their houses were cemented with the blood of the slave. Who can tell how much of the wealth which now freights the ships, and drives the looms of these anti-slavery marts, is the fruit of slave profits? Let the pretended owners disgorge their spoils, and restore them to the Virginian planters, to indemnify them for the worthless and fictitious title to the slaves whom they have been called upon to emancipate; in order that means may be provided to make their new liberty a real blessing to them. Thus we should have a scheme for emancipation, or colonization, which would be just in both its aspects. But will abolitionism assent to this? About as soon as death will surrender its prey. Let them cease, then, for shame's sake, to urge this sophism.

If this principle of a right originated by possession can be sound anywhere, it is sound in its application to our slaves. The title by which the original slave catchers held them may have been iniquitous. But these slave catchers were not citizens of the Southern colonies; these slaves were not brought to our shores by our ships. They were presented by the inhuman captors, dragged in chains from the filthy holds of the slave ships; and the alternative before the planter was, either to purchase them from him who possibly had no right to sell them, or re-consign them to fetters, disease, and death. The slaves themselves hailed the conclusion of a sale with joy, and begged the planters to become their masters, as a means of rescue from their floating prison. The planters, so far as they were concerned, paid a fair commercial equivalent for the labour of the slaves; and the right so acquired passed legally through generations from father to son, or seller to purchaser. The relation, so iniquitously begun in those cases where the persons imported were not slaves already in Africa, has been fairly and justly transferred to subsequent owners, and has resulted in blessings to the slaves. Its dissolution is more mischievous to them than to the masters. Must it not be admitted that the injustice in which the relation originated no longer attaches to it? The difference between the title of the original slave catcher, and that of the late Virginian slave owner, is as great as between the ruffian Norman freebooter, who conquered his fief at Hastings, and his law-abiding descendant, the Christian gentleman of England.

§ 9. THE MORALITY OF SLAVERY VINDICATED BY ITS RESULTS.

To deny the mischievous effects of emancipation upon the Africans themselves, requires an amount of impudence which even abolitionists seldom possess. The experience of Britain has demonstrated, to the satisfaction of all her practical statesmen, that freedom among the whites is ruinous to the blacks. They tell us of the vast decline in the productiveness of their finest colonies, of the lapsing of fruitful plantations into the bush, of the return of the slaves, lately an industrious and useful peasantry, to savage life, and of the imperative necessity for Asiatic labour, to rescue their lands from a return to the wilderness. A comparison between the slaves of the South, and the freed negroes of the North, gives the same results. While the former were cheerful, healthy, progressive, industrious, and multiplying rapidly in numbers, the latter are declared by their white neighbours to be a social nuisance, depressed by indolence and poverty, decimated by hereditary diseases, and tending rapidly to extinction.

We argue hereupon, that it cannot be a moral duty to bestow upon the slave that which is nothing but an injury. It cannot be a sin to do to him that which uniformly and generally is found essential to his well-being in his present condition. We certainly are not required by a benevolent God to ruin him in order to do him justice! No sober and practical mind can hold such an absurdity. Hence we may know, even in advance of examination, that the ethical premises, the theory of human rights, which lead to such preposterous conclusions, must be false. To illustrate this argument, the humane effects of slavery upon the slave should be more fully exhibited. This we propose to attempt in another chapter.

CHAPTER VIII.
ECONOMICAL EFFECTS OF SLAVERY.

We are not propagandists of slavery. The highest wish of Virginia with reference to it was, that now it had been fastened on her against her remonstrances by others, she should be let alone to manage it as she judged the best: a right which had been solemnly pledged to her by her present aggressors. We had no desire to force it on others, or to predict its universal prevalence, as the best organization of society. But having claimed that the Word of God and publick justice authorize it, we admit that it is reasonable we should meet those who assert economical and social results of it so evil, as to render it in credible that a wise and benevolent God should sanction such a mischief. We hope to show that slavery, instead of being wasteful, impoverishing, and mischievous, is so far useful and benevolent as to vindicate the divine wisdom in ordaining it, and to show that we were wisely content with our condition so far as this relation of labour and capital was concerned.

We would also urge this preliminary remark: that the economical effects of American slavery have usually been argued from an amazingly unreasonable point of view. Our enemies persist in discussing it as an election to be made between a system of labour by christianized, enlightened, free yeomen of the same race, on one hand; and a system of labour by African slaves on the other; as though the South had any such election in its power! It was not a thing for us to decide, whether we should have these Africans, or civilized, free, white labour; the former were here; here, not by the choice of our forefathers, but forced upon us by the unprincipled cupidity of the slave-trading ancestors of the Abolitionists of Old and New England who now revile us; forced upon us against the earnest protest of Virginia. Did Abolitionists ever propose a practical mode of removing them, and supplying their places, which would not inflict on both parties more mischief than slavery occasion? They should have showed us some way to charm the four millions of Africans among us, away to some happy Utopia, where they might be more comfortable than we made them; and to repair the shock caused by the abstraction of all this productive labour. Until they did this, the question was not whether it would be wisest for a legislator creating a totally new community, to form it like Scotland or New England; or like Virginia. The true question was, these

Africans being here, and there being no humane or practicable way to remove them, what shall be done with them? If the social condition of Virginia exhibited points of inferiority in its system of labour, to that of its rivals, the true cause of the evil was to be sought in the *presence* of the Africans among us, not in his *enslavement*. We shall indeed assert, and prove, that these points of inferiority were vastly fewer and smaller than our enemies represent. But, we emphatically repeat, the source of the evils apparent in our industrial system was the presence among us of four millions of heterogeneous pagan, uncivilized, indolent, and immoral people; and for that gigantic evil, slavery was, in part at least, the lawful, the potent, the beneficent remedy. Without this, who cannot see that such an *incubus* must have oppressed and blighted every interest of the country? Such an infusion must have tainted the sources of our prosperity. It would have been a curse sufficient to paralyze the industry, to corrupt the morals, and to crush the development of any people on earth, to have such a race spread abroad among them like the frogs of Egypt. And that the South not only delivered itself from this fate, but civilized and christianized this people, making them the most prosperous and comfortable peasantry in the world, developed a magnificent agriculture, and kept pace with the progress of its gigantic rival, attests at once the energy of our people, and the wisdom and righteousness of the expedient by which all this has been accomplished

§ 1. SLAVERY AND REPUBLICAN GOVERNMENT.

Intelligent men at the South found something to reconcile them to their condition, in the wholesome influence of their form of labour, upon their republican institutions. The effect of slavery to make the temper of the ruling caste more honourable, self-governed, reflective, courteous, and chivalrous, and to foster in them an intense love of, and pride in, their free institutions, has been already asserted, and substantiated by resistless facts. The testimony of these facts is concurrent with that of all history. But those qualities are just the ones which fit a people for beneficent self-government. Again: our system disposed, at one potent touch, of that great difficulty which has beset all free governments: the difficulty of either entrusting the full franchises of the ruling caste to, or refusing them to, the moneyless class. The Word of God tells us that the poor shall always be with us. Natural differences of capacity, energy, and thrift, will always cause one part to distance the other part of the society, in the race of acquisition; and the older and denser any population becomes, the larger will be the penniless class, and the more complete their destitution as compared with the moneyed class. Shall they be refused all participation in the suffrage and powers of government? Then, by what means shall the constitution make them secure against the iniquities of class-legislation, which wickedly and selfishly sacrifices their interests and rights to the ruling class? And yet more: by what argument can they be rendered content in their political disfranchisement, when they are of the same race, colour, and class, with their unauthorized oppressors, save as money makes an artificial distinction? The perpetual throes and reluctations of the oppressed class against the oppressors, will agitate and endanger any free government; as witness the strifes of the conservative and radical parties in England, and the slumbering eruptions which the ideas of the democrats of 1848 have kindled under every throne in Western Europe. But on the other hand, if the full franchises of the ruling class be conceded to the moneyless citizens, they seize the balance of power, and virtually hold the reins over the rights, property, and lives of the moneyed classes. But the qualities which have made them continue penniless in a liberal government, together with the pressure of immediate hardship, destitution, ignorance and passion, will ever render them most unsafe hands to hold this power. The man who has "the wolf at his door," who knows not where to-morrow's dinner for his wife and babes is to be obtained, is no safe man to be entrusted with power over others' property, and submitted to all the arts and fiery passions of the demagogue. The inevitable result will be, that his passions will drive him, under the pressure of his destitution, to some of those forms of agrarianism or legislative plunder, by which order and economical prosperity are blighted; and society is compelled, like democratic France and New England, to take refuge from returning anarchy and barbarism, in the despotism of a single will. This truth cannot be more justly stated than in the language of Lord Macaulay, himself once an ardent advocate of British Reform. If the democratic States of America seemed, for a time, to offer an exception to these tendencies, it proves nothing; for in those States, the intense demand for labour, the cheapness of a virgin soil, and the rapid growth of a new and sparse population, rendered the working of the law, for a time, imperceptible. But even there, it had begun to work with a portentous power. Witness the violence and frightful mutations of their parties, the loathsome prevalence of demagogueism, and the great party of free-soil, which is but a form of agrarianism reaching out its plundering hand against the property class across Mason's and Dixon's lines, instead of the property class at home. So completely had the danger we have described been verified, even in these new and prosperous communities, that the moment a serious strain came upon their institutions, the will of the mob burst over constitutions and publick ethics like a deluge, and the pretended republicks rushed into a centralized despotism, with a speed and force which astounded the world. All the pleas of *universal suffrage* have received a damning and final refutation, from the events of this revolution.

But the solution which Southern institutions gave to this great *dilemma* of republicks was happy and potent. The moneyless labouring class was wholly disfranchised of political powers, and thus disarmed of its powers of mischief. Yet this was effected without injustice to them, or cruelty; because they were at the same time made *parts of the families* of the ruling class; and ensured an active protection and competent maintenance, by law, and by motives of affection and self-interest in the masters; which experience proved to be more beneficent in practice to the labouring class, than any political expedient of free countries. The tendency of our African slavery was to diminish, at the same time, the numbers and destitution of the class of white moneyless men, so as to render them a harmless element in the State. It did this by making for them a wider variety of lucrative industrial pursuits; by making acquisition easier for white people; by increasing the total of property, that is to say, of values held as property, vastly, through the addition of the labour of the Africans, and by diffusing a general plenty and prosperity. We very well know that anti-slavery men are accustomed to assert the contrary of all this: but we know also, that they affirm that whereof they know nothing. The census returns of the anti-slavery government of the United States itself stubbornly refute them; showing that the number and average wealth of the property classes at the South were relatively larger, and that white pauperism and destitution were relatively vastly smaller, than at the North. But the violent abolition of slavery here has exploded into thin air every sophism by which it has been argued that it was adverse to the interests of the non-slaveholding whites. The latter have been taught by a hard experience, to know, with a painful completeness of conviction before which the old anti-slavery arguments appear insolent and mocking madness, that they are more injured than the slaveholders. They see, that while the late masters are reduced from country gentlemen to yeomen landholders, they are reduced from a thrifty, reputable middle class, to starving competitors for day labour with still more starving free negroes. The honest abolitionist (if there is such a thing) needs only to take the bitter testimony of the non-slaveholding whites of the South, to unlearn forever this part of his theory. Thus did African slavery among us solve this hard problem; and place before us a hopeful prospect of a long career of freedom and stability.

The comparative history of the free and slaveholding commonwealths of the late United States substantiates every word of the above. The South, as a section, has never, from the foundation of the government, committed itself to any project of unrighteous class legislation, such as tariffs, sectional bounties, or agrarian plunderings of the public domain. The North has been perpetually studying such attempts. The South has ever been remarked, (and strange to say, often twitted,) for the stability and consistency of its political parties. The Northern States have been "all things by turns, and nothing long," save that they have been ever steady in their devotion to their plans of legislative plunder. The South has been a stranger to mobs, rebellions, and fanaticism. When, for instance, the wicked crotchet of Know-nothingism was invented, it seized the brains of the North like an infection. It carried all before it until it came to Virginia, the first of the Southern States which it essayed to enter, when the old Commonwealth quietly arose and placed her foot upon its neck, and the monster expired at once. From the day Virginia cast her vote against it, it never gained another victory, either North or South. But the crowning evidence of the superior stability of our freedom was presented during the recent war. While its stress upon Northern institutions crushed them at once into a pure despotism, the South sustained the tremendous ordeal with the combined energy of a monarchy and the equity of a liberal republick. There was no mob law; no terrorizing of dissentients, no intimidations at elections, nor meddling with their purity and freedom, no infringement of rights by class legislation, no riots nor mobs, save one or two small essays generated by foreigners, and no general suspension of the *Habeas Corpus*, until the pressure of the war had virtually converted the whole country into a camp: and this, even then, was only enacted by the constitutional authority of the Congress. The liberty of the press and of religion was untouched during the whole struggle. Let the contrast be now drawn. Shall the tree be known by its fruits?

We believe, therefore, that we have no cause, in this respect, to lament the condition which Providence had assigned us, in placing this African Race among us. We do not envy the political condition of our detractors, Yankee and British radicals; of the former with their *colluvies gentium*, the off-scouring of all the ignorance and discontent of Europe, and their frantic agrarianism, which will turn, so soon as it has exhausted its expected prey from the homesteads of Southern planters, to ravage at home; and of the latter, with their disorganizing theories of human right, subversive of every bulwark of the time-honored British Constitution, and their increasing mass of turbulent pauperism.

§ 2. SLAVERY AND MALTHUSIANISM.

Taking mankind as they are, and not as we may desire them to be, domestic slavery offered the best relation which has yet been found, between labour and capital. It is not asserted that it would be best for a *Utopia*, where we might imagine the humblest citizen virtuous, intelligent, and provident. But there are no such societies on earth. The business of the legislator, whether human or divine, is with mankind as they are; and while he adapts his institutions to their defects, so as to avoid making them impracticable or mischievous, he should also shape them to elevate and reform as far as possible. The legislator, therefore, in devising a frame of society, should adapt it to a state in which the rich are selfish and the poor indolent and improvident. For, after all that has been boasted of human improvement, this is usually man's condition. Now, in adjusting social institutions, it is all-important to secure physical comfort; because in a state of physical misery and degradation, moral and intellectual improvement are hopeless; and the business of the legislator is more especially to take care of the weak: the strong will take care of themselves. Property is the chief element of political strength; it is this which gives to individuals power in society; for "money answereth all things;" it commands for its possessor whatever he needs for his physical comfort and safety. The great *desideratum* in all benign legislation is to sustain the class which has no property, against the social depression and physical suffering to which they always tend. That there will always be such a class, at least till the *millennium*, is certain, for reasons already stated. Now all civilized communities exhibit a natural law which tends to depress the physical condition of those who have no property, who are, usually, the laboring classes. That law is the tendency of population to increase. The area of a country grows no larger, while the number of people in it is perpetually increasing, unless that tendency is already arrested by extreme physical evils. The same acres have, therefore, more and more mouths to feed, and backs to clothe. Consequently, each person must receive a smaller and smaller share of the total proceeds of the earth. The demand perpetually increases in proportion to the supply; and therefore the price of those productions rises, as compared with the price of labour. Hence in every flourishing community, the relative proportion between the price of land, its rents, and the food and clothing which it produces, on the one hand, and the price of manual labour on the other, is perpetually, though slowly, changing. The former rises, the latter sinks. Improvements in agriculture and the arts, extensive conquests, emigrations, or some other cause, may for a time arrest, or even reverse, this process; but such is the general law, and the constant tendency. The very prosperity and growth of the community work this result. The owners of land become richer: those who live by labour become poorer. Physical depression works moral depression, and these overcrowded and under-fed labourers, becoming more reckless, are familiarized with a lower standard of comfort, and continue to increase. This law has wrought in every growing nation on the globe which is without domestic slavery. It is felt in Great Britain, in spite of her vast colonies, where she has disgorged her superfluous mouths and hands, to occupy and feed them on virgin soils: in spite of her conquests, which have centred in her lap the wealth of continents. It has begun to work in the Northern States of America, notwithstanding the development of the arts, and the proximity of the Great West. Every where it reduces the quantity or quality of food and raiment which a day's labour will earn, and perpetually tends to approximate that lowest grade at which the labouring classes can vegetate, multiply, and toil.

What, now, is the remedy? Not agrarianism: this could only aggravate the evil by taking away the incentive to effort, in making its rewards insecure. Not conquest of new territory: the world is now all occupied; and conquest from our neighbours is unjust. We found the remedy in the much-abused institution of domestic slavery. It simply ended this natural, this universal strife between capital and labour, by making labour the property of capital, and thus investing it with an unfailing claim upon its fair share in the joint products of the two. The manner in which slavery effects this is plain. Where labour is free, competition reduces its price to whatever grade the laws of trade may fix; for labour is then a mere commodity in the market, unprotected, and subject to all the laws of demand and supply. The owner of land or capital pays for the labour he needs, in the shape of wages, just the price fixed by the relation of supply and demand; and if that price implies the severest privation for the labourer or his family, it is no concern of his. Should they perish by the inadequacy of the remuneration, it is not his loss: he has but to hire others from the anxious and competing multitude. Moreover, the ties of compassion and charity are vastly weaker than under our system; for that suffering labourer and his family are no more to that capitalist, than any other among the sons of want. But when we make the labour the property of the same persons to whom the land and capital belong, self-interest inevitably impels them to share with the labourer liberally enough to preserve his life and efficiency, because the labour is also, in the language of Moses, "their money," and if it suffers, they are the losers. By this arrangement also, a special tie and bond of sympathy are established between the capitalist and his labourers. They are members of his family. They not only work, but live, on his premises. A disregard of their wants and destitution is ten-fold more glaring, more difficult to perpetrate, and more promptly avenged by his own conscience and public opinion. The bond of domestic affection ensures to the labourer a comfortable share of the fruits of that capital which his labour fecundates. And the law is enabled to make the employer directly responsible for the welfare of the employed. Thus, by this simple and potent expedient, slavery solved the difficulty, and answered the question raised by the gloomy speculations of Malthus, at whom all anti-slavery philosophers have only been able to rail, while equally impotent to overthrow his premises, or to arrest the evils he predicts. Slavery also presented us with a simple and perfectly efficient preventive of pauperism. The law, public opinion, and natural affection, all joined in compelling each master to support his own sick and superannuated. And the elevation of the free white labourers, which results from slavery, by placing another labouring class below them, by assigning to them higher and more remunerative kinds of labour, and by diffusing a more general prosperity, reduced white pauperism to the smallest possible amount amongst us. In a Virginian slaveholding county, the financial burden of white pauperism was almost inappreciable. Thus, at one touch, our system solved happily, mercifully, justly, the Gordian knot of pauperism, a subject which has completely baffled British wisdom.

The attempt may be made to evade these considerations, by saying that the same law of increase in population will at length operate, in spite of slavery; and that its depressing effects will reveal themselves in this form: that the labouring class will become so numerous, the same alteration between demand and supply of labour will appear, and the slave's labour will be worth no more than his maintenance, when he will cease to sell for any thing. At this stage, it may be urged, self-interest will surely prompt emancipation, and the whole slave system will fall before the evil which it was expected to counteract.

To this there are several answers. The argument implies that the slaves will be, at that stage, relatively very numerous. Then, the political difficulties of emancipation would be proportionably great. The political necessity would overrule the economical tendency, and compel the continuance of the beneficent institution. And while it subsisted, the tie of domestic affection, and the force of law and public opinion, would still secure for slaves a better share in the joint profits of labour and capital, than would be granted to depressed free labour. This was the case in the Roman Empire, where the population of Italy and Sicily was for several centuries as dense as in those modern States where the Malthusian law has worked most deplorably: and yet slavery did not yield, and emancipation did not follow.

But the more complete answer is as follows. We will attempt now to point out an influence which enabled domestic slavery to resist and repair the evils of over-population, vastly better than any other form of labour. As population increases, the size of fortunes which are accumulated increases. Instances of accumulation are more numerous and far more excessive. Density of population, facility of large industrial operations, concentration of number of labourers, with other causes, ensure that rich men will be vastly richer than while population was sparse; and that there will be many more rich men. While a few of these will be misers, as a general rule they will seek to expend their overflowing incomes. But as man's real wants lie within very narrow limits, and the actual necessaries and comforts of life are cheap, the larger part of these overgrown incomes must be spent in superfluities. The money of the many excessively rich men is profusely spent in expensive jewelry, clothing, equipage, ostentatious architecture, useless menials, fine arts, and a thousand similar luxuries. Now the production of all these superfluities absorbs a vast amount of the national labour, and thus diminishes greatly the production of those values which satisfy real wants. A multitude of the labourers are seduced from the production of those more essential values, by the higher prices which luxury and pride are enabled to pay for their objects. Now, although the manufacturers of these superfluities may, individually, secure a better livelihood than those laborers who produce the necessaries of life, yet the result of the withdrawal of so many producing hands is, that the total amount of necessaries produced in the nation is much smaller. There is, then, a less mass of the necessaries of life to divide among the whole number of the citizens; and some people must draw a smaller share from the common stock. Every sensible man knows that these will be the landless, labouring men. The wealth of the rich will, of course, enable them to engross a liberal supply for their own wants, however scant may be that left for the poor. The ability to expend in superfluities is, therefore, a *misdirection* of just so much of the productive labour of the country, from the creation of essential values, to the producing of that which fills no hungry stomach, clothes no naked back, and relieves no actual, bodily want. And here, after all, is the chief cause why the Malthusian law is found a true and efficient one in civilized communities. For, were the increasing labour of a growing nation wisely and beneficiently directed to draw from the soil and from nature all that they can be made to yield, their fecundity would be found to be practically so unlimited, that the means of existence would keep pace with the increase of population, to almost any extent. The operative cause of the growing depression of the poor is, not that the same acres are compelled to feed more mouths, and clothe more backs, so much as this: that the inducements which excessive wealth gives to the production of superfluities, misdirects so much precious labour, that the fruitfulness of those acres is not made to increase with the increase of mouths. This is proved by the simple fact, that in all the old countries the misery of the lowest classes tends to keep pace with the luxury of the highest. It is proved emphatically by the industrial condition of Great Britain. There is no country in which production is so active; none in which agriculture and the arts are more stimulated by science and intelligence; and yet there is a growing mass of destitution, yearly approaching more frightful dimensions, and testing the endurance of human nature by lower grades of physical discomfort. The reason is not to be sought in her limited territory or crowded population; for if the British Islands have not acres enough to grow their own bread for so many, why is it that so productive a people are not able to pay for abundance of imported bread? It is to be found in the existence of their vast incomes, and the excessive luxury practised by the numerous rich. True, these magnates excuse their vast expenditures in superfluities by the plea, that one of the motives is the "encouragement of industry." But they effect, as we have seen, not an encouragement, but a misdirection of industry. The reason why so many British poor have a scanty share of physical comforts is, that there are so many British rich men who, by their lavish expenditure, tempt and seduce so large a multitude of producing hands from the creation of actual comforts to the creation of superfluities.

What safe remedy can the legislator propose for this evil? Not a violent, agrarian leveling of the larger estates. That, as we have shown, would be wicked and foolish. Nor can it be found in sumptuary laws. The world has tried them to its heart's content, and found them impracticable. It is true, that their adoption showed how clear a perception the ancients had of one truth, which modern political science pretends to ignore. That truth is, that luxury is a social evil. We have shown that it is as wasteful of social wealth as it is of morals. The ancients thought thus, and they were right. Legislators now-a-days, in exploding their remedy as no remedy, seem to desire to cheat themselves into the belief that the disease is no disease. But the ancients were not as stupid as men imagine.

Now, we do not boast that we can offer a perfect remedy. But our system of labour certainly gave us a partial one of inestimable value. Where the rich man is a citizen of a hireling State, his accumulated wealth and profuse income are all spent in superfluities, except the small portion needed for the comforts of life for his own family. But when he is a citizen of a slave State, they are first taxed with the comfortable support of his slaves. The law, public opinion, affection for them, and self-interest, all compel him to make the first appropriation out of that profuse income, to feeding and clothing his slaves, before he proceeds to superfluities. Thus, the proceeds of the accumulations which dense population and social prosperity cause, are rescued from a useless and mischievous expenditure in those luxuries, the purchase of which misdirects public industry, and tempts to a deficient production of the necessaries of life; and are directed where benevolence, mercy, and the public good indicate, to the comfortable maintenance of the labouring people. That this is the effect of domestic slavery on the incomes of the rich, is proved by one familiar fact. It is well known at the South how slaveholders usually murmured when comparing their style of living with that of capitalists in the hireling States of equal nominal wealth. The planter who owned fifty thousand dollars worth of fertile lands, and a hundred slaves, while he lived in far more substantial comfort and plenty, displayed in Virginia far less ostentation and luxury than the merchant or manufacturer of the North who owns the same amount of capital. His house was plainly furnished with the old-fashioned goods of his fathers; his family rode in a plain carriage, drawn by a pair of stout nags which, probably, either did a fair share of ploughing also, or drew a large part of the fuel for the household. He himself was dressed partly in "jeans," woven under the superintendence of his wife; and his boys were at school in a log house, with homespun clothing, and, in summer, bare feet. It was not unusual to hear the slaveholder, when he considered this contrast, complain of slavery as a bad institution for the master. But this was its merciful feature, that it in some measure arrested superfluous luxury, and taxed superfluous income with the more comfortable support of the labourers. In a hireling State, these might be left half-starved on the inadequate compensation which the hard law of supply and demand in the labour-market would compel them to accept, while the capitalist was rioting in a mischievous waste of the overgrown profits of his capital.

The question of the productiveness of slave labour may be anticipated, so far as to point out the fact, that this benevolent diversion of the large incomes from luxurious expenditures to the comfortable maintenance of the slaves, was a diversion from unproductive to productive consumption. The slaves were a productive class; and the increased comfort of their living added greatly to their increase, and their ability to labour. No student of political economy need be told how powerfully national wealth is promoted by any cause which substitutes productive consumption for unproductive.

The truth of these views is confirmed by this fact, which is attested by all experienced slaveholders: that the slaves throughout the South lived in far more comfort than they did a generation ago. And this is truest of those Southern communities where population is densest, and the price and rents of land are highest. As these influences, elsewhere so depressing to the poor, advanced, the standard of comfort for our slaves rose rapidly, instead of falling. How can a more splendid vindication of the benevolence of our system be imagined? Our slaves generally ate more meat, wore more and better clothing, and lived in better houses, than their fathers did.

That a palpable view may be given, to those who are not personally acquainted with our system, of its true working, the reader's indulgence will be asked for the statement of a few homely details. In Virginia, all slaves, without exception, had their own private funds, derived from their poultry, gardens, "patches," or the prosecution of some mechanic art, in what is termed "their own time." These funds they expended as they pleased, in Sunday-clothing, or in such additions to their diet and comfort as they liked. The allowances which we proceed to state, are strictly those which the master usually made out of his funds. The allowances fixed by usage in this State were generally these: for clothing of adults, one complete suit of stout woolens, two pair pantaloons of cotton or flax, two shirts, two pair of worsted half-hose, and a hat and a blanket, each year. For shoes, the old rule was, one pair each winter, of the quality of best army shoes or boots, to be replaced at harvest with new ones, in the case of ploughmen and reapers, while the "less able-bodied hands" only got their old shoes repaired. But in latter years, the prevalent custom had come to be, to issue shoes to all adults, as often as is required, to keep them shod throughout the year; while the children were universally shod during the winter only.

For diet, the slaves shared jointly the garden-stuff, fruits and milk of the master's plantation and garden. But their essential and preferred food was a certain daily or weekly allowance of corn meal and bacon, issued in addition to the above. The common rule in Virginia, where these were given in the form of rations, was to allow each adult a half-pound of bacon, and two quarts of meal per day. The meal of Indian corn, when uninjured by the mustiness of a sea-voyage, and properly baked at a bright wood-fire, is an excellent and nutritious food, as is shown by the fact that it fills more than an equal place with bread of wheat, on the tables of the richest planters. In many other families, the allowance of meal was unlimited; and the bacon was not issued in formal rations, the servants living at a common board. The supply laid in was then usually according to the following rule: one hundred and fifty pounds of pork per year, for every soul, white and black. When it is remembered that the sucklings and the white females used almost none of this supply, a simple calculation will show that it is equivalent to at least a half-pound per day for each adult. Such were the customary usages in Virginia. There were probably as many cases where the above rules were exceeded, as where the allowances fell below them. In the new States of the South West, where agriculture is still more profitable, it is said that the allowances were more liberal than in the old slave States.

It happens that the census returns of the United States for 1860, published by our enemies themselves, more than confirm this view of the abundant and comfortable living of our labouring population. According to those returns the free States had in 1860, not quite nineteen millions of people, and the slave States twelve and a quarter millions. Of the cereals used by Americans for human food, the free States raised five hundred and sixty-one millions bushels; and the slave States four hundred and ninety-four millions bushels. That is, while the people of the free States had about *thirty* bushels each of these cereals, those of the slave States had *forty-one* bushels per head. Moreover, the North boasts that breadstuffs are her great export crops, while cotton and tobacco were ours. Our people, including our slaves, must therefore have used more than four bushels each, to their three. In neither country does each person eat either thirty or forty-one bushels per year; because horses and other live stock eat a part, which it is impossible accurately to estimate. Again: of the animals used for human food, (horned cattle, sheep, and swine,) then free States had about *forty* millions, or a little more than *two* per head to each inhabitant; while the slave States had forty and a half millions, or about *three and a half* to each inhabitant. But as bacon or pork is the flesh most commonly consumed by Americans, and especially by farm labourers, the proportion of swine is still more significant. The free States had not quite twelve millions of swine, and the slave States twenty millions six hundred thousand. This gives a little more than *six-tenths of one* swine to each inhabitant of the North, and *one and seven-tenths* to each inhabitant of the South. But this is not all,—for the North (especially the prairie States) exported vast quantities of the flesh of swine to the South, while the slave States exported none to the North. It should in justice be said, that the disparity is not so enormous as would thus appear, because the swine reared in the South are usually smaller than those of the North.

§ 3. COMPARATIVE PRODUCTIVENESS OF SLAVE LABOUR.

From the days of Adam Smith, anti-slavery men have been pleased to consider it as a point perfectly settled, that slave labour is comparatively unfavourable to production, and thus, to publick wealth. So settled is this conviction among the enemies, and so often has it been admitted by the apologists of our system, it will probably be hard to secure even a hearing, while we review the grounds on which the common opinion is based. One would think that the fact that those grounds have usually been urged by men who, like Adam Smith, knew nothing of slavery themselves, should bespeak for us at least a little patience and candour. One of those grounds is, that slavery, by making manual labour the peculiar lot of a servile class, renders it disreputable. This, they suppose, together with the exemption from the law of necessity, fosters indolence in the masters. But, we reply, is manual labour the peculiar lot of the servile class alone, in slave States? Is not this the very question to be settled? Yet it is assumed as the premise from which to settle it. So that the reasoning amounts to no more than this ridiculous *petitio principii*: "Because the slaves do all the work, therefore the masters do none of the work." This should be made a question of fact. And we emphatically deny that Southern masters were an indolent class, as compared with the moneyed classes elsewhere. In fact, the general rule is that rich men do not work, the world over. It was less true, probably, in Virginia, than in any other commonwealth. The wealthy man of the North, with his grown sons, is more indolent, and more a fine gentleman, than the wealthy slaveholder. If it be said that, in free States, a multitude of small farmers cultivate their lands with their own hands, it is equally true that a multitude of small planters in the South, who owned one, three or five slaves, laboured along with them. That the land shall be owned by the very persons who cultivate it, is an exceptional condition of things, resulting, to some extent in New England, from a very peculiar history, origin and condition of society, and not destined to continue general even there. It is as true of hireling as of slave States, that the tendency of civilized institutions is, and ever has been, and ever will be, generally, to collect the lands in larger properties, in the hands of a richer class than that which actually tills them. Nor is there one syllable of truth in the idea, that labour was among us more disreputable, because usually done by slaves. In all countries, there is foolish pride, and importance is attached, by the silly, to empty badges of station. But it was less so among slaveholders than among the rich, or the would-be rich, of other countries. The reason is obvious. In free States there is just as truly a servile class, bearing the servile inferiority of social station, as among us. That class being white, and nominally free, its addiction to manual labour is the only badge of its social condition. Hence whites of the superior class have a far stronger motive, in their pride, to shun labour. But the white master could freely labour among his black servants, without danger of being mistaken by the transient observer for one of the class, because his skin distinguished him: just as the man of unquestioned wealth and fashion can wear a plain coat, which would be shunned as the plague, by the doubtful aspirant to *ton*. We repeat: the planters of Virginia were more often seen performing, not only the labours of superintendence, but actual manual labour, than any wealthy class in America. They were proverbial for perseverance and energy. There is a fact which bears a peculiar testimony to this. While Yankee adventurers and immigrants have intruded themselves into every other calling among us, like the frogs into the Egyptian houses and their very chambers and kneading-troughs, those of them who have attempted to act the tobacco planter have, in almost every case, failed utterly. They lack the requisite energy for the calling.

Another reason of the anti-slavery man is, that the free labourer, stimulated by personal interest in his own success, must be more thrifty, industrious, and economical than the slave, who is stimulated only by fear. We reply: both the premises are absolutely false. Slaves were not stimulated only by fear. They felt at least as much affection as the Red Republican or Chartist hireling. They comprehended their own interest in their master's prosperity as fully as hired labourers do. But, in the second place, the labour of free States is not usually performed by men who have a personal interest in their own success: it is performed, in the main, by a landless class, who are as very hirelings as our slaves were slaves; who need just as much the eye of an overseer, and who must be pricked on in their labour, at least as often, by the threat, not of the birch, but of the more cruel penalty of discharge; which they know is their dismissal to starvation or the work-house. This delusive reasoning proceeds by comparing the yeoman landholder in fee-simple, tilling his own soil with his own hands, with the slave tilling the land of his wealthy master. But are the lands of hireling States prevalently tilled by their yeomen owners? Is this the system to which free society tends? The Englishman will not dare to say so, when he looks around him, and sees how rapidly the small holdings have been swallowed up into larger farms, which are now worked by capitalists with organized gangs of hirelings; nor the Scotchman, with the sight of an old tenant peasantry swept away before the ruthless Bothy-system of his country. And, as we have asserted, the class of yeomen landholders, labouring personally among their few slaves, was at least as large, and as permanent in the South, as in any civilized country.

Here again, the actual experiment of abolition has ridiculously exploded all these baseless reasonings for the superior zeal of the white free labourer, and the thriftless eye-service of the slave. All intelligent men knew before that they were precisely contrary to fact; for they saw all hireling labour at the North obviously required a supervision much more constant and stringent, to prevent the hirelings from bringing the employers to bankruptcy by their worthless eye-service, than the labour of our own merry and affectionate servants. If the white hireling labour was aggregated in masses, we uniformly saw it distributed in gangs, to sturdy "bosses," who stood with their formidable bludgeons in their hands, from morning to night, with just fourfold the persistency of any Southern "head-man" or "overseer," and actually indicted blows on his free white fellow-citizens, as frequently as our overseers on the servant children. If the white hireling labour was employed on their little farms, in small numbers, then the proprietors always informed us, that they must be present in the field all the time, to shame and encourage them by their example, or else their "help" would cheat them to their ruin. But in the South, nothing was more common than to see estates farmed by the faithful slaves, for widows, orphans, professional men, or non-resident proprietors, without any other superintendence than an occasional visit. Now, all this is at an end. The labourers are free hirelings, who, according to the anti-slavery argument, should be so superior in enlightened zeal and fidelity. But lo, the Southern people have found that eye-service has thereby increased ten-fold; and if there is any lesson which the South has effectually learned in these two years, it is, that perpetual and jealous supervision is the sole condition on which a meagre profit can be extracted from this wretched and grinding system; and that else, the impositions of the hired labourers inevitably result in speedy bankruptcy. Hard fact has demonstrated that the truth is precisely opposite to the pretty postulates of the anti-slavery philosophers, so called.

It was currently asserted that one free white labourer did as much work as two or three slaves; and Southern gentlemen used often to be heard assenting to it. But here the reader should be reminded of what has been already shown; that if this industrial evil existed among us, that evil was not slavery, but the presence among us of four millions of recent pagans, characterized by all the listlessness, laziness, and unthrift of savages. Slavery did not make the intelligent and industrious worthless; nor does freedom turn the lazy barbarian into a civilized and diligent citizen. If there ever was any truth in this comparison of the efficiency of the African labourer with the free white, it doubtless existed when the former were newly brought into our country. The estimate then formed became traditionary, and prevailed after the partial training and civilization of the blacks had wholly removed its grounds. Several facts prove that no white agricultural labour was so efficient (especially under our ardent sun) as the Africans, had become. Of this, the crowning proof is, again, given us by the unfortunate experiences of actual abolition. Many Virginian proprietors, having still retained the old, but false prejudice, that the negro slave was a less efficient labourer than the white hireling, and being well assured that the labour of the slaves would be deteriorated by emancipation, procured white labour from the North. What was the result? An almost universal conviction that the freed negro, deteriorated as he was, proved still a better labourer than the white hireling! Consequently, the importation of white labour is totally relinquished. Another of these facts is, that in Middle Virginia, where the best free labour in America exists, and was once almost exclusively used, the slave population was, up to the war, steadily supplanting it in agriculture; and was more and more preferred by the most enlightened agriculturists. Another is, that the great contractors on our public works, many of them Northern men, who came to us provided with white labour, gradually convinced themselves that their works could be executed more cheaply, quickly, and quietly, by slaves. The third fact is, that along the line which separates Virginia and Pennsylvania, or Kentucky and Ohio, the lands immediately south of the line were more valuable than those immediately north of it. This is so well known that Senator Sumner, in his notorious libel on the South, admits its existence, and endeavours to evade its force by the following preposterous solution. He says: freedom, by its proximity, infuses something of its own vigour, virtue, and life, into the adjoining Southern community; so as to stimulate its prosperity; whereas, the blighting slave-power contaminates and palsies freedom along the line of its contact, so as to make it exhibit less than its usual happy effects. That is, we are invited to believe that the indirect influence of free labour is so potent that it can go across Mason's and Dixon's line, or the Ohio River, into the midst of the very blight and curse of slavery, and act so happily as to raise the price of slave-tilled lands to eighty dollars per acre; while its direct influences at home, on a soil uncursed with slavery, cannot sustain the price of exactly similar land at sixty dollars! And we are required to believe that while the mere shadow of slavery, falling across the border, sinks the price of land, otherwise blessed with the most profitable system, to sixty dollars, the actual incubus of the horrid monster on a soil unredeemed by the better system, raises it to eighty dollars! Common sense shows us the true solution. Two farms divided only by the imaginary line of the surveyor, of course differ nothing in the natural advantages of soil, climate and productions. Why, then, did the Virginian farm sell for twenty dollars more per acre? Because the owner could combine all the economy and efficiency of a system of slave labour, with the partial advantages of the system of free labour near him; and thus make his farm more profitable than his Pennsylvanian neighbour.

But we are told that actual inspection showed the labour of the South to be wasteful, shiftless, and expensive, as compared with the free labour of the North. We reply, if it seemed so in any case, it is because the comparison is unfairly made. On the Northern side, the specimen is selected near some great city, in some "crack farming district," where the labour is stimulated by abundant capital, supplied with costly implements, and directed by the best skill of that section. On the Southern side, the specimen was taken from some ill-informed population, or some soil originally thin, and in a community depressed and depleted by the iniquitous taxation of Yankee tariffs. But let the best of each be compared; or the *medium* specimens of each; or the worst of each; and we fearlessly abide the test. Where slave labour was directed by equal skill and capital, it is shown to be as efficient as any in America. There was nowhere on our continent, more beautiful, more economical, or more remunerative farming, than in our densest slaveholding communities.

A third argument against the economy of slave labour, is thus stated by Dr. Wayland: "It removes from both parties, the disposition and the motives to *frugality*. Neither the master learns frugality from the necessity of labour, nor the slave from the benefits which it confers," etc.

Now we emphatically and proudly admit that Southern society has not learned the frugality of New England; which is, among the middle classes, a mean, inhospitable, grinding penuriousness, sacrificing the very comfort of children, and the kindly cheer of the domestic board, to the Yankee *penates*, Mammon and Lucre; and among the upper classes a union of domestic scantiness and stinginess with external ostentation and profusion; a frugality which is "*rich in the parlour, and poor in the kitchen.*" The idea of the Southern planter is the rational and prudent use of wealth to procure the solid comfort of himself, his children, and his servants at home, coupled with a simple and unostentatious equipage abroad, and a generous hospitality to rich and poor. But we fearlessly assert, and will easily prove to every sensible reader, that slavery was peculiarly favourable to the economical application of labour, and of domestic supplies and income. The attempt to carry the freehold tenure of land down to the yeomanry, subdivides land too much for economical farming. The holdings are too small, and the means of the proprietors too scanty, to enable them to use labour-saving machines, or to avail themselves of the vast advantages of combined labour. How can the present proprietor of a farm of five or ten acres in France or Belgium, afford a reaper, a threshing-machine, a three-horse plough, or even any plough at all? The spade, the wheel-barrow, the donkey, and the flail, must do his work, at a wasteful cost of time and toil. But the Southern system, by placing the labour of many at the direction of one more cultivated mind, and that furnished with more abundant capital, secured the most liberal and enlightened employment of machines, and the most convenient "division of labour." Moreover, the administration of the means of living for the whole plantation, by the master and mistress, secured a great economy of supplies. The mistress of Southern households learns far more providence, judgment and method in administering her stores, than are possessed by free labourers or by blacks. The world over, those who have property are more provident than those who have none. For, this providence is the chief reason why they have property; and the improvidence of the poor is the cause of their being poor. But even if the slaveholders had no more of these qualities, all can see that an immense saving is made by having one housekeeper for ten families, with one kitchen, store-house, and laundry, instead of ten kitchens, ten store-houses, and ten varying administrations of stores. A smaller supply of provisions secures a greater amount of comfort to all, and a great saving of labour is effected in preparation of food, and housekeeping cares. A system of slave labour is, therefore, more productive, because it is more economical.

In all this argument, the anti-slavery men keep out of view a simple fact which is decisive of the absurdity of their position. They shall now be made to look it in the face. That fact is, that in free States, a large portion of all those who, from their moneyless condition, ought to pursue manual labour, are too lazy to do so voluntarily. But they must live, and they do it by some expedient which is a virtual preying on the means of the more industrious, by stealing, by begging, by some form of swindling, by perambulating the streets with a barrel-organ and monkey, or by vending toys or superfluities. Their labour is lost to the community; and their maintenance, together with their dishonest arts and crimes, is a perpetual drain from the public wealth. But slavery made the lazy do their part with the industrious, by the wholesome fear of the birch. Slavery allowed no loafers, no swindlers, no "b'hoys," no "plug-uglies," no grinders of hurdy-gurdies, among her labouring class. Who does not see that, even if the average slave in Virginia did only two-thirds of the day's work accomplished by the industrious free labourer in New York, yet, if all the idle classes in that great commonwealth, together with those now industrious, were compelled to do just the tasks of the average Virginia slave, there would be, on the whole, a vast and manifold gain to the public?

Another potent source of the economy of the slave system in its influences upon publick wealth, is found in a fact which Northern men not only admit, but assert with a foolish pride. It is the far greater development of the local traffic of merchants among them. When your down-East commercial traveller, whose only conception of productive industry was of some arts of "living by his wits," saw this contrast between Northern and Southern villages and country neighbourhoods, he pointed to it with undoubting elation, as proof of the vastly superior wealth and productive activity of the North. But in fact, he was a fool; he mistook what was a villainous, eating ulcer upon the public wealth of the North, and on the true prosperity of the people, for a spring of profits. In a farming neighbourhood of the hireling States, he saw at every hamlet and cross-road, pretentious shingle-palaces, occupied as large stores, where great accumulations of farm produce were paraded; sacks of meal, barrels of flour, bins of corn, packs of wool, garners of wheat, tubs of eggs, cans of butter, hogsheads of bacon, and even kegs of home-made soap, together with no little show of cheap finery. In the farming districts of the South, he rode along a quiet, shady road, with the country-seats of the planters reposing at a distance, in the bosoms of their estates; and found at long intervals a little country store, where a few groceries, medicines, and cloths were exposed for sale to sparse customers. Now this narrow trafficker, whose only heaven was buying and selling, very naturally jumped to the conclusion, that the South was so much poorer than the North, as she exhibited less local trade. Whereas in fact, she was just so much richer. And this unpopular assertion is, still, perfectly easy to demonstrate. The necessary labour of distributing commodities from producers to consumers, is a legitimate element of that fair market value, which they have when they finally reach the hand which consumes them. But political economists well know, and uniformly teach, that if any unnecessary middle-men interpose themselves between first producer and ultimate consumer, whose labour is not truly promotive of the economical distribution of commodities, then their industry is misdirected, the wages they draw for it in the shape of increased price of commodities passed through their hands is unproductive consumption, and they are a useless, a mischievous drain upon the common wealth. For instance, if a class of middle-men, retailers, or forwarding merchants, juggle themselves unnecessarily into the importing dry-goods trade of the country; if they place themselves between the manufacturer in England, and the consumer in rural New York, grasping wages for their intervention, in the shape of an additional profit which falls ultimately upon the retail purchaser; while yet they really contribute nothing to the economical distribution of the dry-goods; every one sees that they are a nuisance; they grasp something for nothing; and are preying upon the publick wealth, instead of promoting it like the legitimate merchant. Honest men will speedily require legislation, to expel them and abate the nuisance. Apply now this well-known principle to the case in hand. The simple system of slaveholding distributed that part of the products of farms, which properly went to the labourers' subsistence, direct to the consumers, without taxing it unnecessarily with the profits of the local merchant. The master was himself the retail merchant; and he distributed his commodities to the proper consumers, at wholesale prices, without profit. The consumers were his own servants. He remarked, in the language of the country, that, for this part of his products, he "had his market at home." Now, is it not obvious that the consumer, the slave, got more for his labour, and that the system of hireling labour, by invoking this local storekeeper, instead of the master, to do this work of distribution to consumers, which the master did better without him, and without charge, has brought in a useless middle-man? And his industry being useless and unproductive, its wages are a dead loss to the publick wealth. This coarse fellow behind the counter, retailing the meal and bacon and soap, at extortionate retail prices, to labourers, should be compelled to labour himself, at some really productive task; and the labourers should have gotten these supplies, untaxed with his extortion, on the farms where their own labour produced them, and at the farmer's prices. Is not this true science, and true common sense? But this is just the old Virginian system.

The justice of this view may be seen by a familiar case. A given landholder was, under our beneficent system, a slaveholder. He employed ten labourers; and for them and their families he reserved four hundred bushels of grain in his garners, which their labour and his capital jointly had produced. This grain is worth to him wholesale prices; and it is distributed by him to his servants, throughout the year, without charge. It is, in fact, a part of the virtual wages of their labour; and they get it at the wholesale price. But now, abolition comes: these ten labourers become freemen and householders. They now work the same lands, for the same proprietor; and instead of drawing their wages in the form of a generous subsistence at wholesale prices, they draw money. Out of that money they and their families must be maintained. One result is, that the landholder now has a surplus of four hundred bushels more than before. Of course it goes to the corn-merchant. And there must these labourers go, with their money wages, to buy this same corn, at the enhanced retail price. They get less for their labour. The local merchant, thus unnecessarily invited in, sucks a greedy profit; a vain show of trading activity is made in the community; and all the really producing classes are made actually poorer; while this unproductive consumer, the unnecessary retail trader, congratulates himself on his mischievous prosperity. It is most obvious, that when the advocate of the hireling system attempts to reply to this, by saying that his system has opened a place for an additional branch of industry, that of enlarged traffic, he is preposterous. The answer is, that the additional industry is a loss: it is unproductive. As reasonably might one argue that crime is promotive of publick prosperity, by opening up a new branch of remunerative industry,—that of police and jailors, (a well-paid class!)

But sensible men ever prefer facts to speculations—the language of experience to that of theoretical assertion. Let us then appeal to the fact, as revealed by the statistics furnished of us, by the anti-slavery government of the United States. By the census of 1860, while the population of the Free States was not quite nineteen millions, their total of assessed values, real and personal, was $6,541,000,000: being three hundred and forty-six ($346) dollars to each soul. The free white population of the South was a little more than eight and a quarter millions, and our total of assessed values was $5,465,808,000: being six hundred and sixty ($660) dollars to each soul; nearly double the wealth of the North. But if the four millions of Africans in the South be added, our people still have four hundred and forty-seven ($447) dollars of value for each soul, black and white.

§ 4. EFFECTS OF SLAVERY IN THE SOUTH, COMPARED WITH THOSE OF FREE LABOUR IN THE NORTH.

The citations just made introduce a topic upon which anti-slavery men have usually abounded in sweeping assertion; the actual effects of our system on our industrial concerns. A fair example of these assertions may be seen in Dr. Wayland, Moral Science, p. 210, (Boston, 1838:) "No country, not of great fertility, can long sustain a large slave population. Soils of more than ordinary fertility cannot sustain it long, after the first richness of the soils has been exhausted. Hence, slavery in this country is acknowledged to have impoverished many valuable districts; and hence it is continually migrating from the older settlements to those new and untilled regions, where the accumulated manure of centuries of vegetation has formed a soil, whose productiveness may, for a while, sustain a system at variance with the laws of nature. Many of our free, and of our slaveholding States, were peopled about the same time. The slaveholding States had every advantage, both in soil and climate, over their neighbours; and yet the accumulation of capital has been greatly in favour of the latter," etc.

The points asserted here are, that Northern men have grown rich faster than Southern men; that slavery has so starved itself out by its wasteful nature, as to be compelled to migrate from "many valuable districts," to virgin soils; and that it is slavery which exhausts those virgin soils. Each of these statements is absolutely false. That the first and most important of the three is so, we have just shown, by the overwhelming testimony of fact. Southern citizens have accumulated capital faster than Northern, in the ratio of six hundred and sixty to three hundred and forty-six. And the manner in which these thrice refuted lies are obtruded, may fairly illustrate the morality with which anti-slavery men have usually conducted their argument against us That a conceited, pragmatical Yankee parson should be misled by rancourous prejudice around him, and by the concessions of foolish Southerners, to publish such statements thirty years ago, on a subject of which he knew nothing, is not very surprising. But surely Dr. Wayland, President of Brown University, Christian Divine, Instructor of youth, and Teacher of Ethicks,(!) would hardly have been expected to continue to print the falsehoods in successive editions of his work, after three successive *census returns* had utterly exploded them.

The second statement we contradict by the *census* as categorically as the first. It is not true that slavery was compelled to emigrate, by its own exhaustion, to virgin soils in the South West. For, in fact, slavery has not emigrated at all. Slaves have emigrated, in large numbers; [as we presume, Yankees have.] But the institution has not receded, and, at the beginning of our war, was not receding from its old ground in Virginia and the Carolinas. The slave population of the old States has shown a steady increase at each decennial period, and except where the *penchant* of the Yankees for stealing them had rendered them insecure, they occupied substantially all the old counties, and spread into new ones, as they were settled.

But we shall be asked: can it be possible that the representations so uniformly made by travellers, of the ragged, impoverished, and forlorn appearance of many districts of Eastern Virginia and the Carolinas, and of their poor and slovenly agriculture, are all mistaken? That there is much exhausted, and still more poor land, in these sections; that through extensive districts the soil and crops are now very thin, and the tillage rude, we explicitly admit. But this is by no means the same as admitting that it is slavery which has impoverished those regions. In the first place, of the larger part it is utterly false to say that they have ever been *impoverished*, by any cause; for they never had any fertility to lose. The statement usually made, as to the most of these old lands, is monstrously false. It has been usually represented that the Atlantic slope of Virginia was originally excessively rich, and has been brought to its present condition by slavery and tobacco. But in truth, this region, with the exception of limited spots, was naturally poor and thin; as every sensible person who has examined it knows. A vast proportion of it would scarcely have been judged susceptible of settlement at all, but for the attraction of its healthy climate, and the one or two crops of tobacco which its thin mould would produce. And it is only the thrifty industry of its inhabitants, together with the value of their staple, tobacco, which enabled them to live as plentifully as they did on so poor a soil.

In the next place, the exhaustion is really far less than it appears to the Englishman or New Englander, and the tillage far more judicious and thorough. The agriculture of planting regions is, necessarily, very different from that of farming regions; and especially is the culture of the grasses to a very large extent precluded by the nature of the crops, the soil, and the climate. Hence, excellent lands in the South, especially during fall and winter, often lack that appearance of verdancy, which to the English eye is the chief measure of fertility. But to suppose those lands as exhausted as fields equally bare or brown would be correctly judged in grass regions, would be an amazing mistake. Nor is the management always indolent where it seems slovenly. The Southern planter is proverbially disinclined to consult mere appearances at the cost of substantial advantage. Though the fencing seem rough, and the farm ill kept in many respects, the accurate observer will find his cultivation of the valuable staples, cotton and tobacco, thorough and skillful. There is no neater culture than that of the tobacco fields of Virginia.

Again: wherever the soil was originally fertile, in the Atlantic slope, as in the red lands of the Piedmont region, and the alluvial valleys of the great rivers, there the supposed decline of agriculture is unknown. All those lands which by nature were really fine, are now finer. The tillage was better, the yield per acre larger, the culture more remunerative, at the opening of the war, than at any date since the virgin forests were cleared away.

But so far as there has been an actual exhaustion of Southern soil, [and that there has been is admitted,] it can be proved to be due to other causes than slavery. For an exhaustion precisely similar can be pointed out in many of the free States. In both regions, it has arisen from two causes: the proximity of new and cheap lands, to which the exhausting farmer could easily resort, and the possession of a valuable staple crop, whose profits powerfully stimulated large operations. Those free States which lay under the same circumstances, have undergone the same exhaustion, except in so far as a natural depth of soil has made the process slower. If any parts of our country have escaped the "skinning process" after their first settlement, it has been simply because they were not so fortunate as to possess any valuable staple, or else were too remote from a market. Western Vermont, sixty years ago, was resorted to as a fertile wheat growing district. Long ago it was so exhausted that the culture of wheat was nearly relinquished, and its inhabitants emigrated to the new lands of Western New York to raise wheat; while the wheat fields of Vermont are now sheep-walks, and her farmers buy their flour. But Western New York, in its turn, has declined, till its average crop per acre is only one-half the original; and its farmers have sought the fertile plains of Illinois and Michigan, to subject them in turn to the same exhaustion. Even Ohio, fertile Ohio, the boast of abolitionists, whose black loam seemed able to defy human mismanagement, is proved by the stubborn census tables to have declined one-half, already, in its yield per acre. And her own children acknowledge, that if the appearance of the older parts be compared with that of twenty years ago, the signs of exhaustion are manifest. This vicious system, then, is not traceable to slave labour, seeing it prevails just as often where no slave labour exists; but to the cheapness of new lands, and facility of emigration.

Virginia presents other facts demonstrating the economy and efficiency of slave labour. The great Valley of Virginia (between the Blue Ridge and North Mountain Ranges,) is a farming and grazing region, of fertile soil and prosperous agriculture. In its great extent, some counties are occupied almost exclusively by free labour, and some have a large slave population. Now it is perfectly well known to all intelligent persons here, that precisely in those counties of this beautiful valley where there are most slaves, is the land highest in price, the agriculture most profitable and skillful, the farm buildings most elegant, and the community most prosperous and wealthy. Virginia east of the Blue Ridge is partly a farming and partly a planting region, having a mixed agriculture. Its soil is exceedingly different from that of the great valley, even where as fertile; and consequently the tillage is unlike. But there too, the neatest, most thorough and most profitable agriculture, and the highest priced lands, the finest farm stock, and the most prosperous landholders, are to be found precisely where the slave labour is most prevalent. And there is no agriculture in America superior to that of these favoured regions.

But, in conclusion, even if the industrial pursuits of the South were in the unfavourable condition which the Yankees love to assert, the sufficient cause would be found, not in slavery, but in the exactions and swindlings of their own section, through sectional federal legislation. Let a sober statement of these exactions be weighed, and the wonder will be, not that the South should be depleted, but that she is not bled to death. In the first place, the Federal Government, at its foundation, adopted the policy of giving a fishing bounty, (to encourage, as it said, a school of sailors for the national marine,) which went wholly into the pockets of New Englanders. It is said that the bounties paid are yearly about one and a half millions. Supposing that half only of the sum thus taken from the Federal Treasury was paid in by the South, (which we shall see is less than the truth,) this bounty, with that part of its increase which has accrued by simple interest alone, amounts now to one hundred and seventy-one millions, transferred by this unfair legislation from the South to the North. Next are to be mentioned the tonnage duties on foreign ships carrying between American ports, which, as the South had few ships, constituted a perpetual tax on us for the benefit of the North. Its amount cannot possibly be estimated with exactness, but it must have amounted to millions annually. Next came the oppression of a protective tariff, raising upon imports as high a revenue as sixty or seventy millions annually, in the last years of the government. As the South had few manufactures, and the North many, and as these duties, even where laid for revenue, were discriminating against the cheaper and better foreign manufactures which the South desired, in every case where discrimination was possible; it is manifest that the system constituted a simple robbery of the South of annual millions, for the benefit of the North. But we lost far more than the actual tariff on that portion of the national imports which were consumed at the South; because the restrictive policy, by throwing the balance of trade against the nations which took our grand staples of tobacco and cotton, deprived them of the ability to buy so freely, and at so large prices, as they would have done under a policy of free trade. Thus, the Southern planter not only paid the Northern manufacturer a profit on his goods equal to the protective tariff, but in the process of that robbery, lost several times as much more, in the prices which he should have received for his cotton or tobacco, had he been permitted to go with it to a free European market. This method of legislative plunder was so wasteful, that the Yankee, in stealing one dollar from us, annihilated several other dollars of our values. Next may be mentioned the advantage which the North gained in the funding of the Federal debt incurred at the Revolutionary war. This was so juggled by the Hamilton party, as to give the avails of it chiefly to the North. The enjoyment of that fund, with its increase since, has made a difference of untold millions in favour of the North. Last: the North twice enjoyed the advantage of having the National Bank situated in its midst, and wielding for purposes of traffic a large part of the funds of the Government. This superior command of ready money, acquired in these various ways, enabled the North to develope commercial centres, and to fix the great markets in her territory, thus ensuring to her the countless profits of commissions, freights, etc., on Southern trade.

Is it wonderful that the industry of a people thus swindled and plundered should languish? Who does not know the power of abundant capital, and especially of ready money, in stimulating enterprise and facilitating industry? Yet, under all this *incubus* the South has more than kept pace with its rapacious partner. When, therefore, the Yankee abolitionist points to any unfavourable contrasts in our condition, as evidence of the evil of slavery, he adds insult to falsehood: his own injustice has created the misfortune with which he taunts us, so far as that misfortune exists at all.

§ 5. EFFECTS OF SLAVERY ON POPULATION, DISEASE, AND CRIME.

But our enemies argue that slavery must be an obstacle to national growth and strength; for this is evinced by the very fact that they are nearly nineteen millions, and we only twelve and a quarter; when, at the beginning, the two sections were nearly equal in strength. Let us, therefore, look into this question. The increase of population is usually a sure test of the physical well-being of a people. Hardship and destitution repress population, by obstructing marriages, by breeding diseases, and by increasing the mortality of infants. If the population of the South be found to have a rapid natural increase, it will prove, therefore, the general prosperity of the people; and if the black race be found to multiply rapidly, it will be an evidence that their physical condition is happy, or in other words, that the institution of slavery is a humane one for them. Sufficient access being denied us to the statistics collected in 1860, our remarks must be based in part on the returns of 1850, and previous periods. These returns show that between 1840 and 1850, the whites of the free States increased thirty-nine and a half *per cent.*, (39.42,) and the whites of the slave States increased thirty-four and a fourth *per cent.*, (34.26.) The climate, the occupations, and the African labour of the South, repel almost the whole of that teeming immigration from Europe which has been rushing to our shores; so that making allowance for this source of population, it will be seen that the natural increase of Southern whites is as rapid as that of Northern.

In 1860, the whites in the free States had increased to about eighteen and a half millions; and in the slave States, to about eight and a quarter millions. The increase for the free States was, therefore, forty-two (42) *per cent.*, and for the slave States thirty-three *per cent.*, (33.) The census showed that in the decade between 1840 and 1850, four-fifths of the foreign immigration, for the reasons mentioned, went into the free States. If we suppose the same ratio to have prevailed in the last decade, then the fact that the North has received four-fifths of the immense rush of Europeans who resorted to our shores in the last ten years, will abundantly account for this difference of increase. The South has grown as fast in white population, as the North would have done, left to itself.

But the increase of the slave population of the South is obscured by no such disturbing cause. The South having magnanimously concurred, and even gone before, in suppressing the foreign slave trade, from a conviction of its immorality, the African race has received no accession whatever, in our day, from immigration. Between 1840 and 1850, the increase of the slave population solely from the excess of births over deaths, was twenty-eight and eight-tenths *per cent.*, (28.8,) and between 1850 and 1860, it was twenty-three and three-tenths (23.3) *per cent.* One cause for the diminished rate of increase in the latter decade, was doubtless the growing passion of the Yankees for the abduction of our slaves; which, towards the last, carried off thousands annually. But either rate of increase is more rapid than the whites, either North or South, ever attained without the aid of immigration. The *native increase* of the free States in ten years has probably been between eleven and fifteen *per cent.* So that tried by this well-established test, the physical well-being of the slaves is higher than of any race in the world. Meantime, the miserable free blacks of New England, in the midst of the boasted philanthropy of abolitionism, only increase at the rate of *one and seven-tenths* of one *per cent.* in ten years! Such is the stern and impartial testimony of fact. How calamitous must be that load of social oppression, of disease and destitution, which thus nearly annihilates the increase of this fruitful race! Yet this is the condition to which the benevolent abolitionist would reduce the prosperous servants of the South.

This seems the suitable place to notice the most insulting and preposterous of the abolitionists' slanders. It is that expressed by calling Virginia the "slave-breeding commonwealth." What do these insolent asses mean? Do they intend to revile Virginia, because she did not suppress the natural increase of this peaceful and happy class of her people, by wholesale infanticide? Or because she did not, like the North, subject them to social evils so cruel and murderous, as to kill off that increase by the slow torture of vice, oppression, and destitution? It was the honour of Virginia, that she *was a man-breeding commonwealth*; that her benignant government made existence a blessing, both to the black man and the white, and, consequently, conferred it on many of both. If it has been proved, which we claim, that servitude was the best condition for the blacks, and that it promoted their multiplication, then this is a praise and not a reproach to Virginia. How perverse and absurd is the charge, that Virginia was actuated by a motive beastly and avaricious, in bestowing existence on many black men, and making it a blessing to them; because, forsooth, her wise government of them made them useful to the State and to themselves! By the same reason, the Christian parents who rejoice in children as a gift of the Lord, and a blessing to him "who hath his quiver full of them," are "slave-breeders," because they make their children useful, and hope to find them supports to their old age.

But medical statistics have revealed the fact, that another sure test of the physical well-being and progress of a people may be found, in the *per-centage* of hereditary disease, idiocy, and lunacy among them. The hardships, destitution, and immoralities of a bad state of society have a powerful influence to propagate blindness, deafness, idiocy, scrofula, *cretinism*, and to harass the feebler minds into derangement; while the blessings of good government, abundant food and raiment, and social happiness, strengthen and elevate the "human breed." The returns of the census of 1850 were collected by authority of Congress, on these points, and they show that of whites, North and South, about *one person in every thousand* is either deaf, dumb, blind, insane, or idiotic. Of free blacks in the North, *one person in every five hundred and six* was in one or the other of these sad conditions! Of the black people of the South, *one person among every one thousand four hundred and forty-six*, was thus afflicted. So that, by this test, Southern slaves are three times as prosperous, contented, happy, and moral as Northern free blacks, and once and a half times as much so as the whites themselves. The frightful proportion which these elemental maladies have reached among the wretched free blacks of abolitiondom, does more to reveal the misery of their condition there, than volumes of description.

The statistics of crime and pauperism reveal results yet more astounding for our enemies, and triumphant for us. While the free States had, in 1850, about thirteen and a half millions, including a few hundreds of thousands of free blacks, and the South about nine and a half millions of whites and blacks, there were, in that year (23,664) twenty-three thousand six hundred and sixty-four criminal convictions in the North, and (2,921) two thousand nine hundred and twenty-one in the South. The same year, the North was supporting (114,704) one hundred and fourteen thousand seven hundred and four paupers; and the South (20,563) twenty thousand five hundred and sixty-three. One of the most remarkable things is the great excess of both crime and pauperism in the New England States, "the land of steady habits," not only as compared with the South, but as compared with the remainder of the North, except New York. In Boston and its adjacent county, in Massachusetts, the persons in jails, houses of correction or refuge, and alms-houses, bore, among the blacks, the ratio of *one to every sixteen*: and among the whites, of *one to every thirty-four*. In Richmond, Virginia, the same unhappy classes bore, among the blacks, the ratio of *one to every forty-six*, and among the whites, of *one to every one hundred and twelve*. By this test, then, the white people of Richmond are three times as happy and moral as the white people of Boston, and the negroes of Richmond have proportionably one-third less crime than the white people of Boston, and are nearly three times as moral as the free blacks of that city.

We have thus examined the testimony of facts, as given to us under the unwilling authority of the Congress of the United States. They show that, by all the tests recognized among statesmen, slavery has not made the South less populous, less rich, less moral, less healthy, or less abundant in the resources of living than its boastful rival, in proportion to its opportunities. On this evidence of experience we rest ourselves.

In dismissing this head of our discussion, we would briefly touch two points. One is the annual production of the industry of the North and the South. Without burdening the reader with statistical details, it is sufficient to sum up the annual results of the three great branches, of agriculture, mining, and manufactures. The North exceeds the South in proportion to population, in wheat, hay, dairy products, and manufactures; while the South greatly exceeds the North in the great staples of Indian corn and tobacco, and surpasses it almost immeasurably in rice, cotton, and naval stores. Summing up the varied productions of each section, we find that the industry of the South is, on the whole, more productive than that of the North, relatively to its numbers. And of the great commodities which constitute the basis of foreign commerce, the South yields more than the North, in about the ratio of four to one!

The other point is the relative improvement of the soil. According to the census of 1860, there were *four* acres of improved land to each inhabitant of the North, appraised, with their rateable proportion of stock and implements, at $223. This gives about $56 for each acre and its stock. In the South, on the other hand, each inhabitant claims *nine* acres of improved land, valued, with their stock and implements, at $322. This allows about $36 for each acre and its stock. It has been argued that this evinces the slovenly and imperfect agriculture of the slaveholding States, and the comparative exhaustion of their soils. It is said, their rude tillage is spread over a far wider surface, and conducted with inferiour appointments. And this depreciating result slavery has brought about, they assert, in spite of superiour natural advantages. We remark that, contrary to the usual assertion, the natural fertility was superiour in the free States. The soil of the Middle States had a better natural average than that of the old Atlantic slave States, and the North-western States had a vastly larger proportion of fertile lands than the South-western. In the next place, the agriculture of the South is of such a character that it requires a wider area; and yet this requirement argues nothing of its greater imperfection. It may require more space to fly a kite than to spin a top, and yet it does not follow that the kite-flying is less skillful sport than the top-spinning. An iron manufactory must necessarily cover more ground than a chemical laboratory; but no one argues thence, that the ironmonger is less a master of his trade than the manufacturer of drugs, of his. Last: the fact that the Southern planter accounts the labour of his farm as property, and so, as a part of his invested capital, causes a lower nominal valuation of his lands, though there be no inferiority of actual production. Grain and grass lands in the county of Rockingham have always sold higher than grain and grass lands in the county of Albemarle, which were actually yielding the same products annually. The former were tilled by free labour, and the latter by slave; but the Albemarle farming was confessedly as skillful, as economical, and as profitable, as the Rockingham. The explanation is the following: The Rockingham farmer, hiring his free labour, needed no more capital for this purpose than was sufficient to pay the wages of a few months in advance of the realization of his crop. The Albemarle farmer expended a large portion of his farming capital in the purchase of slaves, and afterwards paid no money in hire. The former, investing twenty thousand dollars in agriculture, could expend the whole sum in land, except what was required to stock it and pay wages for a few months. Thus he would begin by buying three hundred acres of land for eighteen thousand dollars. But the slaveholding farmer began by expending eight thousand dollars in the purchase of servants, leaving him but ten thousand to pay for the three hundred acres of land. For this reason land of the same actual value must be rated at a smaller nominal price among slaveholders than among farmers employing free labour. But the true profits of the farming are not reduced thereby, in the proportion of eighteen thousand to ten thousand. For the slaveholder no longer has to tax his crops, (equal in gross amount to those of the Rockingham farmer,) with the hire of labourers. That tax he pays in the shape of the annual interest on the eight thousand dollars, which, in the first instance, he paid for his servants. Hence the facts do not argue that the land is intrinsically less productive or less profitable; they only argue a different distribution of capital between the two sources of production, land and labour. In consequence of that difference, the land must be represented by less money. This obvious explanation explodes much that has been taught concerning the comparative barrenness of Southern farming.

CHAPTER IX.
CONCLUSION.

These facts, then, have been established beyond question: That slavery was forced upon Virginia against her protests, by the cupidity of New England, and the tyranny and cupidity of Old England: That the African race being thus placed in the State without her agency, she adopted the remedy of domestic slavery, which is proved by the law of God in the Old and New Testaments to be innocent, and shown by events to be beneficent to the Africans: That, according to history, the laws of nations, and the laws of the British Empire inherited by the American States, slaveholding was lawful throughout the territories of the United States, save where it was restrained by State sovereignty: That it was expressly recognized and protected by the Constitution; such recognition having been an essential condition, without which the Southern States would never have accepted the Union: That every department of the government, and all political parties, habitually recognized the political equality of the slaveholding States, and of slaveholding citizens: That the Supreme Court, the authorized expounder of the Constitution, also recognized the equal rights of slaveholders in all the common territories: And that slavery proved itself at once, not only lawful, but eminently promotive of the well-being of the Africans, of the interests of the whole government, and of the publick wealth. Then the North, having ceased to find its own interest in the slave trade and slavery, changed its ground, and began to cast about, merely from a desire of sectional power in the confederacy, for means to destroy the institution. It is unnecessary to argue that the whole free-soil controversy, and the war which grew out of it, were really designed by them to destroy slavery in the States: for they themselves, in the pride of success, have long ceased to conceal that fact.

Now, had slavery been intrinsically a moral and social evil, yet its protection was in the compact between the States; and to the honest mind, there was but one course for the North to adopt when she concluded that she could no longer endure her connexion with slavery. This was, to restore to the South the pledges, the fulfilment of which had become irksome; and to dissolve the Union peacefully and fairly, as it had been formed, leaving us in possession of our own country and rights, to bear our own sin, and pursue our own destiny. It was the federal compact alone, which gave the North any right to govern the South. If they repudiated that contract, it was annihilated equally for both parties. Thenceforward their claim to legislate for the South, or exercise any power over her, was baseless and iniquitous. No fair mind will dispute, that even though slavery had been an indefensible wrong, the South ought not to have permitted herself to be assailed for it, in an equal Union which she had sovereignly entered with this institution expressly recognized. But that basis of argument we utterly repudiate. We will not defend ourselves from such premises. We claim to have been justified, not only by the Constitution of the United States, but by God and the right, in our rights to slaves. Our *status* in the Federal Union was, so far, as equal, as honourable, as legal, as free from ethical taint, as that of any other States with their property in horses, ships, land, and factories.

We have, in another place, (the Life of Jackson,) stated with sufficient fulness, the admitted facts and doctrines of the Constitution, which justified the Southern States in resuming their independence, when the compact, to which they had partially yielded it, was destroyed. The indisputable proofs (now fully admitted by anti-slavery men) might be cited, which showed that their election of a sectional President, with other aggressions, were intended to destroy the most acknowledged and vital rights of the States. Had Virginia assumed her attitude of resistance upon that event, she might have defended it by that maxim, so obvious to every just mind, that it is righteous and wise to meet the first clear aggression, even though its practical mischiefs be unimportant: that "a people should rather contend for their rights upon their threshold than upon their hearthstone." But we had stronger justification still. The aggression intended was practically vast and ruinous in its results. It has been shown in previous chapters, that the destruction of African slavery among us was vital to us, because emancipation by such means would be destructive of the very framework of society, and of our most fundamental rights and interests. All our statesmen, of all parties, had taught us, not only that the reserved rights of the States were the bulwarks of the liberties of the people, but that emancipation by federal aggression would lead to the destruction of all other rights. A Clay, as much as a Calhoun, proclaimed that when abolition overthrew slavery in the South, it also would equally overthrow the Constitution. Calhoun, and other Southern statesmen, with a sagacity which every day confirms, had forewarned us, that when once abolition by federal aggression came, these other sure results would follow: that the same greedy lust of power which had meddled between masters and slaves, would assuredly, and for the stronger reason, desire to use the political weight of the late slaves against their late masters: that having enforced a violent emancipation, they would enforce, of course, negro suffrage, negro eligibility to office, and a full negro equality: that negro equality thus theoretically established would be practical negro superiority: that the tyrant section, as it gave to its victims, the white men of the South, more and more causes of just resentment, would find more and more violent inducements to bribe the negroes, with additional privileges and gifts, to assist them in their domination: that this miserable career must result in one of two things, either a war of races, in which the whites or the blacks would be, one or the other, exterminated; or amalgamation. But while we believe that "God made of one blood all nations of men to dwell under the whole heavens," we know that the African has become, according to a well-known law of natural history, by the manifold influences of the ages, a different, fixed *species* of the race, separated from the white man by traits bodily, mental and moral, almost as rigid and permanent as those of *genus*. Hence the offspring of an amalgamation must be a hybrid race, stamped with all the feebleness of the hybrid, and incapable of the career of civilization and glory as an independent race. And this apparently is the destiny which our conquerors have in view. If indeed they can mix the blood of the heroes of Manassas with this vile stream from the fens of Africa, then they will never again have occasion to tremble before the righteous resistance of Virginian freemen; but will have a race supple and vile enough to fill that position of political subjection, which they desire to fix on the South.

But although Virginia well knew that the very existence of society was assailed by these aggressions, so strict was her loyalty to the Constitution, she refused to make the election of a sectional President the immediate occasion of resistance, because, outrage as it was, it was nominally effected by the forms of the Constitution. When her sisters, more advanced than herself in the spirit of resistance, resumed their independence, she refused to follow them. When, warned by thickening events, she assembled her Convention, immediate embodiment of her own sovereignty, it was not a convention of secessionists. Only twenty-five, out of the hundreds of members, advocated that extreme remedy. But she did by this Convention, what she had already done by her General Assembly: she repeated the assertion of the great principles on which the government was founded; that it was built on the free consent of States originally sovereign, and not on force; that however wrongfully any State might resume its independence without just cause, the only remedy was conciliation, and not force; that therefore the coercion of a sovereign State was unlawful, mischievous, and must be resisted. There Virginia took her stand—on this foundation right, as essential to the well-being of assailant as of assailed. It was not for slavery that she deliberately resolved to draw the sword, cardinal as she knew circumstances rendered slavery at this time; but for this corner-stone of all constitutional liberty, North and South. And this, too, was a principle which she had always held against all assailants, in all ages of the Republick. She had asserted it firmly against her own favourite, Andrew Jackson, in the case of South Carolina, notwithstanding her disapproval of the nullifying doctrine then held by that State. She only asserted her time-honoured creed now. It was not until the claim to subjugate sovereign States was practically applied, that Virginia drew the sword; and then, not for slavery, but for the Constitution, and the liberties of a continent, which it had protected.

It is therefore a great and an odious perversion of the truth, to say that the defensive movement of the South was a war to extend and perpetuate slavery. African slavery was not the *cause*, but the *occasion* of the strife, on either side. On the Northern side it was merely the pretext, employed by that aggressive section to carry out ambitious projects of domination. To the South, it was merely the circumstance of the controversy, that the right assailed was our right to the labour of our servants. It was not the circumstance for which we contended, but the principle—the great cause of moral right, justice, and regulated liberty. It was therefore a gross injustice to burden our cause, in the minds of the rest of the world, with the *odium* which the prejudices of Christendom have attached to the name of slaveholder. Even those who are unable to overcome those prejudices, would, if just and magnanimous, approve our attempt to defend ourselves.

Finally: the means by which this defence has been overpowered were as iniquitous as the attack. A war was waged, precipitated by treachery, aggravated by every measure of barbarity condemned by the laws of nations, by the agency of multitudinous hordes of foreign mercenaries, and semi-civilized slaves seduced from their owners; against captives, women, children, and private property; with the attempt to let loose upon our little community (which they found otherwise unconquerable) a servile insurrection and all the horrors of domestic assassination—an attempt disappointed only by the good feeling and good character which the servants themselves had learned from the humanity of their masters. The impartial and magnanimous mind which weighs these facts cannot but feel itself swelling with an unutterable sense of indignation. The Southern people feel little impulse to give expression to their sense of the enormous wrongs, in reproaches or vituperations of those who have thus destroyed them. When resistance was practicable, they gave a more expressive and seemly utterance to this sentiment, in the energy of their blows. Let the heroick spirit in which the soldiers of Virginia and the South struck for their liberties, and suffered, and died, represent our appreciation of this injustice. A righteous God, for our sins towards Him, has permitted us to be overthrown by our enemies and His. It is vain to complain in the ear of a maddening tempest. Although our people are now oppressed with present sufferings and a prospective destiny more cruel and disastrous than has been visited on any civilized people of modern ages, they suffer silently, disdaining to complain, and only raising to the chastening heavens, the cry, "How long, O Lord?" Their appeal is to history, and to Him. They well know, that in due time, they, although powerless themselves, will be avenged through the same disorganizing heresies under which they now suffer, and through the anarchy and woes which they will bring upon the North. Meantime, let the arrogant and successful wrongdoers flout our defence with disdain: we will meet them with it again, when it will be heard; in the day of their calamity, in the pages of impartial history, and in the Day of Judgment.

THE END

DETAILED HISTORICAL CONTEXT
A DEFENCE OF VIRGINIA

During the period this book was originally written, the world was a very different place. The events of the time produced an impact on the authorship, style and content of this work. In order for you the reader to better appreciate and connect with this book, it is therefore important to have some context on world events during this timeframe. To this end, we have included a detailed events calendar for the *19th* century for your reference.

Please give consideration in particular to the era around *1867*, the year in which this work was first published.

Disclaimer: Some scenes throughout history may not be suitable for children, for example, in relation to war or violence. Please use your own discretion before reading this section to your child or allowing your child to read it.

Ireland was brought under a single monarchy in 1801 by Britain. The Dublin parliament is no more. Ireland's official church will be the Anglican Church. No Catholic may hold elective office.
The Treaty of Amiens was signed in 1802 by exhausted British soldiers.
1803 The $15 million investment in Louisiana Territory, which Napoleon is prepared to sell to raise money for the war, was supported by President Jefferson and others.

The Royal College of Surgeons was founded in London in 1804.

Milan hosted Napoleon's coronation in 1805. He intended to march into England. A French fleet travels up the coast of Spain to Cadiz. From Cadiz, Napoleon dispatched French and Spanish ships to attack the British. At Trafalgar, the British overthrow Napoleon, blocking his plans for an invasion.
West Florida was inundated with Americans in 1810. These settlers rose up in opposition to Spain. President James Madison and Congress

acquired the province in a move that was not accepted globally because they understood Spain's vulnerability as a result of Napoleon's occupation.

1811 Slave plantations outside of New Orleans are aware of the successful slave uprising in Haiti (1791-1804). On January 8, 200 to 500 slaves from various New Orleans-area plantations gather together to rebel against their masters. They kill for freedom. A musket duel was lost by the slaves. A lesson for other slaves, their heads were exhibited on pikes.

1812 Britain has a counter-blockade on the seas. The British navy is instructed by Lord Liverpool, the country's new prime minister, to steer clear of collisions with American commercial ships. Despite the US's wish for peace, Congress declared war on Britain on June 18, 1812.

1817 Due to the conflict with France, real wages in Britain have been declining since the late 1790s. From now until the end of the century, real wages in Britain will increase.

In England, 60,000 people gather in a field to demand universal suffrage. Henry Hunt is sought after by a magistrate, but there are riots and eleven people are killed. a growing reform movement

In order to start a massive uprising, a group of revolutionaries in England intended to assassinate government cabinet members in 1820. The conspiracy on Cato Street. A policeman was among them. Some people utilised the scheme to attack legislative change. The conspirators were found guilty, and five of them were hanged before being beheaded, completing England's decapitations.

French troops are sent into Spain in 1823 by Austria, Russia, and Prussia in order to put an end to the liberal movement and reinstate Ferdinand VII as king. Ferdinand went on a murderous rampage on his fans out of retaliation.

Britain established the Royal Society for the Prevention of Cruelty to Animals in 1824.

Following the death of Louis XVIII, his conservative brother Charles X became king.

1827 Due to Russia's desire to protect Orthodox Christians, Britain, Russia, and France split from Austria over the Greek independence fight. An Egyptian and Turkish fleet is sunk in Navarino Bay on the western coast of the Peloponnesian Peninsula by a combined British, French, and Russian army. In Greece and Arabia, Ottoman power waned.

1833 Crop failures and the Tempo famine in Japan are caused by excessive rain. A famine occurred in Japan about fifty years ago. Prosperity eventually fades. The three-year famine would result in the deaths of 300,000 people.

With the British government prepared to compensate slave owners, the Abolition Slavery Act of 1834 becomes operative. In Canada, many slaves had been freed. Although the remaining 781,000 slaves were freed, no claims for damages were made.

British and Spanish anti-slavery treaty is renewed in 1835. In both Sierra Leone and Havana, suspected Spanish slavers were to be hauled before mixed commissions. Primarily, slave ships carrying extra mess equipment, wood, or food were considered slavers.

Scientists discussed cells in 1838. The concept of the cell is gaining ground as the basic building block of life.

The British are looking for "a trusted friend" on India's western border due to their concern over Russian involvement in Afghanistan. They also sent forth an army of prostitutes, opium and rum sellers, elephants, 38,000 camels, and troops.

In his work Chemistry in Its Application to Agriculture and Physiology, Justus Liebig covered physiology and agriculture in 1840. This will advance industrialisation further and transform agriculture.

1841 Non-explosive cannonballs are fired by naval cannons. High-powered flat-trajectory guns could safely fire explosive shells thanks to a French time-delay technology. Before the decade is up, all three fleets will have them.

1850 Chinese Christians believe that they have been sent by God as his son to redeem the world. He is advocating the Ten Commandments, land distribution, and wealth sharing. He opposes opium use and is in favour of female virginity. The Taiping Rebellion is sparked by him. It extends over eastern China with the intention of driving out other faiths and "Manchu devils."

1855 A majority of Edo is destroyed by an earthquake, a wave, and a fire (Tokyo).

1856 Manchu government agents search a Chinese-owned ship anchored in Guangzhou (Canton) for a known pirate. The ship was registered in Hong Kong. They sent out a ship expedition in search of vengeance along with the French, who were seeking payback for the Manchu death of a French missionary. Unhappiness with China's adherence to the post-Opium War agreements. the Second Opium War has started.

1859 In order to free all the slaves in America, John Brown intended to declare war. His and his supporters' armed rebellion is put down. Brown is found guilty and put to death.

1859 Charles Darwin put off writing Origin of Species for twenty-one years. He made it public.

1859 The atmosphere is heated by the combination of CO_2 and water vapour, claims British scientist John Tyndall. He added that shifting gas concentrations might contribute to climate change.

1860 In America, George Crum created the potato chip. With a basket of potato chips on each table, he opened his first eatery.

1863 Russia's primary cotton supplier was cut off by the American Civil War. Russia has expanded its military presence in Central Asia, which has a sparse, tribal, impoverished, and Muslim population.

Taiping Rebellion leader Hong Xiuchuan declared in 1864 that Tianjin would be saved by God (southeast of Beijing). He passes away just as government soldiers show up. Much of China is taken back by the monarchy. The Taiping insurrection is almost finished.

Tokugawa forces are defeated in Hokkaido in 1869. Military authorities began associating Shinto theology with Emperor Meiji. There were many Shinto shrines on Buddhist temple grounds, and Buddhist images were destroyed in an effort to free Shinto from Buddhist supremacy. A temple's property was taken.

Diamond reserves have been discovered in 1870 near Kimberley, Griqualand, which lies on the northern edge of the British colony. There were throngs of whites and blacks from Europe, Australia, and the Americas.

1873 Japan's ambassador to Europe and America returns with high hopes for the country's future. Confucianism is abandoned by the Meiji government as the official state doctrine.

In what is now Ghana, Britain founds a colony in 1874 that is 400 km wide and 100 km deep. In place of the customary red coats, a British commander instructed his soldiers to don brown jackets and khaki pants during combat.

The Black Hills would always belong to the Sioux, the U.S. administration informed them.

1876 saw the establishment of "redeemed" governments in former Confederate states by Conservatives. To restrict black voting, these regimes created sophisticated voting machines, literacy tests, and poll fees.

Alexander III accuses Jews of causing Christ's death in 1882. All over Russia's empire, there is anti-Semitism. They may have been escaping the empire, according to rumours.

1883 Constance-Baghdad The Orient Express began.

1884 The British army is in charge of coordinating the evacuation of Egypt from Khartoum, which includes 2,500 women, children, ill, and injured people. The army of Muhammad Ahmad surrounds. A warlord and slave trader from Sudan requested military assistance from the British.

1885 saw an international conference on Africa in Berlin. They delegated power to Belgian King Leopold of Congo. Tanzania was given to Germany as a protectorate. The German outposts in Cameroon's interior and what is now Botswana's annexes. A small French colony is founded on Madagascar's northernmost tip.

1894 The emperor Alexander III died. His son, Tsar Nicholas II, was 26 years old. His main passions were for God and a happy family life. A few days after being crowned, the tsar presents the public with gifts. Over a thousand people were crushed to death in an open field. When Nicholas visits churches, he venerates saints and Russian believers fall to their knees at his sight. There is usually a moment of silence followed by loud applause.

1895 Friedrich Engels introduces Marx's Class Struggles in France. Engels claims that "the age of surprise attack, of small conscious minorities leading great mindless masses, has over."

1896 The British worry that the French may seize control of southern Sudan. An army is escorted into Sudan by Horatio Kitchener.

1900 Germany, a global leader in literacy In Germany, it was simple to find a qualified labour, seasoned farmers, and military men. In contrast to China, India, Africa, and Islamic countries, literacy rates were high in Britain, France, Norway, Sweden, and Australia.

In 1900, there were 1.7 billion people, up from a billion in 1800.

This concludes the historical context.

Thank you for your interest in our publications. Please don't forget to check out our other books and leave a review if you enjoyed this book.

Printed in Great Britain
by Amazon

56245469R00136